Third Edition

Revised

deutsch aktuell 1

Wolfgang S. Kraft

Consultants

Chief Consultants

Hans J. König
The Blake Schools
Hopkins, Minnesota

Roland Specht
St. Cloud State University
St. Cloud, Minnesota

Consultants

Gisela Carty
Thomas A. Edison High School, Virginia
Northern Virginia Community College
Alexandria, Virginia

Jack W. Denny
Lyons Township High School
La Grange, Illinois

Linda K. Klein
Waupaca High School
Waupaca, Wisconsin

Cynthia McIver
West Springfield High School
Springfield, Virginia

John Peters
Cardinal O'Hara High School
Springfield, Pennsylvania

Otto Rieger
Claremont High School
Claremont, California

Christiane A. Rudolf
Sycamore High School
Cincinnati, Ohio

EMC Publishing, Saint Paul, Minnesota

ISBN 0-8219-0926-6

© 1993 by EMC Corporation

Published by EMC Publishing
300 York Avenue
St. Paul, Minnesota 55101

Printed in the United States of America
    3 4 5 6 7 8 9 10 XXX 99 98 97 96 95 94

Willkommen!

In today's global economy, knowing a foreign language and culture is a personal and professional asset — one that can open the door to a new world for you. On the personal level, language study will help you to understand other people and their feelings, opinions, and attitudes. It will also heighten your awareness of your own language and culture. On the professional level, international career opportunities will be available to you.

"Why study German? What do I need it for?" you may ask. Did you know German is considered the sister language of English? Did you know that Germans make up the largest single ethnic group in this country? Most major U.S. companies have subsidiaries or branch offices in Germany. Knowing German will give you an advantage with these companies when you apply for a job.

German has long been an important language to study primarily because of the influence of German-speaking countries in political, social, and economic spheres. Present-day political and social changes occurring in Germany have further amplified the need to know more about that country. This new edition of *Deutsch Aktuell* continues the tradition of presenting everyday life in *all* German-speaking countries.

You will learn about the life-styles of German-speaking young people and relate their experiences to your own situation. You will acquire skills to communicate on many topics. As you embark on learning German you will initially listen, then gradually learn to speak on those topics of interest to you.

The strength of *Deutsch Aktuell* is its realistic and up-to-date treatment of the German language and culture. As the word *aktuell* implies, it is a topical, contemporary program. The topics have been carefully selected on the basis of how frequently they occur in the lives of the people from the various countries.

Don't be afraid to express yourself. It is natural to make mistakes, but your language skills will become stronger the more you use the language. In time you will acquire the desire and confidence to communicate in German.

The best of success and have lots of fun, too!

Viel Erfolg und viel Spaß!

Lektion 8
Einkaufen *251*

Lektion 9
Sport *285*

Lektion 10

Musik *321*

Lektion B

Rückblick *351*

Reference

Deutsches
Sprachgebiet

Nordsee

Ostsee

Flensburg

Rügen

Helgoland

Kiel

Fehmarn

Lübeck

Rostock

Inseln

Schwerin

Bremerhaven

Emden

Wilhelmshaven

Hamburg

Elbe

Oldenburg

Bremen

Berlin ★

Oder

Osnabrück

Hannover

Braunschweig

Potsdam

Münster

Bielefeld

Goslar

Magdeburg

Dessau

DEUTSCHLAND

Cottbus

Dortmund

Halle

Essen

Duisburg

Wuppertal

Kassel

Saale

Leipzig

Dresden

Düsseldorf

Rhein

Erfurt

Gera

Köln

Jena

Chemnitz

Aachen

Bonn

Koblenz

Fulda

Thüringer Wald

Erzgebirge

Zwickau

Wiesbaden

Frankfurt/Main

LUXEMBURG

Mainz

Würzburg

Bayreuth

Trier

Darmstadt

Mannheim

Saarbrücken

Heidelberg

Nürnberg

Neustadt

Rothenburg

Donau

Karlsruhe

Regensburg

Baden-Baden

Stuttgart

Passau

Augsburg

München

Linz

Freiburg

Schwarzwald

Chiemsee

Salzburg

Wien ★

Titisee

Konstanz

Oberammergau

Zugspitze

Neusiedlersee

Basel

Bodensee

Garmisch-Partenkirchen

Watzmann

ÖSTERREICH

Zürich

Aare

Innsbruck

Graz

Alpen

Vaduz

LIECHTENSTEIN

Luzern

Rhein

Bern

Grossglockner

SCHWEIZ

Rhone

Genf

Monte Rosa

Deutschland

Stachus in München

Norddeutschland

Markt in Freiburg

Heidelberg

x

Frankfurt

Marienplatz in München

Hafen in Hamburg

Intercity-Zug

Mittenwald

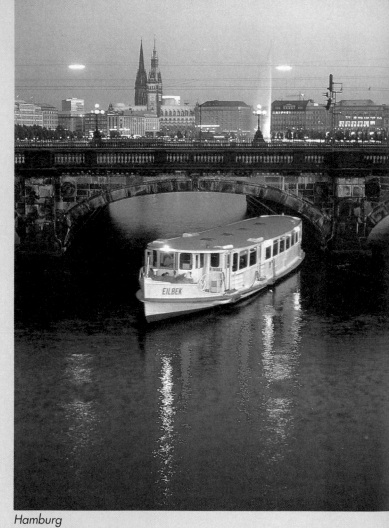

Hamburg

Dortmund

xii

Reit im Winkel

Lüneburg

Karneval in Köln

Schloß Neuschwanstein

Frankfurt

Suhl   Die Elbe in der Sächsischen Schweiz

Köpenick in Berlin

xiv

Schloß Moritzburg
bei Dresden

Erfurt

Mecklenburg

Sportfest in Berlin

Österreich

Salzburg

Altenmarkt

Innsbruck

Schloß Matzen bei Brixlegg

Graz   St. Anton am Arlberg

Maria Luggau im Lesachtal   Seefeld in Tirol   xvii

Die Schweiz

Interlaken

Jodeln

Markt in Bern

Mettenberg bei Grindelwald

Mürren im Berneser Oberland

Kajakfahren

Bern

xix

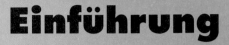

Einführung

E

Communicative Functions

- greeting and saying farewell
- asking and telling names
- counting from 0 to 20
- asking and telling age
- saying the alphabet
- spelling words

Tag, Tina!

Hallo!

All these greetings mean "hello." *Grüß dich!* (southern Germany) and *Tag!* (other parts of Germany) are used among young people, friends and relatives; whereas *Grüß Gott!* (southern Germany) and *Guten Tag!* (other parts of Germany) is the standard form of saying "hello."

In recent years, *Hallo!* has become a popular greeting among children and young adults. *Tschüs!* is a casual form of *Auf Wiedersehen!* — both meaning "good-bye." See the *Kulturecke 1* of Lesson 1 for additional information.

Grüß dich!

1. **Wer ist das?** Imagine that Silke is new in school. She is asking you who the various kids are. *Folge dem Beispiel!* (Follow the example.)

   ☐ Wer ist das? (Dieter)
   Das ist Dieter.

   1. Gabi
   2. Jutta
   3. Klaus
   4. Stefan
   5. Christine
   6. Daniel
   7. Uwe
   8. Diana

2. **Wie heißt er? Wie heißt sie?** It's your first day in school. Ask the person next to you about different students in your class and then introduce yourself to that person. Use either *Tag* or *Grüß dich*.

   Wie heißt sie? (Gisela)
   Sie heißt Gisela.
   Tag, Gisela!

   Wie heißt er? (Ralf)
   Er heißt Ralf.
   Grüß dich, Ralf!

Namen

Namen für Jungen		Namen für Mädchen	
Achim	Jörg	Alexandria	Judith
Alexander	Jürgen	Andrea	Julia
Andreas	Kai	Angelika	Jutta
Axel	Karl	Anita	Karin
Benjamin	Karsten	Anja	Katharina
Bernd	Klaus	Anne	Katja
Bernhard	Kurt	Annette	Katrin
Björn	Lars	Ariane	Kerstin
Boris	Lothar	Astrid	Manuela
Carsten	Ludwig	Barbara	Maren
Christian	Manfred	Bärbel	Margit
Christoph	Manuel	Beate	Marianne
Christopher	Marc	Bettina	Marlis
Daniel	Marco	Bianca	Martina
David	Marcus	Birgit	Melanie
Dennis	Mark	Brigitte	Michaela
Dieter	Matthias	Britta	Miriam
Detlef	Michael	Carmen	Monika
Dirk	Nils	Christa	Nadine
Erich	Norbert	Christiane	Natalie
Erik	Oliver	Christine	Natascha
Ernst	Patrick	Claudia	Nina
Felix	Peter	Cornelia	Nora
Florian	Rainer	Dagmar	Olivia
Frank	Ralf	Daniela	Petra
Franz	Richard	Diana	Regina
Friedrich	Robert	Doris	Renate
Fritz	Rolf	Elfriede	Rita
Georg	Rudolf	Elisabeth	Ruth
Gerd	Rüdiger	Elke	Sabine
Gerhard	Sebastian	Erika	Sabrina
Günter	Simon	Eva	Sandra
Hans	Stefan	Evelyn	Sara
Harald	Steffen	Frieda	Sibylle
Hartmut	Sven	Gabi	Sigrid
Heiko	Thomas	Gabriele	Silke
Heinrich	Thorsten	Gerda	Silvia
Heinz	Timo	Gisela	Simone
Helmut	Tobias	Gudrun	Sonja
Herbert	Toni	Heide	Sophie
Hermann	Torsten	Heidi	Stefanie
Holger	Udo	Heike	Susanne
Horst	Ulli	Helga	Susi
Ingo	Uwe	Ilona	Tanja
Jan	Volker	Ilse	Tina
Jens	Walter	Inge	Ulla
Joachim	Werner	Ingrid	Ulrike
Jochen	Willi	Irene	Ursula
Johann	Wolf	Iris	Waltraud
Johannes	Wolfgang	Jana	Yvonne

3. *Junge oder Mädchen? Folge den Beispielen.* **(Follow the examples.)**

❑ Heike
   Sie ist ein Mädchen.

   Rolf
   Er ist ein Junge.

   1. Dirk
   2. Uwe
   3. Andrea
   4. Christian
   5. Barbara
   6. Sigrid
   7. Birgit
   8. Hartmut

0 null **1** eins **2** zwei **3** drei **4** vier

5 fünf **6** sechs **7** sieben **8** acht

9 neun **10** zehn **11** elf **12** zwölf

13 dreizehn **14** vierzehn **15** fünfzehn **16** sechzehn

17 siebzehn **18** achtzehn **19** neunzehn **20** zwanzig

Wieviel ist drei plus fünf? Drei plus fünf ist acht.
Wieviel ist sieben minus eins? Sieben minus eins ist sechs.

Übung macht den Meister!

Carry on a brief conversational exchange with the person next to you asking *Wie heißt du?* and *Wie alt bist du?* The person next to you will give you an appropriate response to each of your questions.

4. *Wie alt ist er? Wie alt ist sie?* Imagine that an exchange student is meeting your cousins for the first time. Since he or she doesn't know their ages, you are answering his or her question. *Folge dem Beispiel!*

❐ Wie alt ist Dieter? (20)
Er ist zwanzig.

Wie alt ist Petra? (8)
Sie ist acht.

1. Wie alt ist Martina?
(siebzehn)
2. Wie alt ist Ulli?
(neun)
3. Wie alt ist Susanne?
(dreizehn)
4. Wie alt ist Tina?
(fünfzehn)
5. Wie alt ist Wolfgang?
(elf)
6. Wie alt ist Andreas?
(neunzehn)

5. *Wieviel ist...?* Folge den Beispielen.

❐ $1 + 3 = ?$
Eins plus drei ist vier.

$10 - 1 = ?$
Zehn minus eins ist neun.

1. $8 + 11 = ?$
2. $13 - 1 = ?$
3. $5 + 2 = ?$
4. $20 - 6 = ?$
5. $16 - 5 = ?$
6. $7 + 9 = ?$

Das Alphabet

a	ah	k	kah	u	uh
b	beh	l	ell	v	fau
c	tseh	m	emm	w	weh
d	deh	n	enn	x	iks
e	eh	o	oh	y	üpsilon
f	eff	p	peh	z	tset
g	geh	q	kuh	ä	äh
h	hah	r	err	ö	öh
i	ih	s	ess	ü	üh
j	jott	t	teh	ß	ess-tset

6. *Wie buchstabiert man...? Mündlich, bitte!* (How do you spell...? Orally, please.)

1. ist
2. Junge
3. sie
4. Tag
5. heißt
6. fünf
7. Beispiel
8. Mädchen

7. Complete each statement by selecting an appropriate word from the list below.

Wieviel	dich
fünf	Junge
Tschüs	Sie
Guten	heißt
Auf	Mädchen

1. Wie heißen _____?
2. _____ Wiedersehen!
3. Grüß _____, Susanne!
4. Er _____ Dieter.
5. Acht minus _____ ist drei.
6. _____ Tag, Herr Meier.
7. Boris ist ein _____.
8. _____ ist vier plus zwei?
9. Angelika ist ein _____.
10. _____, Astrid.

8. You are trying to demonstrate to your friend that you know some German. Your friend is starting to say something and you finish his or her sentence.

☐ Wie alt bist _____?
Wie alt bist du?

1. Zehn minus vier ist _____.
2. Wie heißen _____?
3. Grüß _____!
4. Auf _____!
5. Er heißt _____.
6. Dirk ist ein _____.

9. You are talking to another student. What are the logical statements to complete this short conversation? You may want to use some of the cues listed below for possible answers.

Ich bin... / Ich heiße... / Tschüs! / Tag! / Sie ist...

Tag!

_____

Wie heißt du?

_____

Wer ist das?

_____

Wie alt ist sie?

_____

Tschüs!

_____

Wer ist das?

Ich heiße Rosi.

Er heißt Rolf.

Tag! Wie geht's?

The following words and expressions will help you in your understanding of the content for this introductory lesson.

Wer ist das?	Who is that?
Das ist...	That is...
Wie heißt er/sie?	What's his/her name?
Er/Sie heißt...	His/Her name is...
Wie heißt du?	What's your name? (informal)
Wie heißen Sie?	What's your name? (formal)
Wie alt bist du?	How old are you?
Ich bin...	I am...
Wie alt ist...?	How old is...?
Wieviel ist...?	How much is...?
ein Junge	a boy
ein Mädchen	a girl

Der Junge heißt Detlef.

Das ist Elke.

Bis bald !

...wieder in Iserlohn

12

Wie geht's?

1

"PFÜA GOTT"

AUF WIEDERSEHEN !

Communicative Functions

- greeting people
- asking and telling how things are going
- asking where someone lives
- asking and telling names

Wo wohnst du?

Holger:	Hallo, Claudia! Wie geht's?
Claudia:	Ganz gut.
Holger:	Was machst du jetzt?
Claudia:	Ich gehe nach Hause.
Holger:	So früh?
Claudia:	Es ist schon spät.

***Richtig oder falsch?* (True or false?) If the statement is false, can you give the correct answer in English?**

1. Claudia doesn't feel too well.
2. Holger says it's already late.
3. Claudia is on the way home.

Hallo, Claudia! Wie geht's?

Ganz gut.

Was machst du jetzt?

Christine:	Wo wohnst du?
Silke:	In der Stadt. Und du?
Christine:	Nicht weit von hier.
Silke:	Und wo genau?
Christine:	Beim Park.
Silke:	Oh, wie schön!

***Richtig oder falsch?* If the statement is false, provide the correct answer in English.**

1. Silke lives downtown.
2. Christine lives far away.
3. Christine lives close to the park.

Christine

Wo wohnt Silke?

Silke

Alex:	Grüß dich, Thomas!
Thomas:	Wo ist deine Freundin?
Alex:	Die Gabi?
Thomas:	Ist da noch eine andere?
Alex:	Vielleicht.

Richtig oder falsch? If the statement is false, give the correct answer in English.

1. Alex most likely lives in northern Germany. Why or why not?
2. Thomas has more than two girlfriends.
3. We don't know if Alex has another girlfriend besides Gabi.

Thomas

Alex

Grüß dich, Thomas!

Fragen

1. Wie geht's Claudia?
2. Wo wohnt Silke?
3. Und Christine?
4. Wie heißt eine Freundin von Alex?

Für dich

In informal conversations or descriptions in which the person referred to is well known, Germans often put the article *der* or *die* in front of the name. *(Wo ist die Gabi? Wo wohnt der Thomas?)*

Kombiniere...

(Combine...) How many sentences can you make using the following words in various combinations? Choose one word or phrase from each column.

Ich	wohne	ein Mädchen
Heike	ist	nach Hause
Du	gehst	in der Stadt
Gerd		weit von hier
		beim Park
		ein Junge

Tag! Wie geht's?

Frau Schmidt ist in der Stadt.

16

Guten Tag, Frau Riegel!

Tag, Petra!

Nützliche Ausdrücke (Useful Expressions)

Hallo, Claudia!   Hi, Claudia!
Grüß dich, Thomas!   Hi, Thomas!
Ich gehe nach Hause.   I'm going home.
Es ist so früh (spät).   It's so early (late).
Wohnst du in der Stadt?   Do you live downtown?
Oh, wie schön!   Oh, how nice!

**Was fehlt hier? (What's missing here?) Complete each
sentence with an appropriate word.**

Oh, wie schön!

1. Oh, wie _____!
2. _____ wohnst du?
3. Es ist _____ so spät.
4. Ich wohne _____ Park.
5. _____ dich, Heike.
6. Wo ist deine _____?
7. Nicht _____ von hier.
8. _____ da noch eine andere?

Lektion 1

Ergänzung

19

Sag's mal!

Wo wohnst du?

dort gleich um die Ecke in Hamburg

nicht weit von hier dort drüben beim Park

in der Lindenstraße

hier in der Stadt da da drüben

Wie geht's?

ausgezeichnet phantastisch nicht so gut

Prima nicht besonders sehr gut

es geht miserabel

übel ganz gut nicht schlecht super

1. *Wie heißt er? Wie heißt sie?* The person next to you is asking you about the names of some of the students in class. Help her or him in identifying each. *Folge den Beispielen!*

❏ Wie heißt sie? (Christine)
Sie heißt Christine.

Wie heißt er? (Dirk)
Er heißt Dirk.

1. Heiko
2. Andrea
3. Georg
4. Christa
5. Helga
6. Günter

Aussprache (Pronunciation)

short /a/	long /a/
ganz	Tag
Stadt	ja
alt	da
zwanzig	Park
das	Gabi
acht	nach
machen	Helga

Übungen (Exercises)

The Familiar Form: *du* (singular) and *ihr* (plural)

The familiar form is used when you speak to relatives, close friends, children and animals.

Beispiele: (Mrs. Schmidt is speaking to a child.)
Wo wohnst du? Where do you live?

(Andreas is talking to his friends.)
Was macht ihr? What are you doing?

Note that *du* is used addressing one person and *ihr* with two or more.

Beispiel: (Andreas and Petra are asked by Kerstin.)
Wohnt ihr in der Stadt? Do you live downtown?

The Formal Form: *Sie* (singular and plural)

The formal form is used when you speak to adults and to those you are not addressing by their first name.

Beispiele: (Thomas is talking to his teacher.)
Wo wohnen Sie, Herr Schulz? Where do you live, Mr. Schulz?

(Mrs. Müller talks to her neighbors.)
Was machen Sie jetzt, Herr und Frau Meier? What are you doing now, Mr. and Mrs. Meier?

The formal form *Sie*, in both singular and plural, is always capitalized.

2. *Du, ihr, Sie?* **Which of these forms would you use in the following situations? You are talking to your...**

1. uncle
2. parents
3. teacher
4. dog
5. customers
6. brother
7. friend
8. horses
9. friend's aunt
10. school principal

du oder Sie?

Personal Pronouns

	Singular		Plural	
1st person	ich	I	wir	we
2nd person	du	you	ihr	you
	er	he		
3rd person	sie }	she	sie	they
	es	it		
formal form	Sie	you	Sie	you

Present Tense Verb Forms

In the present tense in English, there are basically two different verb forms for all persons. For example, *live* is used for all persons, except third person singular where it is *live(s)*. In German, however, the verb has more forms, as can be seen in the chart.

To use the proper form, you need to know the infinitive of the particular verb. The infinitive of the English verb *went*, *gone* or *goes* is *to go*. The infinitive of a German verb ends with *-en* (in a few cases *-n*) as in *gehen*, *wohnen* or *machen*. The infinitive is a combination of the stem of the verb and the ending (infinitive = stem + ending).

When the stem of a verb is known, you need to know the appropriate ending for the particular singular or plural form.

The present tense of regular verbs requires the endings indicated below.

Singular	ich	geh-*e*	I go, I am going
	du	geh-*st*	you go, you are going
	er		he goes, he is going
	sie	} geh-*t*	she goes, she is going
	es		it goes, it is going
Plural	wir geh-*en*		we go, we are going
	ihr geh-*t*		you go, you are going
	sie geh-*en*		they go, they are going
	Sie geh-*en* (sg. & pl.)		you go, you are going

NOTE: Should the stem of the verb in the second person singular end in *s*, *ß*, *x* or *z*, then the *s* of the ending is dropped.

Beispiel: *Heißt du Martina?*
               Is your name Martina?

The Letter ß (ess-tset)

The letter ß is equivalent to ss. The ß is used in these positions:

a. at the end of a word (Grüß dich!)
b. before a consonant (heißt)
c. after a long vowel or vowel combination (Straße, weiß)

The ß is never used when all the letters in a word are capitalized.

Beispiel: Straße but STRASSE

Nouns

All nouns in German (including names and places) are capitalized.

Beispiele: der Tag, die Freundin, die Stadt

Word Order

Similar to English, you can form a short sentence by starting with the subject followed by the verb and then adding other information.

Beispiele: *Ich wohne in der Stadt.* I live downtown.
Der Park ist nicht weit von hier. The park isn't far from here.

3. *Wo wohnst du?* **Assume that you are being asked if you live in a certain location. How might you answer the following questions?** *Folge dem Beispiel!*

❒   Wohnst du hier? (beim Park)
Nein, ich wohne beim Park.

1. Wohnst du in der Stadt?
(dort drüben)
2. Wohnst du da?
(gleich um die Ecke)
3. Wohnst du hier?
(nicht hier)
4. Wohnst du beim Park?
(in der Stadt)

4. Several people are asking you where you live. Answer them with the provided cues and also inquire where they live.

❑ Wo wohnst du? (da drüben)
Ich wohne da drüben. Und du?

1. Wo wohnst du? (dort)
2. Wo wohnst du? (um die Ecke)
3. Wo wohnst du? (beim Park)
4. Wo wohnst du? (nicht weit von hier)
5. Wo wohnst du? (in der Stadt)

5. Your friend is interested in getting to know some students in your school. Tell him or her their names.

❑ Wie heißt sie? (Angelika)   Wie heißt er? (Günter)
Sie heißt Angelika.   Er heißt Günter.

1. Elke
2. Manfred
3. Stefan
4. Julia
5. Anja
6. Ingo

6. You are inquiring what various people are doing now.

❑ Anna
Was macht Anna jetzt?

1. Herr und Frau Schulz
2. ihr
3. Holger
4. Peter und Rolf
5. er

7. *Wer sagt das?* Someone is spreading rumors in school. You are wondering who it is. Your friend tells you the names.

❑ Wer sagt das? (Christine)
Christine sagt das.

1. Felix und Diana
2. Deine Freundin
3. Herr Herder
4. Dein Freund und deine Freundin
5. Wir
6. Helmut

Tschüs, Gabriele!

Wo wohnen sie?

8. Use the cues to answer each question.

❑   Wo wohnen Sie? (in der Stadt)
Ich wohne in der Stadt.

1. Wie heißt sie?
(Christine)
2. Was machst du jetzt?
(nach Hause gehen)
3. Gehst du früh nach Hause?
(nein / spät)
4. Wo ist Gabi?
(da drüben)
5. Wer sagt das?
(Frau Meier)
6. Wie heißt er?
(Paul)

9. Change each of the following questions from the familiar to the formal form.

1. Wie heißt du?
2. Wohnst du weit von hier?
3. Gehst du nach Hause?
4. Was machst du hier?
5. Was sagst du?
6. Wie geht's?

10. *Beantworte diese Fragen!* **(Answer these questions.) Give a complete sentence.**

1. Wohnst du gleich um die Ecke?
2. Wer sagt das?
3. Was machst du jetzt?
4. Wie heißt du?
5. Wie geht's?
6. Ist es spät?
7. Gehst du nach Hause? Ja,...

11. *Was fehlt hier?* (What's missing here.) Select one of the words from the list to complete each sentence.

Stadt	ist
wohnen	das
Tag	sagt
geht	dich
machst	wohnt

1. Wie _____ es Ihnen?
2. Herr Meier _____ beim Park.
3. Guten _____, Herr Holz!
4. Was _____ du hier?
5. Wer _____ das?
6. Grüß _____, Andreas!
7. Wir _____ dort drüben.
8. Frau Schulz sagt _____.
9. Peter wohnt in der _____.
10. Zehn minus drei _____ sieben.

12. Carsten, a German exchange student at your school, meets you for the first time. He is talking to you in German. Can you respond to him?

Carsten:	Tag!
Du:	_____
Carsten:	Wie heißt du?
Du:	_____
Carsten:	Wo wohnst du?
Du:	_____
Carsten:	Ist das deine Freundin?
Du:	_____
Carsten:	Wie heißt sie?
Du:	_____

Übung macht den Meister!

1. Ask the person next to you what his or her name is, where he or she lives and what he or she is doing now.

2. Greet one of your classmates. Make sure that the greeting includes saying "hello" but also an appropriate handshake.

3. Count off numbers 1-20 in your class by saying the numbers first in sequence, then backwards and, finally, skipping either the even or the odd numbers.

Erweiterung (Expansion)

13. **You are agreeing with everything you are asked.**

❑ Wohnst du hier?
Ja, ich wohne hier.

1. Gehst du früh nach Hause?
2. Ist es spät?
3. Wohnst du in der Stadt?
4. Ist drei plus vier sieben?
5. Ist dreizehn minus acht fünf?
6. Heißt er Herr Schulz?
7. Heißt sie Frau Lehmann?

14. *Wieviel ist...?* **Folge dem Beispiel!**

❑ zwei plus vier
Zwei plus vier ist sechs.

1. sieben plus drei
2. zwölf minus fünf
3. acht minus vier
4. zehn plus neun
5. zwanzig minus vierzehn
6. sechs plus elf

15. **State each problem and then answer it.** *Auf deutsch, bitte!* **(In German, please.)**

❑ 4 + 1 = _____
Vier plus eins ist fünf.

1. 5 + 8 = _____
2. 1 + 6 = _____
3. 12 - 3 = _____
4. 20 - 11 = _____
5. 4 + 10 = _____
6. 17 - 15 = _____

16. *Richtig oder falsch?* **Decide whether or not the response to each question or statement is appropriate. If it is inappropriate, give a response that makes sense.**

1. Wie geht's?
Nein.
2. Wo wohnst du?
Da drüben.

3. Was machst du?
   Sie geht nach Hause.
4. Wie heißt er?
   Sie heißt Maria.
5. Guten Tag, Frau Meier.
   Gut.
6. Wohnen Sie in der Stadt?
   Ja.
7. Vier plus fünf ist...?
   Nein.
8. Wo ist deine Freundin?
   Hier.
9. Wie geht es Ihnen, Herr
   Schmidt?
   Nicht schlecht.
10. Heißt du Uwe?
    Ja, gut.

17. Beantworte diese Fragen!

1. Wie heißt dein Freund?
   Deine Freundin?
2. Wo wohnt er? Wo wohnen Sie?
3. Wie heißt du?
4. Wie geht's?
5. Ist es jetzt spät?
6. Was machst du jetzt?
7. Wieviel ist sieben plus drei?
8. Wieviel ist vierzehn minus neun?

Was machst du jetzt?

18. *Wie heißt das auf deutsch?* (What does this mean in German?)

1. What's your name?
2. Where do you live, Mr. Schmidt?
3. Is Angelika your friend?
4. Peter lives at the park.
5. Hello, Claudia!
6. I live downtown.
7. What does he say?
8. How are you, Mrs. Wieland?
9. Are you going home, Hartmut?
10. What are you doing now, Susanne?

Kulturecke 1

Greetings, Farewells and Introductions

The American greeting "Hello" and "Hi" have become almost international greetings these days, and many younger Germans use them when dealing with each other. Their own language, however, did not originally include such short, informal greetings. The normal German greeting is *"Guten Tag."* Often the first word is dropped, and you'll simply hear *"Tag"* or people just mumble *"'n Tag."* In southern Germany you will rarely hear *"Guten Tag"* but rather *"Grüß Gott."* Young people in that region will also greet each other with *"Grüß dich."* In Austria people often greet each other with *"Servus."* Many young people in Germany today are also greeting each other with a simple *"Hallo"* which is similar to our *"Hi."*

In the morning, most Germans greet each other with *"Guten Morgen,"* or simply *"Morgen"* whereas in the evening they say *"Guten Abend"* or again just mumble *"'n Abend."* When entering a town or city, the visitors are often greeted with a sign that says *"Willkommen."*

"Auf Wiedersehen" or simply *"Wiedersehen"* means "good-bye." *"Tschüs"*[*] is a very casual form of *"Wiedersehen,"* primarily used in northern Germany. It comes closest to the American "See you!" or "So long!" Ending a telephone conversation, most Germans say *"Auf Wiederhören"* or simply *"Wiederhören."* It means "Hope to hear you again," just as *"Auf Wiedersehen"* means "Hope to see you again." If a German says *"Bis bald!"* (until soon) or *"Bis dann!"* (until then), he or she usually has a specific time in mind. A German does not need to say "Good-bye, hope to see you again," because *"Auf Wiedersehen"* means exactly that.

On leaving a party at night, when Americans would say "Good night," most Germans will not say *"Gute Nacht"* but *"Auf Wiedersehen."* People living in the same house would say *"Gute Nacht."* And, of course, family members say it when they go to bed.

Germans do a lot more handshaking than Americans. Germans not only shake hands when being introduced, but many still consider a handshake as part of the everyday greeting. To a German, it means little more than saying "Hello." A nod of the head usually accompanies the handshake. When meeting acquaintances in the street, in shops or elsewhere in public, Germans usually shake hands only if they intend to have a little chat.

What do you say when introducing people to each other in Germany? You say *"Darf ich bekannt machen?"* or *"Darf ich vorstellen? — Frau Meier — Frau Schmidt."* The two shake hands, smile and say *"Guten Tag, Frau Meier"* and *"Guten Tag, Frau Schmidt"* to each other. A friendly nod of the head when shaking hands would be in order, too.

Americans who are used to saying "How are you?" when being introduced, may be tempted to say *"Wie geht es Ihnen?"* when being introduced to a German. This is not customary, however, unless you are at the doctor's office and he or she inquires about your health. *"Wie geht es Ihnen?"* or a short *"Wie geht's?"* is a greeting for someone you already know.

*The standard way of spelling *Tschüs* is with *s*. However, Germans will also spell it with *ss* (*Tschüss*) or with *ß* (*Tschüß*).

Was weißt du? (What do you know?) Complete each statement with the appropriate phrase or expression based on the *Kulturecke 1*.

1. "_____ " is a more formal good-bye form than "_____ ."
2. Parents will say "_____" when their children go to bed.
3. The standard greeting in the morning is "_____."
4. When finishing a telephone call, Germans will end it with either "_____" or with the more casual form "_____."
5. In southern Germany, people in the street will greet each other with "_____"; however, young people in that region will say "_____."
6. Germans saying "_____" or "_____" have a specific time in mind of when they will see each other again.
7. The normal German greeting during the day is "_____."
8. "_____" is the typical good-bye phrase.
9. Austrians will often greet one another with "_____."
10. When Germans greet each other in the evening, they will typically say "_____."

Wie heißt die Stadt?

Eine Familie sagt: „Guten Abend!"

Lektion 1

„Du" oder „Sie"?

Both words *du* and *Sie* mean "you." However, *du* is considered the informal mode of address. For Germans, there is nothing stiff about *Sie*. For instance, people may work in the same office for years and still call each other *Sie*, yet the atmosphere can be very friendly and pleasant. So, who calls each other *du*? Primarily blue-collar workers, students and military personnel or police officers say *du* to each other.

In social life, people you know well — called *Bekannte* (acquaintances) — are addressed with *Sie*, while close, personal friends — called *Freunde* — are addressed with *du*. Young people, too, quickly tend to use the *du* form among each other.

Family members always say *du* to each other. Children are always addressed with *du* until mid-adolescence. Among each other, children use the *du* form as well. The *du* form is also used in prayers and church services. Finally, you always address animals with *du*.

***"Du" oder "Sie"?* Indicate which form you as a student in Germany would use if you were to talk to the following.**

1. an acquaintance
2. your doctor
3. a police officer
4. your friend
5. your father or mother
6. a teacher
7. a six-year-old child
8. your cat
9. your aunt
10. your friend's uncle

"Bekannte" are addressed with "Sie."

Friends call each other "du."

Vokabeln

ander(e) other, different
auch also, too
ausgezeichnet excellent
beim (or: bei dem) at, near
  beim Park near the park
da there
  da drüben over there
dein(e) your
dort there
  dort drüben over there
die Ecke,-n corner
es it
die Frau,-en Mrs., woman
der Freund,-e boyfriend
die Freundin,-nen girlfriend
früh early
ganz quite
gehen to go
  Wie geht's? How are you? (familiar)

Wie geht es Ihnen? How are you? (formal)
genau exact(ly)
gleich immediately, right away
  gleich um die Ecke right around the corner
gut good, well, OK
das Haus,-er house
  nach Hause gehen to go home
der Herr,-en Mr., gentleman
hier here
ihr you (familiar plural)
in in
ja yes
jetzt now
machen to do, make
nein no
nicht not
noch still, yet

der Park,-s park
sagen to say
schlecht bad
schon already
schön beautiful, nice
sehr very
so so
spät late
die Stadt,-e city
  in der Stadt downtown
um around, at
  um die Ecke around the corner
und and
vielleicht perhaps
von from
was what
weit far
wir we
wo where
wohnen to live

Wie geht's?

Was macht ihr denn hier?

Wohin gehen sie?

2

Communicative Functions

- answering and talking on the phone
- talking about what to do
- telling the days of the week
- counting from 10 to 1,000
- telling time

Zu Hause

(am Telefon)

Tina:　　Tina Schiller.
Steffie:　Tag, Tina. Hier ist Steffie. Hast du Zeit?
Tina:　　Warum fragst du?
Steffie:　Rolf kommt um sieben. Er bringt viele Kassetten mit.
Tina:　　Gut. Ich komme auch.
Steffie:　Gut, bis dann.

Falsch! The following statements are incorrect. Provide correct statements in German.

1. Tina ist in der Stadt.
2. Ein Mädchen heißt Steffie Schiller.
3. Tina bringt Kassetten mit.
4. Rolf kommt um vier.
5. Tina kommt nicht.

(bei Steffie)

Rolf:　　Ich habe Kassetten und CDs.
Steffie:　Wir hören lieber Kassetten.
Rolf:　　Du, die Rockmusik hier ist toll.
Steffie:　Die Wildcat Band ist besser.
Rolf:　　Na, dann spiel sie mal!
Steffie:　Einen Moment. Tina ist hier.

Wer sagt was? Correct each statement identifying who said what. *Auf deutsch, bitte!*

1. Rolf sagt: „Ich höre lieber CDs."
2. Tina sagt: „Steffie ist hier."
3. Rolf sagt: „Die Wildcat Band ist besser."
4. Steffie sagt: „Ich habe Kassetten."
5. Steffie sagt: „Spiel die Wildcat Band."

(später)

Tina:　　Schon neun Uhr. Ich muß nach Hause.
Rolf:　　Ich auch.
Steffie:　Wir schreiben morgen eine Arbeit.
Tina:　　Keine Angst! Die ist leicht.
Steffie:　Das sagst du immer.
Rolf:　　Sie ist eben klug.

Ich komme auch.

Gut, bis dann.

Die Rockmusik hier ist toll.

Ja oder nein? Agree or disagree with the following statements by giving complete sentences starting with *Ja,...* or *Nein,...*

1. Es ist schon acht Uhr.
2. Rolf, Steffie und Tina schreiben morgen eine Arbeit.
3. Tina sagt: „Die Arbeit ist nicht leicht."
4. Steffie sagt: „Ich muß nach Hause."
5. Tina ist klug.

Was fehlt hier? Complete the following paragraph by providing the missing items based on the previous conversations.

Tina ist zu _____. Sie ist am _____. Steffie fragt: „_____ du Zeit?" Rolf kommt _____ sieben Uhr. Er sagt: „Ich habe _____ und _____. Steffie _____ lieber Kassetten. Die Rockmusik ist _____. Die Wildcat Band ist _____. Tina sagt um _____ Uhr: „Ich muß _____ Hause." Tina, Rolf und Steffie _____ morgen eine Arbeit. Tina sagt: „Die Arbeit ist _____." Tina ist _____.

Steffie hört lieber Kassetten.

Es ist schon zehn vor zwölf.

Nein, Monika ist nicht zu Hause.

Für dich

When Germans answer the phone, they usually will identify themselves by their last and/or first names.

In conversational exchanges, the main verb following a helping (auxiliary) verb (must, should, etc.) can sometimes be dropped and the meaning is perfectly clear. Example: *Ich muß nach Hause (gehen).*

Germans can express future time using the present tense. Example: *Wir schreiben morgen eine Arbeit.* (We'll take a test tomorrow.)

Kombiniere...

Ich muß nach Hause.

How many sentences can you make using the following words in various combinations?

Wir	hört	klug
Helmut	schreiben	CDs
Sofie	haben	ein Mädchen
	ist	eine Arbeit
		Rockmusik
		Kassetten
		hier

Nützliche Ausdrücke

Hast du Zeit?	Do you have time?
Hörst du lieber CDs?	Do you prefer to listen to CDs?
Ich bringe Kassetten mit.	I'll bring cassettes along.
Die Rockmusik ist toll.	The rock music is great.
Na, spiel sie mal!	Well, why don't you play it.
Einen Moment.	Just a moment.
Ich muß nach Hause.	I have to go home.
Ich auch.	Me too.
Keine Angst!	Don't worry! Don't be afraid!

Was paßt hier? (What fits here.) Match each appropriate expression on the left with the best expression on the right.

1. Schreibt sie eine Arbeit?	a. So spät?
2. Hast du jetzt Zeit?	b. Ja, morgen.
3. Kommst du morgen?	c. Rockmusik.
4. Was hörst du?	d. Nein, es ist schon spät.
5. Gisela ist klug.	e. Ja, Erika auch.
6. Es ist schon zehn.	f. Ja, um zehn Uhr.

Ergänzung

Café

Uhren

Montag

Dienstag

Mittwoch

Donnerstag

Freitag

Sonnabend
(Samstag)

Sonntag

Welcher Tag ist heute? Heute ist Montag. Welcher Tag ist morgen? Morgen ist Dienstag.

Wieviel Uhr ist es? (Wie spät ist es?)

Es ist eins. Es ist ein Uhr.

Es ist zwölf. Es ist zwölf Uhr.

Es ist vier. Es ist vier Uhr.

Es ist sieben. Es ist sieben Uhr.

Es ist zehn. Es ist zehn Uhr.

10 zehn	**20** zwanzig	**30** dreißig	**40** vierzig
50 fünfzig	**60** sechzig	**70** siebzig	**80** achtzig
90 neunzig	**100** hundert einhundert	**1000** tausend eintausend	

21 einundzwanzig   **22** zweiundzwanzig

23 dreiundzwanzig   **24** vierundzwanzig

41

1. *Welcher Tag ist morgen? Beantworte diese Fragen!*

   ❐ Heute ist Freitag. Und morgen?
      Morgen ist Sonnabend.

      1. Heute ist Donnerstag.
         Und morgen?
      2. Heute ist Dienstag.
         Und morgen?
      3. Heute ist Samstag.
         Und morgen?
      4. Heute ist Mittwoch.
         Und morgen?
      5. Heute ist Sonntag.
         Und morgen?

2. **Imagine you are working in an office and, throughout the day, several people want to verify the time as they don't have a watch. Try to help them.**

   ❐ Ist es zwei Uhr?
      Ja, es ist schon zwei.

      1. Ist es vier Uhr?
      2. Ist es acht Uhr?
      3. Ist es ein Uhr?
      4. Ist es zwölf Uhr?
      5. Ist es sieben Uhr?

3. *Um wieviel Uhr...?* **Pretend you are in charge of social activities. Various members of your club ask you questions pertaining to time. Give them the proper information.**

   ❐ Um wieviel Uhr geht Paul nach Hause? (acht Uhr)
      Er geht um acht Uhr nach Hause.

      1. Um wieviel Uhr hat Heidi Zeit? (vier Uhr)
      2. Um wieviel Uhr geht Rudi nach Hause? (zehn Uhr)
      3. Um wieviel Uhr hören wir die Musik? (drei Uhr)
      4. Um wieviel Uhr kommen Lisa und Rolf? (zwölf Uhr)
      5. Um wieviel Uhr bringt Gabi die CDs? (sechs Uhr)

Sag's mal!

Wie ist die Rockmusik?

phantastisch

spitze super

miserabel

schlecht gut

echt gut

nicht sehr interessant

soso

toll langweilig

sehr gut klasse zu laut nicht besonders

Aussprache

short /i/	long /i/
ich	sie
mit	wieviel
bist	hier
in	wir
nicht	vier
ist	Ihnen
Christa	Tina
immer	sieben

Wie spät ist es?

Was machen sie?

Übungen

Formation of Questions

To form a question you must use the so-called inverted word order. The subject and the verb of the sentence are interchanged.

Statement: Du kommst morgen. You are coming tomorrow.
Question: Kommst du morgen? Are you coming tomorrow?

Beispiele: *Wohnt Herr Müller in* Does Mr. Müller live downtown?
der Stadt?
Haben wir jetzt Zeit? Do we have time now?
Hören Sie Kassetten? Do you listen to cassettes?

You can readily see that the formation of questions in German is simpler than in English where most questions use a form of "to do" (do you?, does he?, etc.).

The inverted word order is also used with such question words as those listed below:

Wie? (how)   *Wie spät ist es?* (How late is it?)
Wo? (where)   *Wo wohnst du?* (Where do you live?)
Was? (what)   *Was macht Daniela jetzt?* (What is Daniela doing now?)
Wer? (who)   *Wer spielt Rockmusik?* (Who is playing rock music?)
Wieviel? (how much) *Wieviel ist drei plus vier?* (How much is three plus four?)

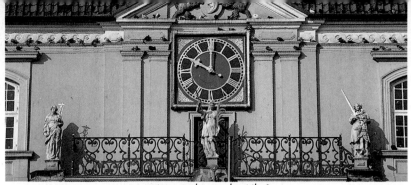

Ist es schon zehn Uhr?

4. Hartmut is quite inquisitive. He is asking you lots of questions which you answer affirmatively.

❑ Ist es schon vier Uhr?
Ja, es ist schon vier Uhr.

1. Hörst du lieber Rockmusik?
2. Heißt sie Heidi?
3. Kommt Holger morgen?
4. Bringst du Kassetten?
5. Ist Gisela klug?
6. Schreibt ihr eine Arbeit?

5. Ask questions about the italicized items.

❑ Er heißt *Holger*.
Wie heißt er?

1. Die Rockmusik ist *toll*.
2. *Peter* kommt spät.
3. Monika ist *zu Hause*.
4. Ich spiele lieber *Kassetten*.
5. Wir schreiben heute *eine Arbeit*.
6. Fünf plus acht ist *dreizehn*.
7. Sie heißt *Marianne*.
8. Tina ist *hier*.

6. Your friend makes a statement. You want to know who else is also involved.

❑ Ich komme. (Peter)
Kommt Peter auch?

1. Ich bringe viele Kassetten. (ihr)
2. Ich höre Rockmusik. (du)
3. Ich wohne in der Stadt. (Claudia)
4. Ich schreibe eine Arbeit. (wir)
5. Ich komme um acht. (er)

Ist Gabi in der Stadt?

7. You are confronted with several questions all of which you answer affirmatively.

❏ Kommst du nach Hause?
   Ja, ich komme nach Hause.

1. Ist Gabi in der Stadt?
2. Wohnst du beim Park?
3. Heißt er Paul?
4. Ist es schon spät?
5. Spielst du Kassetten?
6. Hörst du Rockmusik?
7. Ist Tina klug?
8. Sagst du das?

8. *Wie? Wo? Was? Wer?* oder *Wieviel?*

1. _____ wohnt Herr Schulz?
2. _____ Uhr ist es?
3. _____ kommt?
4. _____ heißt der Junge?
5. _____ ist die Stadt?
6. _____ sagt das?
7. _____ hören Sie?
8. _____ fragt?
9. _____ geht's?
10. _____ macht ihr jetzt?

9. Change each statement to a question.

1. Heute ist Freitag.
2. Holger und Tina kommen.
3. Wir hören Rockmusik.
4. Ihr schreibt eine Arbeit.
5. Du kommst um vier.
6. Heike spielt Kassetten.
7. Sie gehen früh nach Hause, Frau Hoffmann.
8. Er wohnt beim Park.

10. Beantworte diese Fragen!

1. Wieviel Uhr ist es jetzt?
2. Welcher Tag ist heute? Und morgen?
3. Hast du Zeit? Ja,...
4. Wer ist klug?
5. Was hörst du gern?
6. Wer bringt die Kassetten?

Present Tense of *haben* (to have)

Although most verbs show the regular pattern of conjugation (stem + ending), there are several verbs that do not follow this pattern, as in the case with *haben*.

Singular	ich habe	I have
	du hast	you have
	er	he has
	sie } hat	she has
	es	it has
Plural	wir haben	we have
	ihr habt	you have
	sie haben	they have
	Sie haben (sg. & pl.)	you have

Beispiele: *Hast du Zeit?* Do you have time?
Ja, ich habe Zeit. Yes, I have time.
Habt ihr Kassetten zu Hause? Do you have cassettes at home?
Ja, wir haben viele. Yes, we have many.

11. You are agreeing with Peter on several items.

❑ Ich habe viele Kassetten. Und du?
Ich habe auch viele Kassetten.

1. Ich habe Zeit. Und du?
2. Ich habe CDs. Und du?
3. Ich habe Angst. Und du?
4. Ich habe eine Arbeit. Und du?
5. Ich habe eine Freundin. Und du?
6. Ich habe ein Telefon. Und du?

12. *Wer hat heute Zeit?* **You are inquiring who has some time today. Luckily, everyone does.**

❐ Haben Sie heute Zeit, Herr Holz?
   Ja, ich habe heute Zeit.

1. Hast du heute Zeit?
2. Habt ihr heute Zeit?
3. Haben Monika und Maria heute Zeit?
4. Hat Dirk heute Zeit?
5. Hat Frau Werner heute Zeit?

13. Provide the correct form of *haben*.

1. _____ ihr Kassetten?
2. Wir _____ ein Telefon.
3. _____ Sie Rockmusik lieber?
4. Ich _____ keine Angst.
5. _____ du morgen Zeit?
6. Daniela _____ eine Freundin.

Hast du Rockmusik lieber?

The Definite Article (Nominative Singular): *der, die, das* (the)

In German there are three variations of the definite article in the nominative singular, i.e. *der*, *die* and *das*. The nominative is used to identify the subject.

Beispiele: Der Tag ist so schön. The day is so beautiful.
Die Arbeit ist leicht. The work (test) is easy.
Das Telefon ist da drüben. The telephone is over there.

It is extremely important to learn these articles that accompany the individual nouns. We refer to these as masculine (*der*), feminine (*die*) and neuter (*das*). Be aware, however, that the nouns associated with either of the three articles are not necessarily "masculine" or "feminine" or "neuter" by context — i.e., the article for a man's tie (*die Krawatte*) is feminine.

Singular		
masculine	feminine	neuter
nominative der	die	das

14. *der, die oder das?*

❏ Uhr
   die Uhr

   1. Junge
   2. Tag
   3. Park
   4. Stadt
   5. Freund
   6. Mädchen
   7. Ecke
   8. Herr
   9. Telefon
   10. Freundin

die Uhr

15. *Was fehlt hier?* **Supply the proper definite article.**

1. Wo ist _____ Park?
2. Wie heißt _____ Mädchen?
3. _____ Frau wohnt um die Ecke.
4. _____ Telefon ist hier.
5. Wie ist _____ Kassette?
6. Wer ist _____ Junge?
7. Wie ist _____ Rockmusik?
8. Ist _____ Arbeit leicht?
9. _____ Stadt ist schön.
10. Kommt _____ Herr spät?

zu Hause and *nach Hause*

There is a distinct difference in using these two phrases. *Zu Hause* means "at home" (location), whereas *nach Hause* has the meaning "(going) home" (motion).

Beispiele: *Wo ist Heidi?* Where is Heidi?
Sie ist zu Hause? She is at home.

Wohin geht Uwe? Where is Uwe going?
Er geht nach Hause. He is going home.

16. *"zu Hause"* oder *"nach Hause"*? **Are the various people at home (*zu Hause*) or are they going home (*nach Hause*)?**

1. Um wieviel Uhr gehen Sie _____, Herr Lehmann?
2. Heike ist nicht _____.
3. Hast du Kassetten _____?
4. Maria kommt spät _____.
5. Er ist schon früh _____.
6. Ich muß jetzt _____.

Cognates

Words that look alike in German and English and have the same meaning are called *cognates*. Although you can look them up in the vocabulary section, you won't have any problem identifying the meaning of a cognate. Here are some examples of cognates:

Telefon	Diskothek	Bus	Radio	Butter
Jeans	Sweater	Kassette	Auto	Englisch

Katrin und Renate gehen nach Hause

Katrin und Renate wohnen in Jever. Jever ist eine Stadt in Norddeutschland°. Heute ist Sonnabend. Es ist zehn Uhr. Katrin und Renate haben heute viel° Zeit. Da kommt Susanne, Katrins und Renates Freundin.

northern Germany

much

Susanne:	Tag, Katrin. Hallo, Renate.
Katrin:	Was machst du denn hier?
Susanne:	Ich kaufe° ein paar° Kassetten. Sie sind° heute sehr billig°.
Renate:	Kassetten? Du hast aber° schon so viele.
Susanne:	So viele habe ich nicht. Wohin° geht ihr?
Katrin:	Nach Hause. Susanne, ist das Sweatshirt nicht schön?
Susanne:	Und es ist so schick°.
Katrin:	Bis bald.
Susanne:	Vielleicht komme ich später zu dir°.
Katrin:	Bring die Kassetten mit.
Susanne:	Bestimmt°. Tschüs.

I'm buying/a few/ are/cheap

but

where (to)

chic

you (form of du)

definitely

Das Sweatshirt ist sehr schick.

Katrin und Renate sind in der Stadt.

Tag, Katrin. Hallo, Renate.

Was hat Susanne da?

Susanne, Katrin und Renate wohnen in Jever.

Was paßt hier? Complete these sentences by using the words on the right.

1. Heute ist	a. viel Zeit
2. Susanne kauft	b. nach Hause
3. Jever ist	c. schön
4. Katrin ist	d. in Jever
5. Das Sweatshirt ist	e. eine Stadt
6. Die drei Mädchen wohnen	f. ein paar Kassetten
7. Susanne und Renate haben	g. Susannes Freundin
8. Katrin geht	h. Sonnabend

Fragen

1. Wo wohnt Katrin?
2. Welcher Tag ist heute?
3. Wie heißt Katrins und Renates Freundin?
4. Was macht Susanne in der Stadt?
5. Hat sie Kassetten zu Hause?
6. Was ist sehr schick?

Übung macht den Meister!

1. Pretend you are calling your friend. Ask your friend if he/she has cassettes. Your friend tells you that he or she doesn't have many. You mention that you'll buy two or three and that you'll be over at five o'clock.

2. Count from 1 to 50, first counting the odd numbers only and then the even numbers. Try it backwards, too.

3. Ask your classmates what kind of music they like to listen to and how the music is. *Was hörst du gern? Wie ist die Musik?*

Jever ist eine Stadt in Norddeutschland.

Wohin muß Katrin gehen?

Was ist deine Telefonnummer?

Erweiterung

17. *Was ist deine Telefonnummer?* You are meeting several young people from Germany and would like to have their phone numbers. They give you their numbers. Can you say them in German?

    1. 7 13 05
    2. 60 24 19
    3. 9 03 31 82
    4. 12 52 77
    5. 3 22 38
    6. 5 09 83 11

18. *Was fehlt hier?*

elf, _____, dreizehn, vierzehn, _____. sechzehn, _____, achtzehn, neunzehn, _____

Montag, _____, Mittwoch, _____, Freitag, Sonnabend, _____

vier, _____, zwölf, sechzehn, _____, _____ achtundzwanzig, zweiunddreißig, _____, vierzig

19. *Wieviel Uhr ist es?* Give a complete sentence for an answer.

    ❐ 3:00
        Es ist drei Uhr.

    1. 9:00
    2. 1:00
    3. 12:00
    4. 7:00
    5. 10:00
    6. 5:00

20. You are meeting Silke, an acquaintance of yours, in the school cafeteria after school. Respond to Silke based on the information given.

Silke:	Grüß Gott!
Du:	_____
Silke:	Was machst du hier?
Du:	_____
Silke	Wie spät ist es?
Du:	_____
Silke:	Schon so spät?
Du:	_____
Silke:	Ich muß nach Hause.
Du:	_____

21. *Was fehlt hier?* Use one of the words from the list below to complete each sentence.

Kassette	Stadt
hast	sehr
ist	vielleicht
viele	macht

1. Wo _____ Bernd?
2. Er ist in der _____.
3. Was _____ er dort?
4. Er kauft vielleicht eine _____.
5. Sie ist heute _____ billig.
6. Du _____ bestimmt auch Kassetten.
7. Ja, _____ fünfzig oder sechzig.
8. So _____?

22. *Wieviel Uhr ist es?* A number of people don't have a watch. They are asking you for the time. Respond to them by using the cues given.

❏ Wieviel Uhr ist es? (zehn)
  Es ist zehn.

1. Wieviel Uhr ist es? (acht)
2. Wieviel Uhr ist es? (zwölf)
3. Wieviel Uhr ist es? (fünf)
4. Wieviel Uhr ist es? (zwei)
5. Wieviel Uhr ist es? (neun)

23. *Das ist falsch.* **Your cousin's younger brother has difficulties with simple addition and subtraction problems. You help him solve each problem.**

❏   Drei plus vier ist sechs.
     Falsch. Drei plus vier ist sieben.

1. Neun plus drei ist fünf.
2. Zehn minus acht ist null.
3. Zwanzig minus neun ist zehn.
4. Vierzehn plus drei ist dreizehn.
5. Elf plus zwei ist fünfzehn.

24. *Beantworte diese Fragen!* **Use the cues provided in your answers.**

1. Was kaufst du?
   (vier Kassetten)
2. Was macht ihr um drei Uhr?
   (nach Hause gehen)
3. Um wieviel Uhr kommt Peter?
   (zwei Uhr)
4. Was schreibt ihr?
   (eine Arbeit)
5. Was ist heute billig?
   (das Sweatshirt)

Wieviel Uhr ist es in Bremen, in New York und in Moskau?

Um wieviel Uhr kommst du?

Sprachspiegel

25. Imagine that Volker has just moved into your neighborhood. You meet him for the first time and want to get to know him. State how Volker might respond to you.

Du:	Du heißt Volker?
Volker:	_____
Du:	Wie heißt deine Freundin?
Volker:	_____
Du:	Hast du jetzt Zeit?
Volker:	_____
Du:	So früh?
Volker:	_____
Du:	Bis später.
Volker:	_____

26. Wie heißt das auf deutsch?

1. The music is great.
2. Which day is today?
3. I like to listen to music.
4. We are taking a test today.
5. Is the sweatshirt beautiful?
6. Do you have many cassettes?
7. What's your girlfriend's name?
8. What is he doing at home?

Zungenbrecher (Tongue Twister)

Fritz fischt frische Fische.

(Fritz catches fresh fish.)

Kulturecke 1

What Time Is It?

In ancient times, people were just as interested in determining the time of the day as we are today. Different methods and devices such as a sundial were used. Today, of course, we have a more sophisticated way of telling time, not only in our country but all over the world.

One of the most important phrases to know in any language is "What time is it?" In Germany, you will find many clocks that will answer your question immediately. However, sometimes you will need to ask someone for the time. The most common ways to ask the time are *"Wieviel Uhr ist es?"* or *"Wie spät ist es?"* Here are some examples of expressing time in German:

10:00 = Es ist zehn Uhr.
8:00 = Es ist acht.
3:30 = Es ist drei Uhr dreißig. or: Es ist halb vier.
11:30 = Es ist elf Uhr dreißig. or: Es ist halb zwölf.
9:15 = Es ist neun Uhr fünfzehn. or: Es ist Viertel nach neun. or: Es ist ein Viertel zehn.
12:45 = Es ist zwölf Uhr fünfundvierzig. or: Es ist Viertel vor eins. or: Es ist drei Viertel eins.
7:10 = Es ist sieben Uhr zehn. or: Es ist zehn Minuten nach sieben Uhr. or *simply*: Es ist zehn nach sieben.
11:55 = Es ist elf Uhr fünfundfünfzig. or: Es ist fünf vor zwölf.
4:40 = Es ist vier Uhr vierzig. or: Es ist zwanzig vor fünf.
10:20 = Es ist zehn Uhr zwanzig. or: Es ist zwanzig Minuten nach zehn. or: Es ist zehn Minuten vor halb elf.
9:35 = Es ist neun Uhr fünfunddreißig. or: Es ist fünf Minuten nach halb zehn.

Germans do not use the A.M./P.M. system. The traveler will have to become familiar with the 24-hour system in a hurry, particularly when dealing with the official language used on radio and TV or at train stations and airports. The 24-hour system is used primarily to avoid misunderstandings. There is no problem with the numbers 1 to 12, as they designate the A.M. period of time. Figures 13 to 24 indicate the hours that we call *P.M.* A train leaving at 2:21 P.M., for instance, would be announced as *14.21 (vierzehn Uhr einundzwanzig).*

In everyday conversation, Germans often use the time expressions *morgens*, *nachmittags*, and *abends* to avoid misunderstanding. For example, Germans might tell their friends that they are coming to visit them at 8 P.M. by saying, *"Wir kommen um acht Uhr abends."*

Wieviel Uhr ist es? Complete each time expression by providing the missing words.

1. 12:38 = Es ist zwölf Uhr _____.
2. 6:30 = Es ist _____ sieben.
3. 2:52 = Es ist _____ Minuten vor drei.
4. 9:00 = Es ist _____ Uhr.
5. 10:45 = Es ist _____ vor elf.
6. 4:10 = Es ist _____ nach vier.
7. 1:18 = Es ist ein Uhr _____.
8. 7:35 = Es ist _____ Minuten nach halb acht.

Wieviel Uhr ist es jetzt? (Lüneburg)

Um wieviel Uhr ist die nächste Abfahrt? (Boppard)

Kulturecke 2

The Telephone

When answering the phone, whether at home or in the office, it is customary in Germany to give one's family name (*Weber!* or *Hier Weber!*). Young people usually answer the phone with their first and last name.

When calling someone you know, you would say, "*Hier ist...*" If you don't know the person, you should start out with, "*Mein Name ist...*"

Asking to be transferred to someone else, the caller may say, for instance, "*Guten Tag, hier ist Weber. Ich möchte Frau Müller sprechen, bitte!*" (Hello, here is Weber. I would like to speak with Mrs. Müller, please) or "*Könnte ich bitte Frau Müller sprechen?*" (Could I speak with Mrs. Müller, please?) or "*Bitte verbinden Sie mich mit Frau Müller*" (Please connect me with Mrs. Müller).

Company operators often answer calls with an additional "*Guten Tag*" or "*Grüß Gott.*" When transferring a call they will say, "*Moment (Augenblick), bitte*" (Just a moment, please) or "*ich verbinde*" (I'll connect you).

der Fernsprecher

Hier ist Susanne.

Könnte ich bitte Herrn Meier sprechen?

das Telefon

Da sind viele Telefonzellen. (München)

The official word for telephone is *Fernsprecher*, but everyone says *Telefon*. The word for phone booth is *die Telefonzelle*. These public phone booths are easily recognized by their bright yellow color. There are always public phones in local post offices and railroad stations and nowadays even in trains.

Most phones have dialing instructions clearly posted. In calling you should follow these steps:

1. Lift the receiver.
2. Put your coins in the slot (three 10 pfennig coins for local calls).
3. Wait for the dial tone.
4. Dial the number.

Long-distance calls to other German cities or foreign countries can be made from any phone marked "*Ausland*." Of course, these calls can be made from any post office, hotel or private phone. If you place a long-distance call, you should know the *Vorwahl* or *Vorwahlnummer* (area code). In case you don't know this number, you can either look it up in a telephone directory or call the *Auskunft* (information). The number for the *Auskunft* is: 0 11 18 (national) or 0 01 18 (international).

Long-distance calls are measured by pay units (*1 Einheit = 23 Pfennig*) and time. For instance, a person from Munich may call her mother in Hamburg for 1 mark but she can talk to her only for a very short time. If she calls someone in Stuttgart, she can talk longer because Stuttgart is not as far from Munich as Hamburg. The caller must feed the coin-operated phone with additional coins, whenever there is little money left as indicated by lit-up numbers on the telephone coin box; otherwise the caller will be disconnected immediately.

Was weißt du? Match the German words or expressions on the left with their English equivalent meaning on the right.

_____ 1. Ich verbinde.	a. telephone
_____ 2. Auskunft	b. foreign country
_____ 3. Einheit	c. phone booth
_____ 4. Fernsprecher	d. unit
_____ 5. Ausland	e. area code
_____ 6. Ich möchte mit...sprechen.	f. I would like to speak with...
_____ 7. Verbinden Sie mich mit...	g. I'll connect you.
_____ 8. Vorwahl	h. Connect me with...
_____ 9. Telefonzelle	i. information
_____ 10. Augenblick	j. Just a moment.

Vokabeln

aber but
am (or: **an dem**) at the, on the
die **Angst,-e** fear
    Keine Angst! Don't worry! Don't be afraid!
die **Arbeit,-en** work, test
    eine Arbeit schreiben to take a test
bald soon
besser better
bestimmt definitely, for sure
billig cheap, inexpensive
bis until
die **CD,-s** CD, compact disk
dann then
denn used for emphasis
der **Dienstag,-e** Tuesday
der **Donnerstag,-e** Thursday
eben just
fragen to ask
der **Freitag,-e** Friday
gern gladly, with pleasure
    gern hören to like (enjoy) listening to

haben to have
heute today
hören to hear, listen to
hundert hundred
immer always
die **Kassette,-n** cassette
kaufen to buy
kein(e) no
klug smart, intelligent
kommen to come
leicht easy
lieber rather
mitbringen to bring along
der **Mittwoch,-e** Wednesday
der **Moment,-e** moment
der **Montag,-e** Monday
morgen tomorrow
die **Musik** music
muß (form of **müssen**) to have to, must
na well
paar: ein paar a few
die **Rockmusik** rock music
der **Samstag,-e** Saturday
schick chic, fashionable
schreiben to write
der **Sonnabend,-e** Saturday
der **Sonntag,-e** Sunday

spielen to play
das **Sweatshirt,-s** sweatshirt
tausend thousand
das **Telefon,-e** telephone
toll great, terrific, smashing
die **Uhr,-en** clock, watch
    um neun Uhr at nine o'clock
viel much
viele many
warum why
welcher which
wohin where (to)
die **Zeit,-en** time
zu at, to, too

Was sagt er am Telefon?

Wer ist in der Telefonzelle?

Communicative Functions

- naming classroom objects
- talking about school subjects and grades
- telling time
- talking about others
- discussing what to do after school
- describing your classroom schedule

Zur Schule

Jens: Kennst du Jürgen?
Sven: Ist der neu hier?
Jens: Ja, er kommt aus Köln. Ganz sportlich und auch intelligent.
Sven: Du weißt aber viel.

Fragen

1. Kennt Jens Jürgen?
2. Kommt er aus Hamburg?
3. Ist Jürgen klug?

Sven: Die Aufgaben sind wieder sehr schwer.
Jens: Für Englisch oder Mathe?
Sven: Die Englischaufgaben. Hier auf Seite 89.
Jens: Englisch ist doch leicht.
Sven: Du bist ja auch ein Genie.

Wohin gehen Sven und Jens?

Sven

Jens

66

Fragen

1. Ist Englisch für Sven leicht?
2. Und für Jens?
3. Wo sind die Englischaufgaben?

Jens: Schon fünf vor acht. Jetzt schnell!
Sven: Immer langsam! Herr Erhard ist nie pünktlich.
Jens: Heute schreiben wir aber eine Arbeit.
Sven: Stimmt. Dann mal los!

Fragen

1. Wieviel Uhr ist es?
2. Wer ist nie pünktlich?
3. Was schreiben sie heute?

Richtig oder falsch? **Determine whether or not the following statements are correct or incorrect. If they are incorrect, provide a correct statement in German.**

1. Jens kennt Jürgen.
2. Jürgen kommt aus Norddeutschland.
3. Jürgen ist sportlich.
4. Die Matheaufgaben sind auf Seite 89.
5. Jens ist in Englisch sehr klug.
6. Es ist schon acht vor fünf.
7. Herr Erhard ist immer pünktlich.

Sind die Aufgaben schwer?

Jetzt schnell!

Once a person or an object has been mentioned and it is clear who or what is meant, Germans will often use *der* or *die* indicating a person or an object. Example: *Kennst du Jürgen? Ist der neu hier?* (Do you know Jürgen? Is he new here?) or: *Ich habe eine Kassette. Wo ist die?* (I have a cassette. Where is it?)

Kombiniere...

How many sentences can you make using the following words in various combinations? Choose one word or phrase from each column.

Jens und Stefan	haben	heute	fünfzehn
Herr Leber	ist	jetzt	viel Zeit
Ich	habe	nie	pünktlich
Steffie	bin	morgen	eine Arbeit
Wir	kommt		nicht
	schreiben		

Nützliche Ausdrücke

Kennst du...?	Do you know...? (person/place)
Weißt du...?	Do you know...? (fact)
Kommst du aus...?	Do you come from...?
Jetzt schnell!	Let's hurry!
Immer langsam!	Take it easy!
Dann mal los!	Then, let's go!

Was fehlt hier? Complete each sentence with an appropriate word from the list below.

sportlich	pünktlich	Mathe	Uhr	neun
aus	viel	alt	neu	Herr

1. Claudia ist nie _____.
2. Haben wir am Montag _____?
3. Alex ist klug und auch _____.

4. Es ist schon zwölf vor _____.
5. Kommen Sie _____ Köln?
6. Ich bin _____ hier.
7. Sie hat _____ Zeit.
8. Wo wohnt _____ Müller?
9. Wie _____ ist sie? Sechzehn.
10. Wieviel _____ ist es?

Sie lesen die Aufgaben.

Wo sind die Schüler?

Die Schüler kommen aus der Schule.

71

1. *Was hast du heute?* **Beantworte die Fragen!**

❒ Bio / Mathe
Ich habe heute Bio und Mathe.

    1. Deutsch / Englisch
    2. Physik / Mathe
    3. Sport / Musik
    4. Religion / Chemie
    5. Bio / Geschichte
    6. Erdkunde / Kunst

2. *Was ist dein Lieblingsfach?* **Pretend that your favorite subjects are those listed.**

❒ Musik
Mein Lieblingsfach ist Musik.

    1. Kunst
    2. Sport
    3. Deutsch
    4. Chemie
    5. Erdkunde

3. *Was für Noten bekommen sie in...?* **Tell what grades these students are getting in different subjects.**

❒ Sofie / Mathe / zwei
Sofie bekommt in Mathe eine Zwei.

1. Ingo / Deutsch / vier
2. Tina / Englisch / drei
3. Wolfgang und Peter / Chemie / eins
4. Petra / Biologie / zwei
5. Daniel / Religion / zwei
6. Steffie und Jürgen / Erdkunde / drei

Sag's mal!

Wie ist er/sie? Er/Sie ist...

alt ruhig langweilig musikalisch intelligent dumm sportlich freundlich klug jung nett

Aussprache

short /o/	long /o/
noch	groß
von	wo
toll	wohnen
kommst	Montag
Sonntag	schon
dort	vor
sportlich	Note
voll	woher
dort	ohne

Übungen

The Definite Article (Accusative Singular)

In the sentence *Ich frage den Lehrer* (I ask the teacher) *Ich* is called the subject (nominative), *frage* the verb, and *den Lehrer* the direct object (accusative) of the sentence.

Beispiele: Kaufst du den Bleistift?
Ich frage die Lehrerin.
Wir haben das Buch.

Singular			
	masculine	**feminine**	**neuter**
nominative	der	die	das
accusative	den	die	das

From the chart above, you can see that the *die* and *das* articles do not change in the accusative and that *der* changes to *den*.

An *n* is added to certain masculine nouns when they are direct objects (accusative). You know two of these nouns so far: *der Herr, der Junge.*

Beispiele: *Kennst du Herrn Meister?*   Do you know Mr. Meister?
Ich frage den Jungen.   I'm asking the boy.

In informal conversations, names are often preceded by a form of *der* or *die.*

Beispiele: *Kennst du den Peter?*   Do you know Peter?
Fragen Sie doch die Heike.   Why don't you ask Heike.

4. You always seem to misplace some items. Ask where each one is.

Wo ist das Buch?

1.   2.   3.   4.   5.   6.

5. Beantworte die Fragen!

❐ Wo ist die Stadt? (in Deutschland)
  Die Stadt ist in Deutschland.

1. Wo ist die Karte? (da drüben)
2. Wo ist die Aufgabe? (hier)
3. Wo ist der Park? (um die Ecke)
4. Wo ist die Schule? (in der Stadt)
5. Wo ist das Heft? (dort)

6. *Was kaufst du?* **Your sister or brother is asking you what you are buying. Respond to her or him.**

❐ Ich kaufe den Computer.

7. Supply the correct form of the definite article (*der, die, das* or *den*).

1. _____ Lehrerin kommt pünktlich.
2. _____ Mädchen heißt Angelika.
3. Kaufst du _____ Buch?
4. Kennt ihr _____ Lehrer?
5. Haben Sie _____ Kreide?
6. _____ Sweatshirt ist billig.
7. Bekommst du _____ Note?
8. Wir fragen _____ Freund.

HAUPTSCHULE JEVER
MIT ORIENTIERUNGSSTUFE

Question Words: *Wer? Wen? Was?*

Both question words *wer* (who) and *wen* (whom) ask about a person. To inquire about objects, you must use the question word *was* (what).

Wer inquires about the subject of the sentence, whereas *wen* asks about the direct object of the sentence. You can use either word whether masculine, feminine or neuter.

Beispiele: *Heike* wohnt in der Stadt.   *Wer* wohnt in der Stadt?
Ich frage *die Lehrerin.*   *Wen* fragst du?
Wir kaufen *viele Kassetten*.   *Was* kauft ihr?

8. *Wer wohnt dort?* **Pretend that it's quite noisy and you can't hear what is being said about where various people live. Consequently, you inquire whom they are talking about.**

❑   Frau Schiller wohnt in der Stadt.
Wer wohnt in der Stadt?

1. Susanne wohnt beim Park.
2. Der Lehrer wohnt hier.
3. Petra wohnt dort.
4. Karin und Petra wohnen in Hamburg.
5. Frau Tobler wohnt in Deutschland.
6. Wir wohnen in der Stadt.

9. *Ich kaufe das Heft. Und du?* **Your friends and you are going shopping. Everyone seems to be buying something different. Your friends tell you what they are buying, but they also want to know what your purchase is.**

❑   Ich kaufe das Heft. Und du?
Ich kaufe das Buch hier.

1. Ich kaufe das Heft. Und du?

2. Ich kaufe das Heft. Und du?

3. Ich kaufe das Heft. Und du?

4. Ich kaufe das Heft. Und du?

5. Ich kaufe das Heft. Und du?

6. Ich kaufe das Heft. Und du?

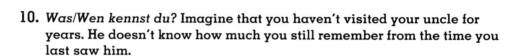

10. *Was/Wen kennst du?* Imagine that you haven't visited your uncle for years. He doesn't know how much you still remember from the time you last saw him.

   ❏ Was kennst du? (Park)
   Ich kenne den Park.

      1. Was kennst du ? (Stadt)
      2. Wen kennst du? (Mädchen)
      3. Wen kennst du? (Frau Kaiser)
      4. Was kennst du? (Rockmusik)
      5. Wen kennst du? (Freund)
      6. Was kennst du? (Schule)

11. *Wen fragen wir?* Your friends want to know whom to ask about a test today. You give the names of those who would know.

   ❏ Wen fragen wir? (Paul)
   Wir fragen den Paul.

      1. Wen fragen wir? (Heike)
      2. Wen fragen wir? (Lehrer)
      3. Wen fragen wir? (Freundin)
      4. Wen fragen wir? (Dieter)
      5. Wen fragen wir? (Lehrerin)

12. *Wer? Wen? oder Was?*

1. _____ ist das? Das ist Herr Schmidt.
2. _____ fragst du? Deine Freundin.
3. _____ kaufen Sie?
4. _____ macht ihr heute?
5. _____ kommt um sieben? Peter und Angelika.
6. _____ kennt er? Frau Meier.
7. _____ hörst du? Rockmusik.
8. _____ hat eine Prüfung?

13. Beantworte diese Fragen!

1. Wen fragst du?
2. Was kaufst du?
3. Wie heißt dein Freund (deine Freundin)?
4. Ist er (sie) sportlich?
5. Woher kommst du?
6. Hast du Deutsch?
7. Wer kommt pünktlich?
8. Hast du Zeit?
9. Was lernst du?

Present Tense of *sein* (to be)

The forms of *sein* are irregular; they do not follow the same pattern as regular verb forms.

Singular		
	ich bin	I am
	du bist	you are
	er	he is
	sie ist }	she is
	es	it is
Plural	wir sind	we are
	ihr seid	you are
	sie sind	they are
	Sie sind (sg. & pl.)	you are

14. Pretend that you are interested to learn about several people at a party. Can you ask some questions using the cues?

❐ er / intelligent
Ist er intelligent?

1. Andrea und Willi / klug
2. Uwe / sportlich
3. du / neu hier
4. ihr / pünktlich
5. der Junge / schon sechzehn

15. *Wer ist nie pünktlich?* State who is never on time.

❐ Herr Lehmann
Herr Lehmann ist nie pünktlich.

1. Herr und Frau Herder
2. ich
3. Birgit und Sven
4. wir
5. du
6. Kerstin

16. Supply the correct form of *sein.*

1. Wieviel Uhr_____ es jetzt?
2. Melanie und Sonja _____ in der Stadt.
3. _____ du um acht Uhr zu Hause?
4. Ihr _____ immer so spät.
5. Ich _____ morgen nicht da.
6. Deutschland _____ weit von hier.
7. Das _____ Steffie.
8. _____ ihr um sieben dort?
9. Wer _____ das Mädchen?
10. Die Aufgaben _____ leicht.

Der Lehrer fragt Peter.

Was machen die Schüler?

kennen and wissen

Both words, *kennen* and *wissen*, mean "to know." However, *kennen* means "to know a person, a place or an item," whereas *wissen* means "to know something" (as a fact).

Beispiele: *Kennst du die Sabine?* Do you know Sabine?
Weißt du, wer Sabine ist? Do you know who Sabine is?

Wir kennen Hamburg. We know Hamburg.
Wir wissen, wo Hamburg ist. We know where Hamburg is.

Kennen Sie dieses Buch? Do you know this book?
Wissen Sie, wo dieses Buch ist? Do you know where this book is?

The verb *wissen* has irregular forms when it is used with *ich*, *du* and *er* (*sie*, *es*). The plural forms are regular.

ich	weiß	wir	wissen
du	weißt	ihr	wißt
er		sie	wissen
sie }	weiß	Sie	wissen
es			

17. *Wer weiß das?* **Tell the class who knows the answer.**

❏   Doris
Doris weiß das.

1. die Lehrerin
2. Angelika und Heinz
3. wir
4. der Junge
5. Stefan und Erich
6. ich

18. **Various people are asked whom they know. Provide an appropriate answer.** *Folge dem Beispiel!*

❏   Wen kennen Sie, Herr Meier? (Frau Priebe)
Ich kenne Frau Priebe.

1. Wen kennt ihr? (Kerstin)
2. Wen kennst du? (das Mädchen)
3. Wen kennt Peter? (Heidi und Monika)
4. Wen kennen Sie? (Thomas)
5. Wen kennt Susanne? (Frau Haller)

19. *Kennen* oder *wissen*? **Provide the correct form of the appropriate verb.**

1. _____ Sie, um wieviel Uhr er kommt?
2. Ich _____ Natalie. Sie ist sehr klug.
3. _____ du den Jungen?
4. _____ ihr, was sie macht?
5. _____ Wolfgang die Physikaufgaben?
6. Wir _____, wo Heiko wohnt.
7. _____ ihr das Mädchen?
8. Ja, wir _____ Herrn Schulz.

Weißt du diese Aufgaben nicht?

Wohin fahren sie?

81

Nach der Schule

Es ist zehn nach eins. Die Schule ist aus°. Kerstin ist froh°. Heute ist Freitag. Sie hat heute und morgen viel Zeit. Kerstin ist siebzehn Jahre alt. Sie geht auf ein Gymnasium° in Köln.

out
glad

secondary school

Kerstin wartet° nur ein paar Minuten, dann sind auch Jana und Timo da. Jeden° Tag fahren sie mit dem Fahrrad° nach Hause.

is waiting
every
go by bike

Kerstin:	Hast du viel für Montag auf°, Timo?
Timo:	Ja. In Englisch und Geschichte habe ich viel zu tun. Und du, Jana?
Jana:	Ich hab' Glück°! Ich muß nur ein paar Seiten für Deutsch lesen°.
Kerstin:	Ich gebe° morgen eine kleine° Party. Kommt ihr?
Timo:	Ich weiß nicht.
Jana:	Wer kommt denn alles?
Kerstin:	Peter, Uwe, Daniela...vielleicht noch drei oder vier andere.
Timo:	Wann geht's denn los?°
Kerstin:	So gegen° sieben.

have a lot of homework

I'm lucky.
read
I'm giving/small

When will it start?
about

Jana muß nur ein paar Seiten lesen.

Jana, Kerstin und Timo sind vor der Schule.

Timo hat viel zu tun.

Viele Schüler° gehen zu Fuß° nach Hause. Kerstin, *many students/walk*
Timo und Jana fahren nur zehn Minuten mit dem Fahrrad
nach Hause. Um diese Zeit ist nicht viel Verkehr°. Sie *traffic*
sprechen wieder über° die Schule und die Party am *talk again about*
Sonnabend.

Kerstin:	Na, kommt ihr morgen?
Jana:	Ich komme bestimmt.
Kerstin:	Und du, Timo?
Timo:	Ich habe aber so viel zu tun. Englisch ist besonders° schwer. *especially*
Kerstin:	Ich habe mein Buch hier. Die Aufgaben auf Seite 53 sind doch nicht schwer.
Timo:	Für dich° nicht. *you (form of du)*
Kerstin:	Wir machen sie schnell vor der Party. Komm um sechs.
Timo:	Gut. Man° sagt ja: „Ohne Fleiß, kein Preis."° *they /No pain, no gain.*
Kerstin:	Bis dann.
Jana:	Tschüs.

Was fehlt hier? *Complete each sentence with the missing item.*

1. Kerstin ist _____ Jahre alt.
2. Sie geht auf ein _____ in Köln.
3. Kerstin wartet ein _____ Minuten.
4. Sie fahren mit dem _____ nach Hause.
5. Timo hat für _____ viel auf.
6. Jana muß ein paar Seiten für _____ lesen.
7. Kerstin hat am _____ eine Party.
8. Die Party ist um _____ Uhr.
9. Kerstin, Timo und Jana fahren _____ Hause.
10. Um Viertel nach eins ist nicht viel _____.
11. Englisch ist für Timo sehr _____.
12. Die Englischaufgaben sind auf _____ 53.

Fragen

1. Um wieviel Uhr ist die Schule aus?
2. Welcher Tag ist heute?
3. Wo geht Kerstin zur Schule?
4. Gehen Kerstin, Timo und Jana nach Hause?
5. Hat Timo viel zu tun?
6. Wer kommt alles zur Party?
7. Um wieviel Uhr ist die Party?
8. Ist gegen ein Uhr viel Verkehr?
9. Was ist für Timo nicht leicht?
10. Wann macht er die Aufgaben?

Übung macht den Meister!

1. Make up a weekly class schedule including days, subjects, class periods. Exchange your schedule with another person and then ask each other such questions as, „*Um wieviel Uhr hast du am Montag Mathe?*", „*Was für ein Fach hast du um acht Uhr am Dienstag?*", „*Um wieviel Uhr ist die Schule aus?*"

2. Ask each other in your class the question, „*Wo ist...?*" (der *Stuhl*, das *Buch*, die *Tafel*, etc.). Vary the answers as much as possible. Example: „*Der Stuhl ist hier.*" (*da*, *dort*, *da drüben*, *dort drüben* or *nicht hier*, *nicht da drüben*, etc.)

3. *Um wieviel Uhr...?* Write down three to five questions dealing with time and pass them to another classmate who will answer them. Your questions could include topics such as asking the time for going home, having a certain class, beginning a party, etc.

Erweiterung

20. *Was paßt hier?* **Use one of the items from below to complete each sentence.**

schwer	Party
ist	Schule
Uhr	aus
Mädchen	viel
pünktlich	Arbeit

1. Wer kommt _____ Bremen?
2. Frau Schmidt ist immer _____.
3. Um ein _____ ist die Schule aus.
4. Heute schreiben wir eine _____.
5. Peter wartet vor der _____.
6. Geschichte ist sehr _____.
7. Herr Wieland kennt das _____.
8. Wir geben am Freitag eine _____.
9. Ich habe _____ zu tun.
10. Die Party _____ um acht.

21. Gerd meets Silvia after school. Take Silvia's part and respond to Gerd in a logical manner.

Gerd:	Grüß dich, Silvia!
Silvia:	_____
Gerd:	Wieviel Uhr ist es jetzt?
Silvia:	_____
Gerd:	Ich muß schnell nach Hause gehen.
Silvia:	_____
Gerd:	Wir schreiben morgen eine Arbeit. Ich habe viel zu tun.
Silvia:	_____
Gerd:	Nein.
Silvia:	_____
Gerd:	Ja, dann habe ich Zeit.
Silvia:	_____
Gerd:	Tschüs.

22. Imagine that your German is at a stage where you can help others who are having difficulties completing conversational exchanges. They start a statement or question but don't know the German words to finish it. Help them out.

1. Wann schreiben wir eine (test) _____?
2. Ich (know) _____ das nicht.
3. Haben wir am Mittwoch (chemistry) _____?
4. Ja, um (half) _____ elf.
5. Warum kommt Marion (never) _____ pünktlich?
6. Sie hat zu viel zu (do) _____.
7. Das (says) _____ sie immer.
8. Ich habe auch viele (exercices) _____ für Mittwoch.
9. Lernst du denn so (much) _____?
10. Ja, besonders für (biology) _____.

23. Respond to each question or statement with a complete question or statement that is meaningful.

1. Die Schule ist um zwei Uhr aus.
2. Die Physikaufgaben sind sehr schwer.
3. Ich habe viel zu tun.
4. Wie weit ist die Schule von hier?
5. Was fragt er?
6. Wo ist die Lehrerin?
7. Monika geht zu Fuß.
8. Ich gebe am Sonntag eine Party.
9. Um acht kommt Daniela.
10. Wir fahren nach Hause.

24. *Was lernst du?* You are talking to several students, asking each what they or others are studying. Use the cues to form a question as well as an appropriate answer.

❐ Walter
Was lernt Walter?
Er lernt Englisch.

1. sie   2. Claudia   3. ihr   4. du   5. Paul

Sprachspiegel

25. Find the responses on the right that answer the questions on the left.

1. Wie ist das Sweatshirt?   a. Nein, nur zwei.
2. Wieviel Uhr ist es denn?   b. Monika.
3. Hast du viele CDs?   c. Ja, er ist nicht dumm.
4. Kommst du später?   d. Schon zehn.
5. Ist Helmut klug?   e. Ja, dann habe ich Zeit.
6. Wer geht jetzt nach Hause?   f. Sehr schick.
7. Warum kaufst du die Kassetten?   g. Sie sind sehr billig.
8. Ist die Arbeit leicht?   h. Ja, er ist da.
9. Hast du jetzt Zeit?   i. Nein, die ist schwer.
10. Ist Peter zu Hause?   j. Nein, aber morgen.

26. *Beantworte die Fragen!* Answer these questions with as much detail as possible, using the vocabulary and expressions you have learned so far.

1. Wer ist am Telefon?
2. Wie ist die Rockmusik?
3. Hörst du gern Rockmusik?
4. Welcher Tag ist heute?
5. Hast du viele Kassetten?
6. Um wieviel Uhr kommst du nach Hause?
7. Wo wohnst du?
8. Was machst du jetzt?

27. *Wir gehen zur Schule.* Describe (in narrative and/or dialog style) the following sequence, using the cues merely as a guideline.

You are walking to school...picking up your friend on the way...waiting several minutes before he or she comes out of the house...greeting him or her...talking about several items concerning school...arriving at school...hurrying because the first class begins soon.

28. *Wie sagt man's?* **From the list below, select the appropriate word to complete the various short conversational exchanges.**

intelligent	noch	das
neunzehn	aus	nicht
schon	pünktlich	nach
siebzehn	ist	leicht

1. Woher kommst du?
   Ich komme _____ Bremen.
2. Wie alt bist du?
   Ich bin _____. Und du?
   Schon _____.
3. Chemie ist schwer.
   Nein, es ist sehr _____.
   Du bist _____.
4. Frau Reimer kommt um acht.
   Ja, sie ist immer _____.
5. Kennst du Daniel?
   Ja, er _____ Sofies Freund.
6. Kommst du am Mittwoch zur Party?
   Ich weiß _____ nicht.
7. Was macht ihr jetzt?
   Wir fahren _____ Hause.
   Und dann?
   Das wissen wir noch _____.
8. Das Gymnasium ist gleich um die Ecke.
   Ich weiß _____.
9. Ich warte _____ fünfzehn Minuten hier.

29. **Wie heißt das auf deutsch?**

1. Chemistry is very hard.
2. Why isn't she punctual?
3. Mr. Meier knows that.
4. Rainer comes at seven minutes after ten.
5. I have time.
6. When are you taking the test, Heike?
7. You are always late, Volker.
8. We know Mrs. Holland.

Rückblick (Review)

I. Provide the proper form of *haben* or *sein*.

1. Er _____ sehr sportlich.
2. _____ du etwas Zeit?
3. Um elf Uhr _____ wir da?
4. Wir _____ viele Kassetten.
5. _____ ihr eine Party?
6. Ich _____ aus Köln.
7. Ihr _____ nie pünktlich.
8. Monika und Stefan _____ klug.
9. Wolfgang _____ um zehn Mathe.
10. Ich _____ ein Telefon.

II. *Wieviel Uhr ist es?* Give the complete answer (including numbers) to this question. Use the 24-hour system.

❐ 1:30 P.M.
Es ist dreizehn Uhr dreißig.

1. 6:00 P.M.
2. 10:00 P.M.
3. 11:30 A.M.
4. 3:15 A.M.
5. 11:15 P.M.
6. 2:26 P.M.
7. 7:12 A.M.
8. 9:55 A.M.
9. 4:13 P.M.
10. 1:45 P.M.

III. *Wieviel ist...?* Write out the complete answer in German.

❐ $6 + 8 = ?$
Sechs plus acht ist vierzehn.

1. $5 + 9 = ?$
2. $26 - 17 = ?$
3. $15 + 18 = ?$
4. $60 - 20 = ?$
5. $100 - 91 = ?$
6. $31 + 25 = ?$

IV. *Wer? Wen? Was? Wie? Wo?* Use the appropriate question word to form a question about the italicized part in each sentence. Be sure to ask the complete question.

❐ Wir wohnen *in Hamburg.*
Wo wohnen wir?

1. Sie kennt *Julia und Christa* sehr gut.
2. Er heißt *Jörg.*
3. Achim und Renate wohnen *in Deutschland.*
4. Wir schreiben *eine Arbeit.*
5. *Günter und ich* gehen nach Hause.
6. Bremen ist *in Norddeutschland.*
7. Ihr hört *Musik.*
8. Wir fragen *Frau Müller.*

Dirk kennt Michael gut.

Sie schreiben an die Tafel.

Land und Leute (Country and People)

Deutschland — Land und Fläche

Deutschland hat ungefähr° 78 Millionen Einwohner°. Deutschland paßt° 22 mal° in die USA (Vereinigten Staaten von Amerika), ohne° Alaska und Hawaii. Das Land ist ungefähr halb so groß wie° der Staat Texas. Die weiteste Entfernung° von Norden nach Süden ist 830 km (Kilometer), von Osten nach Westen 630 km.

approximately/inhabitants fits/times without as big as farthest distance

Berlin ist die Hauptstadt° von Deutschland. Diese Stadt liegt° im Osten und ist auch die größte° Stadt. Andere große Städte sind Hamburg, München, Köln, Düsseldorf, Frankfurt, Leipzig, Stuttgart, Hannover, Chemnitz, Bonn und Dresden. Wo liegen diese Städte? Im Norden, Süden, Osten oder Westen?

capital is located/biggest

Leipzig

Berlin

München

Dresden

Was paßt hier? **Complete each statement on the left by matching it with the appropriate item on the right. You will not need all the items on the right.**

1. Berlin ist
2. Deutschland ist
3. In Deutschland wohnen
4. Deutschland paßt 22 mal in die
5. Die weiteste Entfernung
   von Norden nach Süden ist
6. Berlin liegt
7. Die weiteste Entfernung
   von Westen nach Osten ist

a. eine kleine Stadt
b. 78 Millionen Einwohner
c. im Osten
d. 830 km
e. halb so groß wie Texas
f. 630 km
g. USA (ohne Alaska und
   Hawaii
h. im Westen
i. die Hauptstadt von
   Deutschland

Zungenbrecher

Es klapperten die Klapperschlangen
bis die Klappern schlapper klangen.
(The rattlesnakes rattled until the
rattles sounded weaker.)

Wo sind die zwei Jungen? (Limburg)

Was macht er?

Kulturecke

School Life

School life in the Federal Republic of Germany is considerably different from our own. There is practically no social life at a German school. Although schools offer physical education classes — and many have modern facilities — students wishing to participate in various sports activities usually join local sports clubs.

Although not part of the school system, more than 80 percent of three to six-year olds attend the *Kindergarten*. The kindergarten is a German institution adopted by many countries — the very word, in fact, has become assimilated in many languages.

Formal education begins at age six when children are required to attend the *Grundschule* for a period of four years. It has been a tradition for parents to give their first grader on the first day of school a *Schultüte*, which is a huge cone filled with candies and cookies. These younger children usually carry briefcases or satchels strapped to their backs when going to and coming from school. During their years in the *Grundschule*, children are already accustomed to a sizeable stack of homework.

At the age of 10, or after fourth grade, most children and their parents face the difficult decision of which of three different schools to attend. Many students go to the *Hauptschule* where they receive a basic education for the next five to six years. Upon completion of the *Hauptschule* many students enter the work force full time; others become apprentices and continue their education at a vocational school called *Berufsschule*.

A second choice after fourth grade is the *Realschule*. Here the students will remain for the next six years and receive training for higher level but non-academic occupations of all kinds.

Finally, study at the *Gymnasium*, grades 5 to 13, leads to the *Abitur*, the final certificate that is a prerequisite for attending a university. Students going to the *Gymnasium* have a very concentrated curriculum. It is not uncommon for these students to take as many as 10 or more different subjects a week. A typical schedule readily shows the emphasis on academic subjects.

During the past decade, the *Orientierungsstufe* has become the answer for many children whose parents and teachers cannot make the proper choice of which school to attend after fourth grade. The *Orientierungsstufe* is an orientation for grades five and six, the two years following the *Grundschule*. It gives students an opportunity to switch, based on their ability, to any of the other three schools after sixth grade.

Sie haben Große Pause.   *Sie hat viel auf.*

A special problem has arisen from the numerous children of foreign workers living in Germany many of whom have now made Germany their adopted country. These children have become immersed in the German language and culture at a rapid pace. Many schools offer special classes for these children.

Furthermore, a comprehensive school called *Gesamtschule* has been introduced in some parts of Germany for students in grades five to ten. Depending on their ability, parents and students decide which courses to take — ranging from basic to more advanced courses.

How do students get to school? In recent years, school buses have become quite common in larger cities. Many students walk to school. Others take public transportation or ride their bikes. Some of the older students ride their mopeds, which are usually parked in a specially designated area in the parking lot. There are also a few cars in the parking lot that students over 18 years of age have been allowed to drive. However, the teachers have their own designated parking area.

Most school buildings were built during the past 20 to 30 years. Let's visit the *Nicolaus Cusanus Gymnasium* in Bergisch-Gladbach. This school is just celebrating its 100th anniversary. Of course, a newer school stands now in place of the older building. Upon entering the school, the visitors

Wo sind die Schüler?

Viele Schüler kommen mit Fahrrädern.

94

Sie haben heute keine Schule.

Wohin gehen diese Schüler?

are reminded of this special occasion. Numerous posters made by the students attest to the fact. Furthermore, several events have been scheduled to commemorate the anniversary. Students have also spent numerous hours making mummies to recreate a classroom scene from years gone by.

In the main hallway are bulletin boards that are used by the students and administrators to make various announcements. Although many German schools now offer a warm snack or small meal, students at this high school bring their own bag lunches or buy some snacks and cold beverages from vending machines located in the main hallway. During the *Große Pause*, a 20-minute recess, students usually congregate in the school yard to eat their snacks and chat with their friends.

It is still customary, particularly for younger students, to get up when the teacher enters the room. Teachers do not have a classroom of their own. For most subjects, students stay with the same classmates in the same room. The earlier grades at the *Gymnasium* offer rather general subjects, while upper grades introduce such subjects as English literature and philosophy.

Lektion 3

Sie sind im Gymnasium.

Wo warten sie?

At the *Gymnasium*, students must prove themselves. Only one-fourth of all students receive their *Abitur*.

German students generally spend fewer hours at school than American students, staying only until noon or 1:00 to 2:00 P.M. However, some of them today still have school for two or three hours on Saturday as well. And, of course, after school, students must spend considerable time doing their homework.

Was weißt du? Match the items on the left with those on the right. You will not need all the items.

_____ 1. Große Pause
_____ 2. Gymnasium
_____ 3. Abitur
_____ 4. Orientierungsstufe
_____ 5. Grundschule
_____ 6. Realschule
_____ 7. Hauptschule

a. orientation level for 5th and 6th graders
b. grades 10-13
c. final diploma
d. grades 1-4
e. grades 5-10
f. orientation after age 14
g. recess
h. basic education for 5 to 6 years after 4th grade
i. grades 5-13

Vokabeln

alles all, everything
auf on, to
die Aufgabe,-n problem, exercise, assignment
aufhaben to have homework to do
aus from, out of, out
ausreichend sufficient
befriedigend satisfactory
bekommen to get, receive
besonders especially, special
die Biologie biology
der Bleistift,-e pencil
das Buch,-̈er book
die Chemie chemistry
der Computer,- computer
das Deutsch German
dich (form of du) you
diese (form of dieser) this
doch used for emphasis
das Englisch English
die Erdkunde geography
das Fach,-̈er (school) subject
fahren to drive, go
das Fahrrad,-̈er bicycle
froh glad
der Fuß,-̈e foot
zu Fuß gehen to walk
geben to give
eine Party geben to give a party
gegen about, around
das Genie,-s genius
die Geschichte history
das Glück luck
Glück haben to be lucky
das Gymnasium,-sien secondary school

halb half
das Heft,-e notebook
intelligent intelligent
jeden (form of jeder) every, each
kennen to know (person, place)
klein small, little
die Kreide,-n chalk
der Kuli,-s (ballpoint) pen
die Kunst art
die Landkarte,-n map
langsam slow
der Lehrer,- teacher (male)
die Lehrerin,-nen teacher (female)
lernen to learn, study
lesen to read
das Lieblingsfach,-̈er favorite (school) subject
das Lineal,-e ruler
los: Dann mal los! Then let's go!
Wann geht's los? When will it start?
man one, they, people
mangelhaft inadequate
die Mathematik (or: Mathe) mathematics
mein my
die Minute,-n minute
mit with
nach to, after
neu new
nie never
die Note,-n (school) grade, mark
das Papier paper
die Party,-s party
die Physik physics

pünktlich punctual, on time
der Radiergummi,-s eraser
die Religion religion
schnell fast
die Schulbank,-̈e school desk
die Schule,-n school
der Schüler,- pupil, student (secondary school)
die Schultasche,-n school bag, satchel
schwer hard, difficult
die Seite,-n page
der Sport sport
sportlich athletic
sprechen über to talk about
stimmen to be correct
Stimmt. That's right (correct).
der Stundenplan,-̈e class schedule
die Tafel,-n blackboard
der Tafellappen,- rag (to wipe off blackboard)
tun to do
die Uhr,-en clock, watch
ungefähr approximately
ungenügend unsatisfactory
der Verkehr traffic
das Viertel,- quarter
vor before, in front of
wann when
warten to wait
wenig little
wieder again
wissen to know (a fact)
woher where from

Unterhaltung

Communicative Functions

- talking about a movie
- expressing likes and dislikes of a movie
- naming neighboring countries
- telling months and seasons
- talking about the weather
- expressing opinion about a rock concert

99

Was machst du heute?

Ich möchte ins Kino gehen.

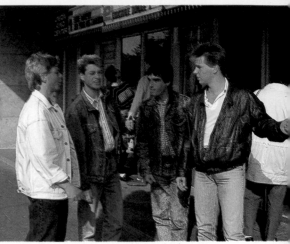
Kommt doch mit!

Gehen wir ins Kino!

(am Telefon)

Peter:	Was machst du heute?
Jens:	Ich möchte ins Kino gehen.
Peter:	Gute Idee. Was läuft im Union-Kino?
Jens:	*Frantic*, ein Film aus Amerika. Wirklich spitze!
Peter:	Wann beginnt der Film?
Jens:	Einen Moment. Hier steht's. Um halb vier.
Peter:	Ich komme gleich rüber.
Jens:	Gut. Beeil dich!

Fragen

1. Welcher Film läuft im Union-Kino?
2. Wie ist der Film?
3. Um wieviel Uhr beginnt der Film?
4. Wer kommt gleich rüber?

(beim Kino)

Gerd:	Hallo, Peter und Jens.
Sven:	Wohin geht ihr denn?
Jens:	Ins Kino. Kommt doch mit!
Gerd:	Die Karten kosten neun Mark. Ich habe nicht genug Geld.
Jens:	Das macht nichts. Ich habe genug. Kommt! Gehen wir!

Fragen

1. Kennt Gerd Peter und Jens?
2. Wieviel kostet eine Karte?
3. Hat Gerd genug Geld?
4. Wer hat genug Geld für Gerd?

(im Kino)

Jens:	Vier Karten, bitte.
Verkäuferin:	Das macht sechsunddreißig Mark.
Jens:	Hier sind vierzig.
Verkäuferin:	Und vier Mark zurück. Beeilt euch! Der Film läuft schon.

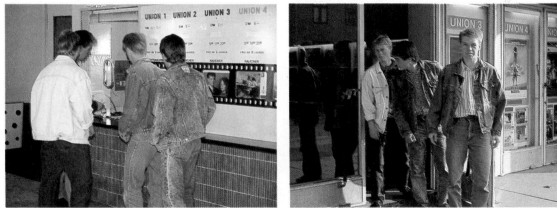

Wieviel kosten vier Karten?   *Wie ist der Film?*

Fragen

1. Wieviel kosten die vier Karten?
2. Wieviel Geld hat Jens?
3. Wer bekommt das Geld?

(später)

Peter:	Der Film ist klasse. Was meinst du, Jens?
Jens:	Ja, der ist sehr spannend.
Sven:	Für mich etwas langweilig.
Gerd:	Du bist viel zu kritisch. Ich gehe gern noch einmal.

Frage

Wie ist der Film? Was sagen oder meinen Peter, Jens und Sven?

Peter sagt: „_____."
Jens meint: „_____."
Sven sagt: „_____."

Wer sagt oder fragt das? (Who says or asks that?) Identify the speakers of the following statements.

❑ Was läuft im Union-Kino?
Peter fragt das.

1. Der Film ist klasse.
2. Wann beginnt der Film?
3. Das macht sechsundreißig Mark.
4. Ich gehe gern noch einmal.
5. Ich möchte ins Kino gehen.
6. Wohin geht ihr denn?
7. Die Karten kosten neun Mark.
8. Der Film läuft schon.
9. Ich komme gleich rüber.
10. Der ist sehr spannend.

At least one-third of all movies shown in Germany comes from the U.S. Almost all U.S. movies are synchronized with a German sound track — there are no subtitles, as the English has been carefully translated into German to match the lip movements with its original sound track. In the synchronized sound track you will always hear the voice of the same German actor or actress for a particular American actor or actress.

Movie theaters are required by law to indicate the age of admittance to each movie. The standard phrase, for example, is *frei ab 14 Jahren* (admittance 14 years or older).

Kombiniere...

How many questions can you form by using one item from each column for each question.

Ist	Peter und Jens	wirklich	ins Kino
Gehen	der Film	um sieben	pünktlich
Beginnt	du	heute	spannend
Hast		genug	zur Schule
			Zeit
			Geld
			langweilig

Hier steht's.

Gehen wir ins Café!

Nützliche Ausdrücke

Gehen wir ins Kino!	Let's go to the movie (theater).
Ein Film aus Deutschland läuft dort.	A movie from Germany is playing there.
Sie kommt gleich rüber.	She'll come over right away.
Hier steht's.	Here it is.
Beeil dich! Beeilt euch!	Hurry up!
Wieviel kostet...?	How much is...?
Das macht nichts.	That doesn't matter.
Das macht zehn Mark.	That costs (comes to) ten marks.
Was meinst du?	What do you think? What's your opinion?
Ich gehe gern noch einmal.	I (would) like to go again.

Was paßt hier? **Match each expression on the left with an appropriate response on the right.**

1. Beeilt euch!	a. Um wieviel Uhr?
2. Was läuft im Kino?	b. Ja, ich habe viel Zeit.
3. Kommst du rüber?	c. Um acht Uhr.
4. Drei Karten, bitte.	d. Ja, er ist spitze.
5. Ist der Film spannend?	e. Ein Film aus Deutschland.
6. Wann beginnt das Konzert?	f. Das macht 24 Mark.
7. Wie ist der Film?	g. Nicht so schnell.
8. Wir gehen heute ins Kino.	h. Sehr langweilig.

Ergänzung

105

1. **Wo liegt...?** Answer this question by locating the following cities. You may want to use the map in the front section of this book.

❏ Hamburg
Hamburg liegt im Norden.

Leipzig
Leipzig liegt im Osten.

1. Stuttgart
2. Bonn
3. Bremen
4. Berlin
5. Kiel
6. Dresden
7. München
8. Rostock
9. Düsseldorf
10. Gera

2. **Im Frühling, Sommer, Herbst oder Winter?** Relate the months to the seasons.

❏ Januar
Januar ist im Winter.

1. Juli
2. März
3. Dezember
4. September
5. Mai
6. August

3. **Wie ist das Wetter?** Looking at the illustrations below, indicate with a complete sentence what the weather is like. There may be more than one expression for each scene.

Sag's mal!

Wie ist dieser Film? Er ist...

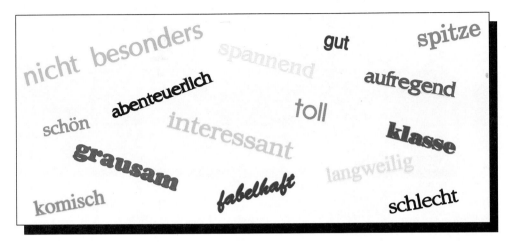

nicht besonders   spannend   gut   spitze

abenteuerlich   aufregend

schön   interessant   toll   klasse

grausam   langweilig

komisch   fabelhaft   schlecht

Aussprache

/x/	/ch/
Bu**ch**	i**ch**
a**ch**t	ni**ch**t
do**ch**	Mäd**ch**en
au**ch**	glei**ch**
ma**ch**en	schle**ch**t
Fa**ch**	lei**ch**t
na**ch**	wel**ch**er
einfa**ch**	di**ch**
no**ch**	spre**ch**en
Wo**ch**e	wirkli**ch**

Übungen

Indefinite Article (Nominative and Accusative Singular)

	Singular		
	masculine	**feminine**	**neuter**
nominative	ein	eine	ein
accusative	einen	eine	ein

The articles in the *ein*-group are called indefinite because they do not specifically identify the noun with which they are associated. All articles you have learned so far, i.e., *der, die, das*, are *der*-words (definite articles). In English the indefinite article is either "a" or "an."

Beispiele: *ein Junge* (a boy), *eine Aufgabe* (an exercise), *ein Buch* (a book)

From the above you can see that only the accusative of the masculine article differs from the nominative (*ein, einen*). This is also true of the definite article (*der, den*).

4. *Was ist das?* **Your friends want to learn some German words. They point to different items. Help them identify each.**

☐   Das ist ein Heft.

1.   2.   3.   4.   5.   6.

5. *Wo ist...?* Several people are asking your help in locating specific objects, places or people. Can you help them?

◻ die Schule / da drüben
　 Eine Schule ist da drüben.

　1. das Kino / nicht weit von hier
　2. die Stadt / im Süden
　3. die Verkäuferin / dort
　4. der Lehrer / am Telefon
　5. das Auto/ zu Hause
　6. die Freundin / in Deutschland

6. *Was hast du?* Tell your classmates that you have the following. Use the cues provided.

◻

Ich habe eine Schultasche.

1.　　2.　　3.　　4.　　5.　　6.　　7.

7. Complete the following sentences.

　1. Kaufst du (a cassette) _____ ?
　2. Wir fragen (a teacher) _____.
　3. Hören Sie (a girl) _____?
　4. Ich habe (a favorite subject) _____.
　5. Hast du (a girlfriend) _____?
　6. Schreibt ihr heute (a test) _____?
　7. Frau Meier wartet (a moment) _____.
　8. Sie lesen (a book) _____.
　9. Wann hast du (a party) _____?
　10. Er macht (an exercise) _____.

8. Form complete sentences (statements or questions) using the indefinite article.

❑ ich / haben / Freund
Ich habe einen Freund.

1. wir / kaufen / Telefon
2. wer / haben / Party
3. fragen / ihr / Lehrer
4. ich / lesen / Buch
5. Katrin / wissen / Aufgabe
6. hören / Dieter / Kassette
7. kennen / du / Mädchen
8 Helga / haben / Mark
9. kaufen / wir / Heft
10. ich / fragen / Verkäuferin

The Command Form

Familiar Command

To form commands in English, the speaker simply takes the infinitive without "to," e.g., "go," "run" or "write." In German, the familiar command form in the singular is constructed by eliminating the *en* from the infinitive, i.e.,by maintaining the stem. In German, commands (imperative sentences) are always followed by an exclamation point.

Beispiele: *Geh! geh(en)* Go!
Schreib! schreib(en) Write!
Frag! frag(en) Ask!

NOTE: Frequently an e is added to the stem so that it would also be correct to say *Schreibe!, Gehe!, Frage!* However, an e must be added if the stem ends in *-d* or *-t*.

Beispiel: *Warte!* Wait!

When you address more than one person, the familiar (plural) form is as follows: *Geht! Schreibt! Fragt!*

It is helpful to remember that the familiar plural command is the same as the second person plural without *ihr*.

NOTE: The ending *et* instead of just *t* is added to a verb stem that ends with *-d* or *-t*.

Beispiel: Wartet hier!

Formal Command

The singular and the plural formal command are formed by inverting subject and verb.

Gehen Sie! Schreiben Sie! Fragen Sie!

You will notice right away that this formation is identical to the construction of a question. There is, however, a distinct difference in the intonation of a question and a formal command.

Command Forms of *haben* and *sein*

The following are the command forms for *haben* and *sein*:

Hab keine Angst, Karin!
Habt keine Angst, Ingo und Tina!
Haben Sie keine Angst, Herr Schmidt!
Sei pünktlich!
Seid pünktlich!
Seien Sie pünktlich!

The *wir*-Command Form (Let's...)

The *wir*-command form is used when asking for some action in the sense of *Let's* (do something)...!

Beispiele: *Gehen wir!* (Let's go!)
Fragen wir die Verkäuferin! (Let's ask the saleslady!)

Command Form Used in Public or Official Language

Besides the common forms listed above, you may also encounter another command form used mostly in official announcements such as legal notices printed on documents or signs or at train stations, airports, etc.

Beispiele: (sign in front of a house or driveway)
Bitte nicht parken! (Please don't park here!)

(sign inside a train or airport)
Nicht rauchen! (Don't smoke!)

(announcement of train departure)
Türen schließen! (Close doors.)

Notice that the above commands use the infinitive verb form.

9. Pretend that you are giving several instructions to one of your friends.

❐ die Arbeit schreiben
Schreib die Arbeit!

    1. die Musik hören
    2. ein Buch kaufen
    3. nach Hause gehen
    4. die Aufgabe machen
    5. zu Daniela kommen
    6. eine Kassette spielen
    7. die Lehrerin fragen
    8. Deutsch lernen

10. Change these statements to command forms.

❐ Du sagst das nicht.
Sag das nicht!

    1. Du kaufst die Karte billig.
    2. Du schreibst die Aufgabe.
    3. Du gehst ins Kino.
    4. Du kommst zur Party.
    5. Du lernst Englisch.
    6. Du wartest beim Park.
    7. Du bringst die Kassetten.
    8. Du hörst die Musik.

11. You are talking to more than one friend. Give proper instructions.

❐ nach Hause gehen
Geht nach Hause!

    1. Deutsch schreiben
    2. nicht spielen
    3. viel lernen
    4. schnell kommen
    5. das Buch lesen
    6. eine Party geben

12. Pretend you are addressing adults instead of your friends. How would you change the informal to the more formal command forms?

❐ Sag das, bitte!
Sagen Sie das, bitte!

1. Komm zur Party, bitte!
2. Spiel die Kassette, bitte!
3. Warte zu Hause, bitte!
4. Geh doch ins Kino, bitte!
5. Kauf die Karten, bitte!
6. Fahr etwas schneller, bitte!

13. Convert these sentences to commands.

❐ Du bist sehr pünktlich.
Sei pünktlich!

1. Sie gehen nach Hause, Frau Holz.
2. Ihr hört die Musik.
3. Du lernst es schnell.
4. Ihr fragt die Verkäuferin.
5. Du bist klug.
6. Sie kaufen kein Fahrrad.
7. Du hast keine Angst.
8. Ihr schreibt die Arbeit.

14. Can you figure out what these instructions mean?

1. Wasser nicht trinken!
2. Bitte aussteigen!
3. Etwas lauter sprechen!
4. Fleißiger lernen!
5. Langsamer fahren!
6. Drücken/Ziehen!

Negation

The word *kein* means "no" and negates nouns.

Beispiele: *Ich habe kein Buch.* (I have no book.)
Sie kauft keine Karte. (She doesn't buy a ticket.)

The endings of *kein* are identical to those of *ein*-words.

Beispiele: *Peter kauft ein Fahrrad. Peter kauft kein Fahrrad.*
Ich habe einen Bleistift. Ich habe keinen Bleistift.

The word *nicht* means "not" and negates verbs, adjectives and adverbs.

Beispiele: *Ich komme nicht.* (I am not coming.)
Er weiß das nicht. (He doesn't know that.)

Usually, *nicht* appears after the subject, verb, all objects and expressions of time, whichever comes last in the sentence. Therefore, you will find *nicht* at the end of many sentences.

Beispiele: *Wir fragen nicht.* (We aren't asking.)
Wir fragen den Lehrer nicht. (We aren't asking the teacher.)
Wir fragen den Lehrer heute nicht. (We aren't asking the teacher today.)

15. **Susanne is wondering what Andrea is buying. Andrea responds to each of her questions negatively.**

❏ Kaufst du ein Fahrrad?
Nein, ich kaufe kein Fahrrad.

1. Kaufst du ein Heft?
2. Kaufst du einen Kuli?
3. Kaufst du ein Buch?
4. Kaufst du eine Karte?
5. Kaufst du eine Kassette?
6. Kaufst du eine Schultasche?

16. **Answer each of the following questions in the negative.**

❏ Kennt Peter eine Verkäuferin?
Nein, er kennt keine Verkäuferin.

1. Lernt Heidi eine Aufgabe?
2. Bringt Dieter ein Buch?
3. Fragen Ingo und Hans einen Lehrer?
4. Hast du eine Schultasche?
5. Bekommt Heidi in Mathe eine Eins?
6. Hört ihr eine Kassette?
7. Kaufst du einen Kuli?

17. **Pretend that you are hearing some statements but you don't agree with them.**

❏ Wir fahren schnell.
Nein, wir fahren nicht schnell.

1. Sabine geht morgen ins Kino.
2. Der Film beginnt um acht Uhr.
3. Monika kommt aus Österreich.
4. Die Lehrerin weiß es.
5. Es regnet heute.
6. Die Sonne scheint.
7. Günter sagt das.

114

18. Your classmates are asking you some questions, all of which you answer negatively.

❏ Hast du heute Zeit?
Nein, ich habe heute keine Zeit.

Kommst du um vier?
Nein, ich komme nicht um vier.

1. Bist du um eins zu Hause?
2. Gehst du pünktlich zur Party?
3. Schreibst du morgen eine Arbeit?
4. Kaufst du ein Sweatshirt?
5. Weißt du das?
6. Kennst du einen Lehrer?
7. Lernst du viel?
8. Hast du eine Freundin?
9. Kommst du um drei nach Hause.
10. Bist du sportlich?

Wo, wohin and woher

Wo (where) is a question word asking about a location, whereas *wohin* (where to) and *woher* (where from) are question words asking about direction.

Beispiele: *Wo wohnst du?* Where are you living?
Wohin gehst du? Where are you going (to)?
Woher kommst du? Where are you (coming) from?

19. Form questions asking for the italicized words.

❏ Frau Schneider geht *nach Hause*.
Wohin geht Frau Schneider?

1. Herbert wohnt *in der Stadt*.
2. Inge und Lotte fahren *nach Deutschland*.
3. Holger kommt *aus Mainz*.
4. Das Kino ist *gleich um die Ecke*.
5. Herr Schmidt wohnt *in Köln*.
6. Sie gehen *zur Party*.

20. Complete each question and then answer it. Provide different questions and statements for each.

❑ Wo _____?
  Wo wohnt Paul?
  Er wohnt nicht weit von hier.

  1. Wohin _____?
  2. Woher _____?
  3. Wo _____?
  4. Woher _____?
  5. Wo _____?
  6. Wohin _____?

gern

The word *gern* used with a verb indicates liking something or someone.

Beispiele: *Ich lese gern.* I like to read.
  Gehst du gern ins Kino? Do you like to go to the movie theater?
  Hat er das Mädchen gern? Does he like the girl?

21. *Was machst du gern?* Your classmates are asking you what you like to do. Respond accordingly.

❑ ein Buch lesen
  Ich lese gern ein Buch.

  1. Musik hören
  2. nach Deutschland fahren
  3. ins Kino gehen
  4. Kassetten spielen
  5. eine Party geben
  6. Deutsch sprechen
  7. die Lehrerin fragen

22. Answer these questions by using *gern* in your answers.

  1. Was machst du gern?
  2. Wohin gehst du gern?
  3. Was lernst du gern?
  4. Was hörst du gern?
  5. Wen fragst du gern?

Zum Rockkonzert

Warum sind Heidi und Tina so aufgeregt°? In der   *excited*
Konzerthalle gibt's° heute ein Rockkonzert. Herbert Gröne-   *there is*
meyer und seine Band sind da. Grönemeyer ist in
Deutschland sehr bekannt°. Heidi und Tina haben schon   *well known*
ein paar Wochen° zwei Karten für dieses Konzert. Heute   *weeks*
gibt es keine Karten mehr°. Sie sind schon lange   *There are no more...*
ausverkauft°.   *long sold out*

Tina hat Rockmusik gern°. Sie hat viele Kassetten.   *likes*
Auch von Grönemeyer hat sie ein paar. Heute kommt
Heidi schon früh vor dem Konzert zu Tina und bringt
ihre° Kassetten mit. Sie hören noch einmal Grönemey-   *her*
ers Hits.

Herbert Grönemeyer

Sie haben zwei Karten für das Rockkonzert.

Um halb sieben gehen sie in die Stadt. Das Konzert beginnt um acht Uhr. Viele Fans sind schon vor sieben da. Alle kennen Grönemeyers Rockmusik.

Schon eine Stunde vor dem Konzert machen sie die Türen auf°. In der Konzerthalle ist jetzt viel los°. Die Jugendlichen° sind sehr laut und drängeln°. Genau um acht beginnt das Rockkonzert. Grönemeyer singt einen bekannten Hit. Die Jungen und Mädchen jubeln und schreien°. Tina sagt etwas° zu Heidi, aber beide verstehen° nichts. Es ist einfach° zu laut. Die Musik ist ganz toll. Nach einer Stunde° gibt es eine Pause°.

they open the doors/
is much going on/
young people/
pushing

cheer and scream/
something
understand/simply

hour/intermission

Nach der Pause singt Grönemeyer andere Hits. Die Jugendlichen sind jetzt noch lauter. Viele stehen und klatschen im Rhythmus°. Es ist einfach ganz toll. Ein paar Jugendliche fotografieren° die Show. Nach zehn Uhr singt Grönemeyer den letzten° und populärsten Hit. Alle stehen, klatschen, jubeln und schreien. Für Tina und Heidi war° dieser Tag super.

stand and clap in
rhythm/take pictures
last

was

Was machen die Jugendlichen?

Grönemeyer singt den populärsten Hit.

Was paßt hier? Match the items on the left with the most appropriate ones on the right.

1. Heute
2. Die Karten
3. Grönemeyer
4. Heidi
5. In der Konzerthalle
6. Tina und Heidi
7. Das Konzert
8. Ein paar Jugendliche

a. fotografieren die Show
b. ist viel los
c. singt nach der Pause andere Hits
d. sind schon ausverkauft
e. haben Karten für das Rockkonzert
f. kommt vor dem Konzert zu Tina
g. gibt's ein Rockkonzert
h. beginnt um acht

1. Warum sind Tina und Heidi aufgeregt?
2. Bekommen die Jugendlichen heute noch Karten?
3. Was machen Tina und Heidi vor dem Rockkonzert?
4. Wie kommen Heidi und Tina zur Konzerthalle?
5. Um wieviel Uhr beginnt das Rockkonzert?
6. Warum verstehen Tina und Heidi kein Wort?
7. Wann gibt es eine Pause?
8. Was machen ein paar Jugendliche?
9. Was macht Grönemeyer nach zehn Uhr?

Übung macht den Meister!

1. Ask your classmates which movie they would like to see, what time it starts and when you should leave in order to be on time.

2. Find out from one of your classmates which movie he or she would like to see and why.

3. Discuss the weather in your area during the different seasons and/or months of the year.

4. Cut out the national weather report and use it to ask such questions as, *„Wie ist das Wetter in ...?"* (New York, Los Angeles, Miami, Chicago, etc.).

5. Pick a German city and ask a question like, *„Wo liegt Köln...?"* Your classmates should provide an answer such as *„Köln liegt im Westen."*

6. Pretend you are going to a rock concert. Describe such details as preparation to buy tickets, going there, the crowd, the musicians, etc.

Wie ist das Wetter heute? (Hamburg)

Erweiterung

23. *Was paßt hier?* **Match each word from the list below with the most appropriate word on the left.**

Physik	Mittwoch	Uhr	Wetter
Kilometer	Mädchen und Jungen	Film	Stuttgart
Lehrerin	Musik	Juni	Zwei

1. die Band
2. der Tag
3. das Kino
4. die Zeit
5. der Monat
6. die Stadt
7. die Schule
8. die Jugendlichen
9. die Note
10. das Fach
11. die Sonne
12. die Entfernung

Die Stadt Heidelberg

24. **Susanne is calling Julia and wants to find out if she is interested in going to a movie this evening. Can you take Susanne's part and complete the conversation logically?**

Susanne:	_____
Julia:	Meine Hausaufgaben.
Susanne:	_____
Julia:	Welcher Film läuft heute?
Susanne:	_____
Julia:	Um wieviel Uhr beginnt der Film?
Susanne:	_____
Julia:	Kommt Günter auch?
Susanne:	_____
Julia:	Dann gehen wir zwei.
Susanne:	_____
Julia:	Bis später.

25. Complete each word by adding another noun of one or more syllables which corresponds to the definite article.

❏   die Haus_____
    die Hausaufgabe

1. das Rock_____
2. die Haupt_____
3. das Fahr_____
4. die Konzert_____
5. der Tafel _____
6. die Schul_____
7. das Lieblings_____
8. das Nachbar_____

26. Beantworte diese Fragen!

1. Gehst du gern ins Kino?
2. Wie ist das Wetter heute?
3. Wo liegt Kiel?
4. Wohin gehst du?
5. Was machst du nicht gern?
6. Was kaufst du in der Stadt?
7. Was machst du am Sonntag?

Sprachspiegel

27. *Wie sagt man's?* From the list below, select the appropriate words to complete the short conversational exchanges.

schnell	bekannt	Fahrrad	Sonne
Deutsch	schön	beginnt	stimmt
Geld	gern	Juli	ist
Sonntag	Herbst	kosten	Konzerthalle

1. Hast du eine Karte?
   Nein, ich habe nicht genug _____.
2. Der Film ist aus München.
   Verstehst du denn _____?
3. Gehst du gern ins Kino?
   Ja, besonders am _____.
   Warum nicht am Freitag?
   Dann _____ die Karten zehn Mark.
4. Wir haben noch viel Zeit.
   Nein, das _____ nicht. Es ist schon halb fünf.

5. Am Donnerstag gehen wir zum Rockkonzert.
   Wo _____ das denn?
   In der _____.
6. Die Band ist in Amerika ganz _____.
   Ich kenne sie nicht.
   Hörst du nie Musik?
   Nein, ich habe diese Rockmusik nicht _____.
7. Wie ist das Wetter heute?
   Es ist _____. Die _____ scheint.
   Dann gehe ich zu Fuß und fahre nicht mit dem _____.
8. Kommst du im _____?
   Ja, dann ist es nicht so heiß.
9. Woher kommt Ingo?
   Aus Österreich. Er wohnt einen Monat bei Helmut.
   Wann kommt er?
   Im _____.
10. Beeil dich!
    Warum so _____?
    Der Film _____ bald.

28. **Develop your own dialog, using the information given strictly as a guideline. Be as creative as possible!**

You suggest to your two friends that you go to a movie. Friend A wants to see a movie from France, but Friend B prefers one from Germany. Friend B wins this argument, especially since the tickets won't cost as much. You inquire about the movie schedule. Friend B suggests that you go at four o'clock. The tickets will not be very expensive at that time. Friend A mentions that you should ask Friend C to come along. You talk to him or her over the phone, but he or she tells you that he or she has too much homework. Friend A indicates that you'll take the bicycle, because otherwise you won't be on time. All of you agree to ride your bicycles to the movie theater.

Ist diese Band klasse?

29. *Beantworte diese Fragen!* **Answer these questions with as much detail as possible, using the vocabulary and expressions you have learned so far.**

    1. Was läuft im Kino in der Stadt?
    2. Wer spielt in der Konzerthalle?
    3. Warum bist du so aufgeregt?
    4. Wann beginnt die Vorstellung?
    5. Kommst du später rüber?
    6. Wieviel kosten drei Karten?
    7. Wie ist der Film?
    8. Ist diese Band klasse?

30. Wie heißt das auf deutsch?

    1. I would like to go to a movie.
    2. Where are you going (to)?
    3. The movie is boring.
    4. The weather is beautiful.
    5. What are you doing tomorrow?
    6. Are you coming to the party?

Rückblick

I. Provide the proper verb form.

    1. (kaufen) _____ ihr die Kassetten?
    2. (warten) Peter und Dieter _____ schon.
    3. (wissen) Das _____ ich nicht.
    4. (fragen) _____ doch Frau Lohmann, Andreas!
    5. (sein) _____ Sie sportlich, Herr Tobler?
    6. (lesen) Was _____ ihr denn?
    7. (haben) _____ du heute Zeit?
    8. (geben) Wir _____ am Samstag eine Party.
    9. (kennen) Ich _____ das Mädchen nicht.
    10. (beginnen) Das Konzert _____ um sechs Uhr.
    11. (bekommen) Maria _____ keine gute Note.
    12. (gehen) _____ Sie bitte zu Fuß!

II. Form questions from these statements.

❐ Er heißt Walter.
   Heißt er Walter?

1. Lübeck liegt im Norden.
2. Ihr schreibt das Wort.
3. Die Schule beginnt um acht.
4. Peter hat eine Freundin.
5. Er weiß das nicht.
6. Berlin ist die Hauptstadt.
7. Die Jugendlichen hören die Musik.
8. Sie kennt die Lehrerin nicht.
9. Du kommst nicht zur Party.
10. Heinz fragt dasMädchen.

III. Form questions by asking for the italicized words. Use these question words: *wer, wen, wo, woher, wohin.*

1. Das Kino ist *in der Stadt.*
2. *Frau Gruber* wartet da drüben.
3. Beide fahren *nach Hause.*
4. Maria kommt *aus Österreich.*
5. Wir fragen *eine Verkäuferin.*
6. Sie gehen *ins Kino.*
7. Herbert kennt *Jutta.*
8. Die Rockband ist schon *da.*
9. *Herr Riebe* wohnt hier.
10. Essen liegt *im Westen der Bundesrepublik.*

IV. Complete the following sentences.

1. Wir gehen gern _____.
2. Der Film _____.
3. Die Karten sind _____.
4. Heute fahren wir _____.
5. Ich kaufe _____.
6. Wieviel ist _____?
7. Er lernt _____.
8. Wohnst du _____?

124

V. *Haben, sein, kennen* oder *wissen*? Fill in the proper verb form in the following sentences.

1. _____ du Herrn Schmidt?
2. Morgen _____ ich keine Schule.
3. Warum _____ ihr so aufgeregt?
4. _____ Monika Mathe gern?
5. Ich _____ nicht, um wieviel Uhr sie kommt.
6. Lisel und Helmut _____ sechzehn.
7. Frau Holz ist neu hier. Ich _____ sie nicht.
8. Kommt er später? _____ du das?
9. Wir _____ zwei Karten.
10. Ich _____ nicht sehr sportlich.

VI. Supply the correct form of the definite article.

❐ _____ Stadt liegt weit von hier.
Die Stadt liegt weit von hier.

1. Frag doch _____ Lehrer!
2. Hörst du _____ Musik?
3. Wo ist _____ Rockkonzert?
4. _____ Buch ist dort.
5. Ich kaufe _____ Kassette.
6. Wir wissen _____ Aufgabe.
7. Kennt ihr _____ Jungen?
8. _____ Herr kommt pünktlich.

Zungenbrecher

Brauchbare Bierbrauerburschen brauen brausendes Braunbier.
(Useful beer brewery fellows are brewing foaming brown beer.)

Jugendliche hören gern Schallplatten (records) von Grönemeyer.

Der Zirkus kommt.

Auf dem Oktoberfest in München.

Sie machen Musik.

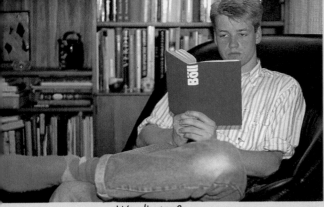
Was liest er?

Das Festspielhaus in Bayreuth

Kulturecke

Entertainment and Leisure-Time Activities

Entertainment in Germany is a national pastime for almost everyone. Put simply — Germans love to be entertained.

This is obvious to the visitor who sees numerous round columns (*Litfaßsäulen*) covered with posters announcing the various events taking place in town.

The larger cities provide the most opportunities for different types of entertainment. Internationally known stars tour Germany throughout the year. American rock stars have made a long-lasting impact, particularly among the younger generation.

Neighborhood movie theaters feature both German and foreign films. American movies are particularly popular. There are more than 185 theaters that receive subsidies from state and local governments. Many of the theaters today, as in Berlin, for example, have performances that will suit almost everyone. Most Germans buy their theater tickets well in advance or they subscribe to season tickets. Besides the major city theaters, there are also the small theaters that cater to specific tastes. The big cities also pride themselves on offering major musical performances such as in the city of Bayreuth where it is always difficult to get tickets for performances.

Outdoor theaters present plays during the summer months for local audiences, tourists and vacationers. Small-time entertainment is provided by various groups, especially university students. To the delight of shoppers, most shopping areas attract musicians who depend on the audience's enjoyment and consequent gratuity. Every large city has a zoo, which caters to all ages. American and European circus troupes tour the country every year. As in the U.S., German cities hold fairs at least once or twice a year offering carnival attractions of many types and the traditional rides for thrill-seekers.

There are numerous festivals in Germany throughout the year. Dressed in their folk costumes, these groups provide color and entertainment for the townspeople and visitors. The largest bands and crowds can be seen at the annual *Oktoberfest* in München, where over a million people congregate in an atmosphere that the Germans call *Gemütlichkeit*. The *Oktoberfest* takes place from late September to early October, but the famous *Karneval* in Köln is usually held during the month of February. Hundreds of thousands of people line the streets to witness the parade.

The German people enjoy many leisure-time activities. From September through May, millions of German fans watch the major and minor soccer matches throughout the country every week. During the summer, many Germans head for the water for swimming, sailing or fishing. Some rent boats of various types and explore the rivers and lakes on their own. Every city has one or more outdoor swimming pools that are modern and offer many facilities to the public.

The winter months offer other entertainment opportunities. Ice-skating, for example, has become very popular in recent years, particularly among the young. Furthermore, Germans head south to the mountainous area and go skiing — downhill or cross-country.

Every eighth German is a hiker. Major parks and forests have numerous hiking paths that are usually outlined on large boards right at the entrance of the path. The hiking paths are also well marked. Bicycling has always been a favorite diversion among all age groups. There are many well-marked bicycle paths in the cities and towns and throughout the countryside. Some people enjoy horseback riding in the city parks and in the country, or being pulled in a horse-drawn wagon.

People who don't care to exert themselves in active sports can stroll around the beautifully landscaped parks found throughout Germany. After a long walk, it is no problem to find a place to sit down. Benches have been provided all over for people to relax and watch the world go by. Ice cream stands, stationary or even mobile, add further delight for people of all ages. Outdoor cafés have long been traditional German gathering places. Here, people order a cup of coffee or cola and sit for an hour or two

Viele fahren gern nach Rothenburg.

Wohin kann man in Gera gehen?

Bühnen der Stadt **Gera**
Dimitroffallee 2 ☎ 6940
Informationen und Kartenerwerb im Besucherservice Sorge 33

Oper
Operette   Ballett
   Musical   Schauspiel
Konzert   Puppentheater

without an obligation to order anything else. Outdoor chess games are quite popular. Chess figures two or three feet high are moved on one-foot squares. Minigolf courses can be found throughout Germany. Unusual to Americans are the concrete putting areas. Most Germans consider yard work a leisure-time activity. Those who are not fortunate enough to have their own yard may have a *Kleingarten* (sometimes called *Schrebergarten*) on the edge of town. On this rented plot, they can spend hours and hours tending flowers, trees, fruits and vegetables.

Germans enjoy reading. There are newspaper stands scattered all over. Many Germans, regardless of age, can be seen reading outdoors on benches or, as a matter of fact, anyplace where they can find a spot to sit down.

The most common leisure-time activity in Germany is watching television. Although most Germans have a wide range of interests, more than one-fourth consider television viewing as their only pastime. Similar to American teenagers, many young people in Germany enjoy listening to popular music. Others learn and practice playing their own instruments.

Perhaps the most increasingly popular leisure-time activity is the computer. Germans enjoy the variety of challenging games and the education value which the computer has to offer.

Wie heißt diese Stadt?

Titisee im Schwarzwald (Black Forest) ist sehr bekannt.

Was weißt du? Complete each sentence by selecting the appropriate items from the list below. You will not need all the items listed.

posters	concrete	bicycle paths	Köln
streets	going to theaters	München	watching TV
grass	town	nine	squares
skiing	eight	hiking paths	boards
Bayreuth	café	theater tickets	photos

1. _____ is the most common leisure-time activity.
2. The *Oktoberfest* is an annual celebration in _____.
3. One out of _____ Germans is a hiker.
4. The soccer season in Germany lasts _____ months.
5. *Litfaßsäulen* are usually covered with _____.
6. The famous *Karneval* takes place in _____.
7. Most Germans buy their _____ in advance.
8. The *Kleingarten* is usually found right outside of _____.
9. Many cities have well-marked _____.
10. Germans can sit for a long time in a _____ while drinking a cup of coffee.
11. _____ are usually indicated on large boards.
12. Big chess figures are moved on one-foot _____.
13. Many German minigolf courses are _____.
14. Major musical performances take place in _____.

Vokabeln

alle all, everyone
Amerika America
der April April
aufgeregt excited
aufmachen to open
der August August
ausverkauft sold out
die Band,-s band
sich beeilen to hurry
    Beeil dich! Hurry (up)! (singular)
    Beeilt euch! Hurry (up)! (plural)
beginnen to begin
beide both
bekannt well-known
bitte please
der Dezember December
drängeln to push, shove
einfach simple
einmal once
    noch einmal once more
etwas some, a little, something
der Fan,-s fan
der Februar February
der Film,-e film, movie
fotografieren to take pictures
der Frühling,-e spring
geben to give
    es gibt there is (are)
das Geld money
genug enough
heiß hot
der Herbst,-e fall, autumn
der Hit,-s hit (song, tune)
die Idee,-n idea
ihre (form of ihr) her
der Januar January
jubeln to cheer
der Jugendliche,-n youngster, teenager, youth
der Juli July

der Juni June
kalt cold
die Karte,-n ticket
das Kino,-s movie theater
klasse super, fantastic
klatschen to clap, applaud
das Konzert,-e concert
die Konzerthalle,-n concert hall
kosten to cost
kritisch critical
kühl cool
lange long, long time
langweilig boring
laufen to run
    Der Film läuft schon. The movie is running already.
laut loud
letzt- last
los sein to be going on
    Da ist viel los. There's a lot going on.
machen to do, make
    Das macht 5 Mark. That comes to 5 marks.
    Das macht nichts. That doesn't matter.
der Mai May
die Mark mark (German monetary unit)
der März March
mehr more
    nicht mehr no more
meinen to mean, think
mitkommen to come along
möchten to would like to
    Ich möchte... I would like to...
der Monat,-e month

das Nachbarland,-̈er neighboring country
nichts nothing
der November November
der Oktober October
Österreich Austria
die Pause,-n intermission, break
populär popular
regnen to rain
der Rhythmus rhythm
die Rockband,-s rock band
das Rockkonzert,-e rock concert
rüberkommen to come over
scheinen to shine
schneien to snow
schreien to scream, shout, yell
die Schweiz Switzerland
seine (form of sein) his
singen to sing
der September September
die Show,-s show
spannend exciting, thrilling
spitze hot, super
der Sommer,- summer
die Sonne sun
die Stunde,-n hour
super super, great
die Tür,-en door
die Verkäuferin,-nen saleslady, clerk
verstehen to understand
war (past tense of sein) was
warm warm
das Wetter weather
der Winter,- winter
wirklich really
die Woche,-n week
zurück back

Communicative Functions

- ordering in a café
- talking about what to do today
- naming beverages and various ice creams
- giving directions
- expressing how food tastes
- talking about going to a dance

Ein Eis, bitte!

(auf dem Weg)

Marc: Sollen wir ein Eis essen?
Gabi: Gute Idee.
Ali: Ich komme auch mit.
Gabi: Gehen wir doch zum Eiscafé Rialto.
Marc: Ja, die haben italienisches Eis.
Ali: Das schmeckt besonders gut.

Falsch! **The following statements are incorrect. Provide the correct statements in German.**

1. Marc, Gabi und Ali sind zu Hause.
2. Ali kommt nicht mit.
3. Im Eiscafé gibt es nur deutsches Eis.

Sollen wir Eis essen?

Gute Idee!

Gehen wir doch zum Eiscafé!

(vor dem Eiscafé)

Marc: Die Auswahl ist hier immer groß.
Ali: Aber es ist nicht billig. Oh, ich habe zu wenig Geld.
Marc: Macht nichts. Ich kann dir ein paar Mark leihen.
Ali: Es ist schon halb vier.
Gabi: Ja und? Die Heike kann ja warten.
Marc: Ich glaube auch.
Ali: Na, wie ihr meint. Dann mal los!

Wer sagt das? **Indicate who makes reference to the following.**

1. Es ist drei Uhr dreißig.
2. Gehen wir!
3. Im Eiscafé gibt's eine große Auswahl.
4. Ich habe nicht genug Geld.
5. Heike muß warten.

(im Eiscafé)

Gabi: Ich möchte ein Milchmix.

Ali: Und ich einen Hawaiibecher.

Kellner: Bitte?

Marc: Bringen Sie bitte ein Milchmix, einen Hawaiibecher und ein Schokoeis mit Schlagsahne.

Kellner: Ich bringe es sofort. *(später)* So, bitte sehr. Hoffentlich schmeckt's.

Wie schmeckt das Eis?

Was bringt der Kellner?

Wer möchte was? Indicate what each of the three orders.

1. Ali
2. Gabi
3. Marc

(später)

Ali: Was wirst du später machen?

Marc: Du gehst ja zu Heike. Gabi, warum kommst du nicht rüber.

Gabi: Ja, ich habe nichts vor.

Marc: Im Fernsehen gibt's heute eine Quizshow.

Gabi: Toll! Dann komme ich bestimmt.

Ali: Mmmh, das Eis schmeckt sehr gut.

Marc: Zahlen, bitte.

Gabi: Ihr eßt aber schnell!

Ja oder nein? Agree or disagree with the following statements by giving complete sentences starting with *Ja,...* or *Nein,...*

1. Ali geht später zu Gabi.
2. Gabi hat heute viel zu tun.
3. Marc und Ali essen das Eis schnell.
4. Das Eis schmeckt gut.

Was machen die Jungen?

Dort bekommt man Eis.

Zahlen, bitte!

Für dich

Italian ice creams have become quite popular among Germans. A *Hawaiibecher* consists of lemon and pineapple ice cream as well as frozen yogurt. The *Milchmix* is similar to our milk shake.

Except for several cable stations and local TV stations, there are two major national TV networks in Germany, the *ARD* (*Arbeitsgemeinschaft der öffentlich-rechtlichen Rundfunkanstalten Deutschlands*) referred to as *Erstes Programm* (Channel One) and the *ZDF* (*Zweites Deutsches Fernsehen*) referred to as *Zweites Programm* (Channel Two).

Kombiniere...

Wie viele Sätze kannst du bilden? (How many sentences can you form?)

Die Auswahl	schmeckt	es	viel vor
Das Eis	gibt	später	Eis essen
Im Fernsehen	ist	immer	eine Quizshow
Gabi und Marc	möchten	nicht	besonders gut
Wir	haben	heute	groß

Es schmeckt besonders gut.

Bitte sehr.

Nützliche Ausdrücke

Wie schmeckt's?	How does it taste?
Es schmeckt besonders gut.	It tastes especially good.
Wie ist die Auswahl?	How is the selection?
Ich leihe dir zehn Mark.	I'll lend you ten marks.
Ja und?	So what?
Bitte?	May I help you?
Bitte sehr.	Here you are.
Was hast du vor?	What are you planning to do?
Zahlen, bitte!	The check, please.

Was paßt hier? **Match each expression on the left with the most appropriate response on the right.**

1. Gehen wir zum Eiscafé, Frau Tegel!
2. Bringen Sie bitte Schokoeis.
3. Ich habe nur zwei Mark.
4. Zahlen, bitte.
5. Wie ist die Auswahl?
6. Ich möchte Vanilleeis.
7. Was habt ihr heute vor?
8. Möchten Sie deutsches Eis?

a. Ich kann dir Geld leihen.
b. Achtzehn Mark, bitte.
c. Nein, wir möchten italienisches Eis.
d. Wir gehen zu Dieter.
e. Gute Idee. Dort ist die Auswahl besonders gut.
f. Ich auch.
g. Sofort.
h. Ausgezeichnet.

Ergänzung

1. *Wir sind im Eiscafé.* You joined several friends in an ice cream parlor. When the waiter comes, you're telling him what everyone wants to order.

   ❏ Heidi / ein Milchmix
     Heidi möchte ein Milchmix.

   1. Rolf / eine Cola
   2. Uwe / Vanilleeis
   3. Tina und Ulla / Apfelsaft
   4. Gisela / Zitroneneis
   5. Dieter und Hartmut / Vanilleeis mit Schlagsahne
   6. Katrin / Erdbeereis

2. Imagine you've been living in a small town in Germany for several months and have become familiar with the area. Can you help the tourists who need some assistance?

   ❏ Wo ist der Schillerpark? (gleich um die Ecke)
     Der Schillerpark ist gleich um die Ecke.

   1. Wo ist die Schule?
      (nur drei Minuten zu Fuß)
   2. Wo ist die Herderstraße?
      (nicht weit von hier)
   3. Wo ist das Eiscafé Rialto?
      (fünf Ecken vom Park)

4. Wo ist Meiers Haus?
   (um die Ecke)
5. Wo ist das Kino?
   (im Norden der Stadt)

Sag's mal!

Wie schmeckt's?

Aussprache

short /u/	long /u/
mu**ß**	**g**ut
und	**Uh**r
z**um**	Fu**ß**
um	t**u**n
M**u**sik	s**u**per
St**u**nde	kl**u**g
short /e/	**long /e/**
b**e**sser	g**eh**en
etwas	w**e**r
g**e**rn	Id**ee**
Ecke	W**e**g
H**e**rbst	l**e**st
G**e**ld	s**eh**r

Übungen

The Modal Auxiliaries: *dürfen, können, mögen, müssen, sollen, wollen*

Modal auxiliaries (sometimes called helping verbs) help to set the mood of the particular sentence in which they occur. Let's take one sentence in English and change the modal auxiliary.

He *is allowed to* go to the movie.	Er *darf* ins Kino gehen.
He *can (is able to)* go to the movie.	Er *kann* ins Kino gehen.
He *likes* to go to the movie.	Er *mag* ins Kino gehen.
He *must (has to)* go to the movie.	Er *muß* ins Kino gehen.
He *is supposed to* go to the movie.	Er *soll* ins Kino gehen.
He *wants to* go to the movie.	Er *will* ins Kino gehen.

As you can see, the meaning or "mood" in each of these sentences is different. The same is true in German. You will notice, however, that the word order remains constant in these sentences.

It is very important to remember that the infinitive of the main verb is placed at the end of the sentence. The modal auxiliary appears in the position normally held by the verb when it is a single word.

Beispiel:

		modal auxiliary		infinitive
statement	Tina	will	in die Stadt	gehen.
question		Will	Tina in die Stadt	gehen?

If a modal auxiliary is used with a verb containing a separable prefix, the prefix is not separated from the verb.

Beispiel: Uwe will ins Kino mitkommen.
Uwe wants to come along to the movie theater.

Sometimes, the main verb can be eliminated provided that the meaning is clear by using only the modal auxiliary.

Beispiele: Ich muß schon um sieben Uhr in die Schule.
I have to go to school already at seven o'clock.

Möchtest du ein Glas Milch?
Would you like (to have) a glass of milk?

Except for *sollen*, all other modal auxiliaries show a stem vowel change from the singular to the plural.

	dürfen may, to be permitted to	**können** can, to be able to	**mögen** to like	**müssen** must, to have to	**sollen** to be supposed to, should	**wollen** to want to
ich	darf	kann	mag	muß	soll	will
du	darfst	kannst	magst	mußt	sollst	willst
er sie es	darf	kann	mag	muß	soll	will
wir	dürfen	können	mögen	müssen	sollen	wollen
ihr	dürft	könnt	mögt	müßt	sollt	wollt
sie	dürfen	können	mögen	müssen	sollen	wollen
Sie	dürfen	können	mögen	müssen	sollen	wollen

Mögen is used most commonly to express liking or preference in the sense of *gern haben* (like to have), *gern essen* or *trinken* (like to eat or drink). Today it is quite frequently used in the negative, often without the main verb: *Er mag das Buch nicht.* (He doesn't like the book). A more common form derived from *mögen* is *möchten* (would like to). *Sie möchte nach Deutschland fahren.* (She would like to go to Germany).

The forms of *möchten* (would like to) are: *ich, er, sie, es möchte; du möchtest; wir, sie* (plural), *Sie möchten; ihr möchtet.*

3. ***Was wollt ihr denn machen?*** **You and your friend are considering to do a number of things. Respond accordingly.**

   ◻ ein Schokoeis essen
   Wir wollen vielleicht ein Schokoeis essen.

   1. auf Marc warten
   2. zu Fuß gehen
   3. mit dem Fahrrad fahren
   4. ein Buch lesen
   5. die Musik hören

4. Sie möchten das nicht. No one would like to do the things suggested. *Folge dem Beispiel!*

❑ Möchtest du ins Kino gehen?
Nein, ich möchte nicht ins Kino gehen.

1. Möchtet ihr nach Hause fahren?
2. Möchte Rainer jetzt essen?
3. Möchten Lisa und Gabi zu Fuß gehen?
4. Möchtest du singen?
5. Möchte Daniela die Karte kaufen?
6. Möchtet ihr fotografieren?

5. Du sollst das tun. A list of things has been left at home for you to do. Express what you are supposed to do.

❑ zu Peter gehen
Ich soll zu Peter gehen.

1. mit dem Fahrrad in die Stadt fahren
2. ein paar Minuten warten
3. am Sonnabend eine Party geben
4. ein paar Kassetten kaufen
5. das Buch lesen

6. Wer kann das? Several of your classmates are able to do the items as indicated. Tell who can do what.

❑ Uwe / fotografieren
Uwe kann fotografieren.

1. Karin und Timo / die Aufgabe machen
2. Monika / nach München fahren
3. Günter / drei Karten kaufen
4. ihr / zu Fuß gehen
5. wir / laut sprechen
6. du / schon früh kommen

7. Beantworte diese Fragen!

1. Wohin möchtest du fahren?
2. Was sollst du nicht tun?
3. Wer will zum Eiscafé gehen?
4. Was mag Wolfgang nicht?
5. Was muß er heute noch machen?
6. Wen kann er nicht hören?
7. Was dürft ihr später machen?

8. *Was fehlt hier?* In the following sentences, provide the proper form of the modal auxiliaries as well as the main verb of the sentence.

1. _____ ihr die Musik _____?
   (want to hear)
2. Herr Meier _____ bald in der Stadt _____.
   (have to be)
3. Wann _____ das Konzert _____?
   (supposed to begin)
4. Ich _____ das Fahrrad _____.
   (would like to buy)
5. Wir _____ die Arbeit _____.
   (have to write)
6. _____ Diana zur Party _____?
   (supposed to come along)
7. Was _____ du denn _____?
   (want to read)
8. Heiko _____ schon um neun _____.
   (can come)
9. Du _____ das nicht _____.
   (permitted to do)
10. _____ Sie den Kellner _____?
    (can ask)

9. *Das können wir nicht verstehen. Warum kommt sie nicht mit?* Construct meaningful sentences using the information given.

1. Was / wollen / wir / heute / tun
2. Sollen / wir / vielleicht / ins Kino gehen
3. Ich / können / nicht / in die Stadt fahren
4. Warum / können / du / nicht / mitkommen
5. Susanne und ich / müssen / die Englischaufgaben lernen
6. Möchten / du / Film / aus Italien sehen
7. Ich / wollen / Film / gern sehen
8. Heute / dürfen / ich / nicht / aus dem Haus gehen
9. Das / können / ich / nicht / verstehen

Future Tense

In trying to express events that will take place any time from the present, we may use the future tense.

Beispiel: I will read a book.
         Ich werde ein Buch lesen.

Similar to the modal auxiliaries, *werden* requires the same word order.

werden		
ich	werde	I will
du	wirst	you will
er		he will
sie }	wird	she will
es		it will
wir	werden	we will
ihr	werdet	you will
sie	werden	they will
Sie	werden	you will

Should the content of the conversation or description imply future events, often the present tense is used.

Beispiel: Morgen komme ich zu dir.
Im Herbst fahren wir nach Frankreich.

10. *Wer wird nach Deutschland fahren?* **Announce who will be going to Germany.**

❏ Herr Schulz
Herr Schulz wird nach Deutschland fahren.

    1. Holger und Alex
    2. die vier Jugendlichen
    3. mein Freund
    4. ich
    5. Karin
    6. meine Lehrerin

11. *Wann passiert das?* **(When does this take place?) Indicate when the various events take place.** *Folge dem Beispiel!*

❏ Der Film beginnt. (um acht)
Der Film wird um acht beginnen.

    1. Wir geben eine Party.
       (am Freitag)
    2. In der Stadt ist viel
       Verkehr. (immer)

3. Susi geht zum Konzert.
   (um sieben Uhr)
4. Fahren Sie zum Eiscafé?
   (später)
5. Ich kaufe die Karten.
   (im August)

12. *Bilde Sätze!* (Form sentences.)

❏ Diana / eine gute Note bekommen
   Diana wird eine gute Note bekommen.

1. ich / für das Eis zahlen
2. wir / Erdbeereis essen
3. Udo / Margit fotografieren
4. Die Lehrerin / das wissen
5. Hans und Rudi / mit dem Fahrrad kommen
6. ihr / Petra nicht kennen

13. Change the following sentences from the present to the future tense.

❏ Ich sage das nicht.
   Ich werde das nicht sagen.

1. Sie hören die Musik.
2. Oliver weiß viel.
3. Das Schokoeis schmeckt gut.
4. Die Karten sind ausverkauft.
5. Die Jugendlichen klatschen.
6. Er singt diesen Hit sehr gern.
7. Das Konzert beginnt um acht.
8. Alle kennen die Musik.
9. Ich habe keine Zeit.
10. Du verstehst kein Wort.

14. Beantworte diese Fragen!

❏ Regnet es? Ja, es...
   Ja, es wird regnen.

   Verstehst du das? Nein,...
   Nein, ich werde das nicht verstehen.

1. Hast du Angst? Nein, ich...
2. Gehen sie zu Fuß? Ja, sie...
3. Lernt ihr viel? Ja, wir...
4. Bekommst du einen Computer? Nein, ich...
5. Hört ihr diese Musik gern? Nein, wir...

6. Ist die Auswahl groß? Ja,...
7. Wartest du ein paar Minuten? Ja, ich...
8. Schmeckt das Eis dort gut? Nein, es...
9. Spielt ihr diese Kassette? Ja, wir...
10. Beginnt der Film um drei? Nein, der Film...

Plural Forms of Nouns

For singular nouns you must know the gender, that is to say, you must know whether the noun is a *der-, die-,* or *das*-word. You will have to learn these, of course. In the plural, however, all nouns are *die* in the nominative and accusative, regardless of their gender.

As you can see from the list below, most nouns undergo certain changes from the singular to the plural. There is no definite rule for the formation of plural nouns. You must learn the plural form when you learn a new noun. For simplification, all important nouns that you have learned up to this lesson, have been placed into groups whenever the change from the singular to the plural follows certain patterns.

	Singular			Plural
	masculine	**feminine**	**neuter**	
nominative	der	die	das	die
accusative	den	die	das	die

Plural of Nouns

no change	
der Computer	die Computer
der Kellner	die Kellner
der Lehrer	die Lehrer
das Mädchen	die Mädchen
der Schüler	die Schüler
der Tafellappen	die Tafellappen

add -n, -en or -nen	
die Aufgabe	die Aufgaben
die Ecke	die Ecken
die Idee	die Ideen
der Jugendliche	die Jugendlichen
der Junge	die Jungen
die Karte	die Karten
die Kassette	die Kassetten
die Minute	die Minuten
der Name	die Namen
die Note	die Noten
die Pause	die Pausen
die Schule	die Schulen
die Schultasche	die Schultaschen
die Seite	die Seiten
die Stunde	die Stunden
die Tafel	die Tafeln
die Tasse	die Tassen
die Woche	die Wochen
die Arbeit	die Arbeiten
die Frau	die Frauen
der Herr	die Herren
die Tür	die Türen
die Uhr	die Uhren
die Freundin*	die Freundinnen
die Lehrerin*	die Lehrerinnen
die Verkäuferin*	die Verkäuferinnen

*In most cases, -in is added to indicate a female person (Freund/Freundin, Lehrer/Lehrerin, Verkäufer/Verkäuferin).

add -e or ⸚e	
der Bleistift	die Bleistifte
der Film	die Filme
der Freund	die Freunde
das Heft	die Hefte
das Konzert	die Konzerte
das Lineal	die Lineale
das Telefon	die Telefone
der Fuß	die Füße
die Schulbank	die Schulbänke
die Stadt	die Städte

add ⸚er	
das Buch	die Bücher
das Fach	die Fächer
das Fahrrad	die Fahrräder
das Glas	die Gläser
das Haus	die Häuser
das Land	die Länder

add -s	
die Band	die Bands
die CD	die CDs
der Fan	die Fans
der Hit	die Hits
das Kino	die Kinos
der Kuli	die Kulis
der Park	die Parks
der Radiergummi	die Radiergummis
die Show	die Shows
das Sweatshirt	die Sweatshirts

15. *Und ihr?* **You are comparing various items with your friends.** *Folge dem Beispiel!*

❐ Ich habe ein Buch hier. Und ihr? (fünf)
Wir haben fünf Bücher hier.

1. Ich habe ein Fahrrad zu Hause. Und ihr? (ein paar)
2. Ich spiele eine Kassette. Und ihr? (viele)
3. Ich kaufe einen Kuli. Und ihr? (drei)
4. Ich lese eine Seite. Und ihr? (vierzig)
5. Ich frage einen Lehrer. Und ihr? (zwei)
6. Ich höre ein Konzert. Und ihr? (vier)

16. *Was oder wen verstehst du gut?* **Indicate what or whom you understand well.**

❐ die Frau
Ich verstehe die Frauen gut.

1. das Mädchen
2. die Aufgabe
3. den Lehrer

4. die Verkäuferin
5. den Computer
6. den Jungen

17. *Was möchtest du kaufen?* Describe what you would like to buy.

❒ Ich möchte Hefte kaufen.

1.   2.   3.   4.   5.   6.

18. **Change the following sentences from the singular to the plural.**

❒ Ich lese das Buch.
Wir lesen die Bücher.

1. Hörst du die Band?
2. Die Kassette ist toll.
3. Ich frage die Frau.
4. Der Junge kauft die Karte.
5. Die Lehrerin kennt das Mädchen.
6. Kaufst du nicht den Kuli?
7. Ich schreibe die Arbeit.
8. Wie heißt der Lehrer?

19. **Provide the plural form as indicated.**

❒ eine Freundin: ein paar _____
ein paar Freundinnen

1. ein Haus: drei _____
2. ein Fahrrad: viele _____
3. eine Woche: zwei _____
4. ein Schüler: zehn _____
5. eine Stunde: sechs _____
6. eine Show: acht _____
7. ein Computer: so viele _____
8. eine Seite: ein paar _____
9. ein Fach: sieben _____
10. eine Tür: nicht viele _____

Steht da ein Fahrrad?

Words Used for Emphasis

A number of German words are used strictly for emphasis. Such words are *aber, auch, denn, doch* and *ja*. These words cannot be translated literally but are particularly important in conversational usage.

Beispiele:	*Du bist klug.*	You're smart.
	Du bist aber klug.	Aren't you smart!
	Warum kommst du so spät?	Why are you coming so late?
	Warum kommst du auch so spät?	Why *did* you have to come so late?
	Wer kommt zur Party?	Who is coming to the party?
	Wer kommt denn zur Party?	Who *is* coming to the party? (or: Tell me, who is coming to the party.)
	Gehen wir zu Monika.	Let's go to Monika.
	Gehen wir doch zu Monika.	Why don't we go to Monika?
	Ich habe keinen Bleistift.	I don't have a pencil.
	Ich habe ja keinen Bleistift.	But I don't have a pencil.

Der Jugendklub in Altenburg

Wohin wollen sie gehen?

Britta soll singen.

Der Björn kann zeigen, was er kann.

Hoffentlich spielt der Diskjockey heute tolle Hits.

Die Musik ist super.

Lesestück

Im Jugendklub

Warum gehen Björn, Andreas, Natascha und Katja gern
zum Jugendklub°? Dort ist immer viel los, besonders   *youth club*
jeden Donnerstag. Auch heute wollen sie wieder zum
Jugendklub. Schon um halb sieben sind sie dort. Sie
können aber erst° um sieben hineingehen°.   *only/go inside*

Andreas:	Wir müssen noch eine halbe Stunde warten.
Björn:	Macht nichts. Wir haben ja Zeit.
Natascha:	Hoffentlich spielt der Diskjockey heute tolle Hits.
Katja:	Dann kann der Björn zeigen°, wie gut er tanzt°.
Andreas:	Das möchte ich wirklich sehen°.

show
dances
see

Die vier warten noch ein paar Minuten. Es sind schon andere Jugendliche vor dem Jugendklub. Um sieben Uhr machen sie die Tür auf°. Jetzt wollen auch die beiden Jungen und Mädchen hinein. Im Klub finden° sie gleich einen Tisch°. Es wird immer erst um acht voll°.

open up
find
table/full

Andreas:	Ich habe Durst°. Und ihr?
Natascha:	Ich auch.
Katja:	Wie immer, bring doch Cola.
Andreas:	Mach ich.
Natascha:	Andreas ist mal wieder° ein Kavalier°.
Björn:	Das stimmt. Ich habe heute nicht genug Geld. Nächste° Woche bin ich dran°.
Andreas:	So, vier Colas.
Katja:	Prost°!
Björn:	Mmmh, die schmeckt gut.

I'm thirsty.
once again/gentleman
next
It's my turn.
Cheers!

Peter, der Diskjockey, ist heute mit seiner Freundin Britta da. Britta ist eine gute Sängerin°. Die Jugendlichen wollen nicht, daß° Peter Kassetten spielt. Britta soll singen. Sie singt ein paar bekannte Hits. Die Jugendlichen klatschen. Britta ist im Jugendklub sehr beliebt.

singer
that

Andreas:	Warum sitzen° wir hier?
Katja:	Das möchte ich auch wissen.
Björn:	Viele tanzen schon. Dann mal los!
Andreas:	Die Musik ist super.
Katja:	Und auch schnell.
Natascha:	Es ist hier sehr heiß.
Andreas:	Ja, ich schwitze° auch. Zurück zur Cola! Die ist noch kalt.

are sitting
sweating

Wer...? Identify the person or persons each phrase refers to based on the Lesestück.

❏ zum Jugendklub gehen
  Björn, Andreas, Natascha und Katja gehen zum Jugendklub.

1. sehr schwitzen
2. nächste Woche dran sein
3. Durst haben
4. ein paar Hits singen
5. mit seiner Freundin da sein
6. nicht genug Geld haben
7. klatschen
8. ein Kavalier sein

1. Wer geht gern zum Jugendklub?
2. Um wieviel Uhr können sie in den Jugendklub hineingehen?
3. Wie lange müssen die vier warten?
4. Bekommen sie gleich einen Tisch?
5. Was bringt Andreas?
6. Warum kauft Björn die Cola nicht?
7. Wie schmeckt die Cola?
8. Wie heißt der Diskjockey?
9. Was wollen die Jugendlichen nicht?
10. Was singt Britta?
11. Haben die Jugendlichen Britta gern?
12. Warum will Andreas nicht mehr tanzen?

Übung macht den Meister!

1. *Ich möchte...* Tell one of your classmates that you would like to have some ice cream and ask if he or she would like to come along. Determine when and where you should meet.

2. Make up a list of your favorite ice creams and include the price for each in German marks (DM). Pretend that you are the waiter/waitress. Your customers (classmates) are asking you what ice creams you have today. You tell them what they are and the cost. Some additional words and expressions you may find useful are: *Wieviel kostet...?* (How much is...?), *Es kostet...* (it costs...), *Ananaseis* (pineapple ice cream), *Pfirsicheis* (peach ice cream), *Nußeis* (nut ice cream).

3. *Wo ist...?* Pretend that you are in Germany and several people (your classmates) want to know the location of various places. Help them out. *Beispiel: Wo ist die Schule? Fünf Minuten zu Fuß von hier.*

4. *Gehen wir zur Disko!* Describe your intention of going to a disco. In your description include the following information: the name of the place you're going to, time the dance starts, who is coming along, whether or not they have a DJ or a live band, etc.

Erweiterung

20. *Kannst du die Sätze ergänzen?* (Can you complete the sentences?) Be sure that each sentence is meaningful.

1. Das Eis _____.
2. Um wieviel Uhr _____?
3. Wir gehen _____.
4. Müßt ihr _____?
5. Die Jugendlichen _____.
6. Im Jugendklub _____.
7. Ich habe _____.
8. Die Jungen bekommen _____.

21. *Was paßt hier?* Use the items below to complete each sentence.

später	groß	voll	Durst	Mark
lange	Sängerin	Klub	sehr	gut

1. Das Schokoeis schmeckt _____ gut.
2. Die Auswahl ist _____.
3. Willst du die Cola? Ja, ich habe _____.
4. Im _____ ist immer viel los.
5. Ich kann dir ein paar _____ leihen.
6. Um neun Uhr ist es dort immer _____.
7. Was machst du _____?
8. Angelika ist eine gute _____.
9. Wir müssen _____ vor der Tür warten.
10. Ich zeige Rainer, wie _____ sie tanzt.

22. *Ich möchte mit dir tanzen.* Imagine you are at a school dance. You have your eyes set on one particular person and would like to ask that person to dance. Complete the following conversation accordingly.

_____

Hallo!

_____

Ganz gut.

_____

Ja, jeden Freitag.

_____

Ja, die Rockmusik ist immer gut.

_____

Ja, gern.

23. Beantworte diese Fragen!

1. Wohin gehst du heute?
2. Was trinkst du gern?
3. Wo ist der Jugendklub?
4. Was spielt der Diskjockey?
5. Was möchtest du machen?
6. Wo mußt du warten?
7. Wie ist die Auswahl im Eiscafé?
8. Was willst du denn sehen?

Sprachspiegel

24. *Was paßt hier?* Find the responses on the right that answer the questions on the left.

1. Was ist dort los?
2. Möchtest du den Film sehen?
3. Was macht ihr morgen?
4. Wann machen sie die Tür auf?
5. Hast du Durst?
6. Kennst du die Sängerin?
7. Wo sollst du sitzen?
8. Singt er viele Hits?
9. Warum schwitzt ihr denn?
10. Willst du das Buch nicht lesen?

a. Um sechs Uhr.
b. Ja, sie ist ganz bekannt.
c. Wir werden ins Kino gehen.
d. Am Tisch hier.
e. Ja, es soll interessant sein.
f. Viele Jugendliche tanzen.
g. Nein, aber ich möchte etwas essen.
h. Ja, er kommt aus Frankreich.
i. Nein, nur ein paar.
j. Es ist so heiß.

25. *Gehen wir tanzen!* Describe (in narrative and/or dialog style) the following sequence, using the cues merely as a guideline.

You're planning to go to a dance. You call your friend to find out if he or she would like to come along. Your friend tells you that he or she would like to go but doesn't have enough money. You indicate that you have enough and that you'll lend him or her the money. He or she agrees and you'll determine a time and place to meet.

26. *Wie sagt man's?* From the list below, select the appropriate words to complete the various short conversational exchanges.

habe   schon   heiß   vor   hier
schmeckt singt   viele   gehst   zwei
los   spät   zu   macht   bekannt

1. Warum sitzt ihr hier?
   Es ist hier nicht so _____.
2. Kennst du diesen Hit?
   Ja, er ist ganz _____.
3. Wo ist die Adenauerstraße, bitte?
   Ungefähr acht Ecken von _____.
   Fährst du mit dem Fahrrad?
   Nein, ich gehe _____ Fuß.

4. Wie _____ die Cola?
   Nicht schlecht.
   Kannst du _____ kaufen?
   Ja, ich habe fünf Mark.
5. Ich _____ nicht genug Geld.
   Ich auch nicht.
6. Ist heute viel _____?
   Nein, nur jeden Sonnabend.
7. Was _____ sie denn?
   Ich kenne diesen Hit nicht.
8. Wieviel Uhr ist es _____?
   Elf Uhr.
   So _____ schon?
   Na, dann mal los!
9. Was _____ ihr im Jugendklub?
   Wir singen dort gern.
   Kommen immer _____?
   Ja, dreißig oder vierzig.
10. Ich habe nichts _____.
    Möchtest du zu Heike mitkommen?
    Wann _____ du zu Heike?
    In ein oder zwei Stunden.

27. *Beantworte diese Fragen!*

1. Was ist hier los?
2. Was macht ihr nach der Schule?
3. Warum klatschen sie so laut?
4. Was habt ihr morgen vor?
5. Wie ist die Musik?
6. Hast du viel zu tun?
7. Warum schwitzt du denn?
8. Möchtest du ein Milchmix?

Rückblick

I. *Nein, das stimmt nicht.* **You don't agree with what is being said.**

❑ Paul hat ein Fahrrad.
Nein, er hat kein Fahrrad.

Wir schreiben das.
Nein, wir schreiben das nicht.

1. Die Jugendlichen tanzen gern.
2. Wir essen Eis gern.
3. Britta möchte ein Milchmix.
4. Die Auswahl ist sehr groß.
5. Björn geht oft zum Jugendklub.
6. Wir bringen einen Freund.
7. Er kann einen Tisch finden.
8. Der Kellner hat eine Mark.

II. *Wer, Wen, Was, Wo, Wohin?*

1. _____ weißt du?
2. _____ sind sie denn? Zu Hause.
3. _____ fragst du den Verkäufer?
4. _____ wohnen Sie?
5. _____ kennst du? Peter und Susi.
6. _____ fahren wir? In die Stadt.
7. _____ ist das? Sie heißt Tina.
8. _____ wartet ihr später?
9. _____ bringst du zur Party mit, Rolf?
10. _____ tanzt dort so toll?

III. *Kennen, wissen, sein* **oder** *haben?* **Complete each sentence by providing the correct form of one of these verbs.**

1. _____ ihr, wo ich Maria finden kann?
2. _____ du am Sonntag etwas Zeit?

3. Die Karten _____ sehr teuer.
4. Herr Haller _____ die Schüler gut.
5. Wo _____ denn Jens jetzt wieder?
6. Die Jugendlichen _____ diesen Tanz gern.
7. Um wieviel Uhr kommt ihr aus der Schule? Das _____ich nicht.
8. Ich _____ diese Verkäuferin nicht. Sie ist neu hier.

IV. *Was ist das Gegenteil von diesen Wörtern?* (What are the opposites of these words?)

1. gut
2. groß
3. wenig
4. schwer
5. hier
6. spät
7. ohne
8. spannend
9. gegen
10. heiß
11. nein
12. nach

V. **Supply the missing words. Keep the proper sequence.**

Dezember, _____, _____, September, August, _____, Juni, Mai, _____, März, _____, Januar

vier, _____, _____, sechzehn, zwanzig, _____, achtundzwanzig, _____, sechsunddreißig, _____

Mittwoch, _____, Freitag, Sonnabend, _____, _____, Dienstag

VI. **Wie heißen die vier Jahreszeiten?**

VII. *Wieviel Uhr ist es?* **Express the time differently from what is provided.**

❐   Es ist Viertel vor fünf.
    Es ist fünfzehn Minuten vor fünf.

1. Es ist halb neun.
2. Es ist Viertel nach elf.
3. Es ist sieben vor drei.
4. Es ist sechs Uhr dreißig.
5. Es ist fünf nach acht.
6. Es ist vier Minuten vor halb zwei.

Innsbruck

Land und Leute

Österreich

Österreich ist eine Republik. Das Land liegt in der Mitte° von Europa. Österreich ist ungefähr so groß wie der Staat Maine. Es hat mehr als° sieben Millionen Einwohner. Fast° 99% sprechen Deutsch. Österreich hat sieben Nachbarländer — die Schweiz, Liechtenstein, Italien, Jugoslawien, Ungarn, die Tschechoslowakei und die Bundesrepublik Deutschland. In Österreich gibt es neun Bundesländer°. Die Nationalfahne° ist rot-weiß-rot°.

Das Land liegt zum größten Teil° in den Alpen. Die Berge° verlaufen° von Westen nach Osten. Der höchste° Berg ist der Großglockner. Er ist 3 798 m (Meter) hoch. Die Donau ist der längste Fluß°. Sie fließt° von Westen nach Osten und hat in Österreich eine Länge° von 347 Kilometern.

Die Hauptstadt von Österreich ist Wien. Mehr als 20% der Österreicher wohnen in der Hauptstadt. Wien liegt

center

more than

almost

Federal States
national flag/red-white-red

mostly
mountains/run/highest

longest river/flows
length

Das Land liegt zum größten Teil in den Alpen.

Wien, die Hauptstadt

In Österreich ist es sehr schön.

im Osten Österreichs. Dort ist das Land flach°. Die
Donau fließt durch° Wien. Im Süden liegt Graz, eine
andere große Stadt. Linz liegt im Nordosten. Die Donau
fließt auch durch Linz. Nach Wien, Graz, und Linz
kommt Salzburg im Nordwesten. Salzburg ist eine be-
liebte° Stadt. Viele Touristen kommen jedes Jahr im
Sommer zum Musikfest° nach Salzburg. Innsbruck ist
die fünftgrößte Stadt in Österreich. Diese Stadt liegt im

flat
through

popular
music festival

Westen und ist während° jeder Jahreszeit° beliebt. *during/season*
Besonders schön ist es dort im Winter. Viele Winter-
sportler besuchen° dann Innsbruck und Umgebung°. *winter athletes visit/area*

Welche Städte möchtest du in Österreich besuchen?
Wien, Graz, Linz, Salzburg oder Innsbruck? Warum
möchtest du sie gern sehen?

Was weißt du? Beantworte diese Fragen!

1. Wie groß ist Österreich?
2. Wo liegt das Land?
3. Wie viele Nachbarländer hat Österreich?
4. Wie heißen sie?
5. Wie viele Bundesländer gibt es?
6. Wie heißt der höchste Berg? Wie hoch ist er?
7. Fließt die Donau von Norden nach Süden?
8. Wo liegt Wien?
9. Warum ist Salzburg so beliebt?
10. Wo liegt Innsbruck?

Was paßt hier?

1. Wien ist
2. Die Donau ist
3. Viele Wintersportler kommen
4. Der höchste Berg heißt
5. Österreich ist
6. Viele Touristen kommen
7. Österreich liegt
8. Die Donau fließt
9. Graz liegt
10. In der Umgebung von Wien gibt es

a. durch Linz und Wien
b. eine Republik
c. nach Salzburg
d. die Hauptstadt
e. nach Innsbruck
f. keine Berge
g. im Westen von Ungarn
h. Großglockner
i. im Süden
j. der längste Fluß

Zungenbrecher

In Ulm und um Ulm und um Ulm herum.
(In Ulm and around Ulm and all around Ulm.)

Youth Activities

Young people in Germany today have more leisure time (*Freizeit*) than youth did a generation ago. Leisure time plays a big part in the lives of young people. What do young people like to do? Their interests are not much different from those of young people in other countries.

According to a national survey, 45 percent participate in sports (*Sport*), ranging from organized sports sponsored by local clubs to neighborhood get-togethers. Swimming and soccer clubs (*Schwimm- und Fußballklubs*) are the most popular. Many are content to remain sideline spectators (*Zuschauer*) and cheer on their teams (*Mannschaften*) and friends to victory.

Thirty-seven percent of those surveyed enjoy hanging around town and talking to friends about which fashion designers are "in" and all the things you *can't* afford on an average monthly allowance (*Taschengeld*) of 40 DM.

Im Sommer haben sie viel Freizeit.

eine Reisende

zwei Fußballklubs

Hat er viel
Zeit?

Zum Zeitvertreib sitzen sie im Café.

Was macht er?

Television (*Fernsehen*) occupies a tremendous amount of time as do videocassette recorders. One in three German families owns one. Young people are crazy about computers, which they effortlessly learn to operate. Going to the movies is still the favorite pastime (*Zeitvertreib*). And this is followed by cruising around by bike or *Mofa* and going to the disco.

For most young people, the "clique," is all-important. Membership means you play by the rules...share the same interests, adopt the same slang and wear the same clothes. Twenty years ago, only 14 percent of the girls and 24 percent of the boys said they belonged to a clique. Today it is 66 percent of the boys. The girls are slightly ahead of the boys.

There is no lack of leisure-time activities available to young people by the local communities (*Gemeinschaften*), churches (*Kirchen*), social clubs (*Gesellschaftsklubs*) and youth organizations (*Jugendorganisationen*). Many other countries envy the many sports facilities, hobby centers, libraries, continuing education courses, trips and youth exchanges offered young people in Germany.

165

German youth are particularly avid travelers (*Reisende*) — no wonder in a country which shares its borders with nine other countries. Very few young people in Germany have never ventured outside their own country — and this is made easier by hitchhiking (per *Anhalter fahren*), traveling on the inexpensive youth passes issued by the European train systems, or participating in trips (*Reisen*) arranged by youth organizations. Their frequent travels facilitate international understanding and tolerance of other cultures, religions, social systems, ways of life and political views.

Was weißt du?

1. Twenty years ago, about one-fourth of the ____ indicated that they belonged to a clique.
2. The German equivalent for "hitchhiking" is ____.
3. About 33 percent of all German families own a ____.
4. Germany has its border with ____ countries.
5. German teenagers like to ride around on their bikes or on ____.
6. Many of the surveyed teenagers receive a *Taschengeld* of ____ a month.
7. About two-thirds of the boys surveyed recently say that they belong to a ____.
8. One of the favorite pastime activities, in German called ____, is going to the movies.

Das wird gut schmecken!

im Jugendklub

Vokabeln

als than
mehr als more than
der Apfelsaft apple juice
die Auswahl selection, choice
Bitte? May I help you?
Bitte sehr. Here you are.
bringen to bring
die Cola,-s cola
der Diskjockey,-s disc jockey, DJ
dran sein to be one's turn
Ich bin dran. It's my turn.
dürfen to be permitted to, may
der Durst thirst
Durst haben to be thirsty
das Eis ice, ice cream
das Eiscafé,-s ice cream parlor, café
der Eistee ice tea
das Erdbeereis strawberry ice cream
erst just
essen to eat
das Fernsehen television
finden to find

das Glas,-er glass
glauben to believe, think
der Hawaiibecher,- kind of ice cream sundae
hineingehen to go inside
hoffentlich hopefully
italienisch Italian
der Jugendklub,-s youth club
der Kaffee coffee
der Kakao hot chocolate
der Kavalier,-e gentleman
der Kellner,- waiter
können to be able to, can
lang long
längst- longest
leihen to loan, lend
mal times
mal wieder once again
das Milchmix,-e milk shake
mögen to like
müssen to have to, must
nächst- next
Prost! Cheers!
die Quizshow,-s quiz show
rot red
die Sängerin,-nen singer
die Schlagsahne whipped cream

schmecken to taste
das Schokoeis chocolate ice cream
schwitzen to sweat
sitzen to sit
sofort right away, immediately
sollen to be supposed to, should
tanzen to dance
die Tasse,-n cup
der Tisch,-e table
trinken to drink
das Vanilleeis vanilla ice cream
voll full
vorhaben to plan, intend
was what
was für what kind of
der Weg,-e way
auf dem Weg on the way
werden will, shall
wollen to want to
zahlen to pay
Zahlen, bitte. The check, please.
das Zitroneneis lemon ice cream

Hat sie viel zu tun?

Was machen sie gern in ihrer Freizeit?

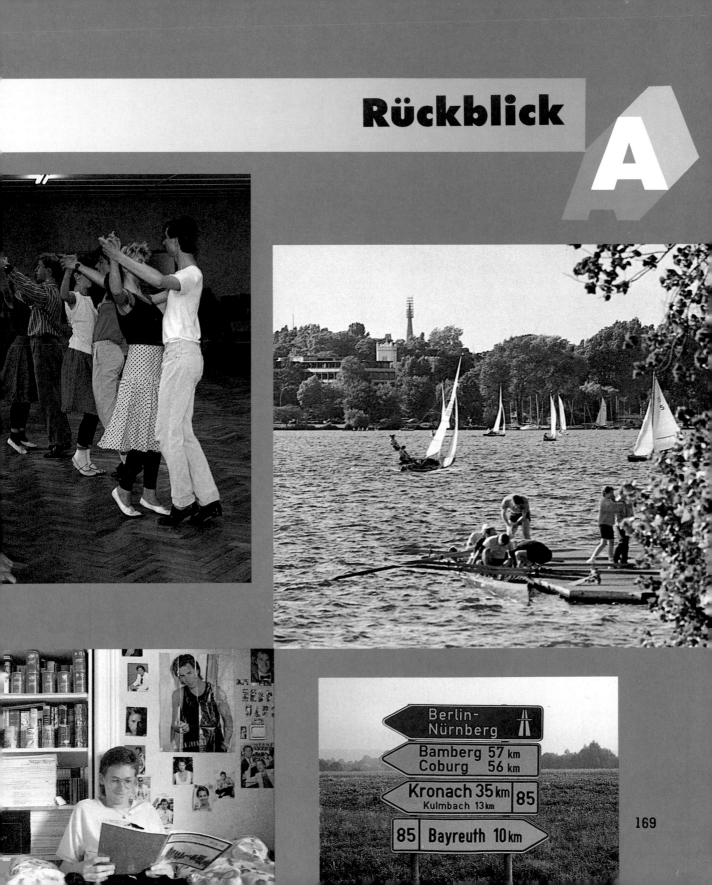

Rückblick

A

Etwas über uns!

Mein Name ist Ulli Schreiber. Ich komme aus Wilhelmshaven. Das ist eine Stadt in Norddeutschland. Ich bin sechzehn Jahre alt und gehe auf das Schiller Gymnasium, ungefähr drei Kilometer von wo ich wohne. Meine Lieblingsfächer sind Mathe und Englisch. In Mathe bekomme ich immer eine Eins, in Englisch eine Eins oder eine Zwei. Meine Freunde sind Sven und Bernd. Ich habe auch eine Freundin. Sie heißt Susi und ist sechzehn. Mein Hobby ist Briefmarken sammeln°. Wo wohnst du und was sind deine Lieblingsfächer?

Ich heiße Lisel Haller, bin fünfzehn und wohne in Chur, einer kleinen Stadt im Osten der Schweiz. Bei uns gibt es viele Berge. Jeden Winter laufen meine Freundinnen und ich oft Ski°. Das ist mein Lieblingssport. Meine Freundinnen sagen immer: „Die Lisel ist ganz sportlich." Bestimmt weißt du, was mein Lieblingsfach in der Schule ist. Ja, Sport. Ich habe auch ein Hobby. Ich höre gern Rockmusik aus Amerika. Hast du auch ein Hobby?

Ich bin Dieter Rösler und komme aus Chemnitz. Das ist eine große Stadt im Osten Deutschlands. Ich bin sechzehn. Ich gehe auf ein Gymnasium. Meine Schule ist direkt in der Stadt. Ich fahre immer mit der Straßenbahn° zur Schule. Ich habe drei Lieblingsfächer: Physik, Chemie und Deutsch. Meine Hobbys sind Bücher lesen (besonders Romane°) und Poster sammeln. Mein bester Freund ist Joachim. Er sammelt auch Poster. Wie heißt deine Schule? Wie kommst du zur Schule?

Ich heiße Rosi Steiner, bin fünfzehn und wohne in Salzburg. Weißt du, wo Salzburg liegt? Diese Stadt liegt nicht weit von Deutschland. Salzburg ist sehr bekannt und populär. Jedes Jahr kommen viele Ausländer° nach Salzburg, besonders Amerikaner. Musik ist mein Lieblingsfach. Ich spiele Gitarre sehr gern. Meine Freundinnen und ich singen oft Volkslieder°. Singst du auch gern oder spielst du ein Musikinstrument?

(*Briefmarken sammeln* to collect stamps; *laufen...Ski* to ski; *Straßenbahn* streetcar; *Romane* novels; *Ausländer* foreigners; *Volkslieder* folk-songs)

Was weißt du von Ulli, Lisel, Dieter und Rosi? **The following sentences contain information which Ulli, Lisel, Dieter and Rosi provided in their short description about themselves. For each item, state** *„Das ist..."*

❏ Diese Person wohnt in Salzburg.
Das ist Rosi.

Diese Person... Das ist...

1. sammelt gern Poster.
2. wohnt in der Schweiz.
3. spielt Gitarre gern.
4. läuft gern Ski.
5. wohnt in Wilhelmshaven.
6. bekommt in Mathe immer eine Eins.
7. hat drei Lieblingsfächer.
8. hört gern Rockmusik.
9. singt oft Volkslieder.
10. wohnt im Osten Deutschlands.
11. hat eine Freundin. Sie heißt Susi.
12. wohnt nicht weit von den Bergen.
13. kommt mit der Straßenbahn zur Schule.
14. hat einen Freund. Er heißt Joachim.
15. sammelt Briefmarken.

Du bist dran! (It's your turn!)

1. Make up a list of personal details, including such items as your name, age, address, name of school, favorite subjects, friends' names and hobbies. Use this information to introduce yourself to other classmates. To vary responses and create more interest (and a bit of humor), you may want to list items/details that don't necessarily reflect your personal data.

2. *Ein Interview.* Make up a list of personal questions using the vocabulary from the descriptions of the four young people. Address a classmate with these questions. Then, reverse the roles — your classmate will ask you questions and you answer them.

Übungen

1. **Supply the correct form of the appropriate verb from the list below.**

heißen	sagen	kennen	hören	wohnen
warten	haben	sein	kommen	kaufen

   1. _____ du ein Lieblingsfach?
   2. Frau Rabe _____ in München.
   3. Wir _____ um vier Uhr.
   4. _____ Sie gern Musik?
   5. Wie alt _____ du?
   6. Weißt du, wie er _____?
   7. Das ist Paul. _____ ihr Paul?
   8. Heidi _____ vor der Schule. Sie hat viel Zeit.
   9. Wir _____ drei Karten.
   10. Der Lehrer _____: „Es ist schon spät."

2. **Select the proper question word (*wer, wen, was, wie, wieviel, wo, woher*).**

   1. _____ wartet Kerstin?
   2. _____ kommt am Montag?
   3. _____ ist acht plus drei?
   4. _____ heißt sie?
   5. _____ fragen wir? Herrn Schmidt.
   6. _____ kommt Monika? Aus Köln.
   7. _____ kennst du? Peter.
   8. _____ liegt München?
   9. _____ sagt der Lehrer?
   10. _____ alt bist du?

3. **Change each statement to a question.**

   1. Ich lerne Deutsch.
   2. Das ist sehr leicht.
   3. Morgen schreiben wir eine Arbeit.
   4. Er hat viel zu tun.
   5. Heute geben wir eine Party.
   6. Wir kommen um acht.

4. Supply the correct form of the definite article.

1. Kennst du _____ Stadt?
2. Um wieviel Uhr kommt _____ Straßenbahn?
3. _____ Junge wohnt dort drüben.
4. Ich habe _____ Bleistift.
5. Wir fragen _____ Mädchen.
6. Karin kauft _____ Kassette.
7. Wo ist _____ Park?
8. Wir kennen _____ Lehrer.
9. Kaufen sie _____ Heft?
10. _____ Rockmusik ist toll.

5. Complete each sentence.

1. Er geht _____.
2. Was machst du _____?
3. Um wieviel Uhr _____?
4. Heute kommen _____.
5. Wir kaufen _____.
6. Hört ihr _____?

6. Beantworte diese Fragen!

1. Wie heißt du?
2. Wie heißt dein Lehrer oder deine Lehrerin?
3. Wie alt bist du?
4. Wo wohnst du?
5. Was ist dein Lieblingsfach?
6. Um wieviel Uhr ist die Schule aus?

7. Form questions by asking for the italicized words. Use the question words *wer, wen, was, wo* and *woher*.

❏ Wir wohnen *in Hamburg.*
  Wo wohnen wir?

1. Angelika kauft *ein paar Sweatshirts.*
2. Ich frage *die Lehrerin.*
3. Sie wartet *beim Park.*
4. *Andreas* ist intelligent.
5. Wir verstehen *das* nicht.
6. Tina kommt *aus Deutschland.*
7. *Frau Schmidt* weiß es.
8. Bremen liegt *im Norden.*
9. Peter und Uwe schreiben *eine Arbeit.*
10. Herr Meier kennt *Doris.*

8. *zu Hause* oder *nach Hause*?

1. Ich bin heute schon früh _____.
2. Peter hat die Schultasche _____.
3. Wir kommen am Sonntag spät _____.
4. Gehst du nach der Schule _____?
5. Wartest du _____?
6. Sie fahren _____.

9. Wieviel kannst du verstehen?

Jürgen und Oliver

Jürgen ist siebzehn Jahre alt. Er wohnt in Neustadt. Diese Stadt ist nicht groß. Sie ist klein. Jürgen ist sehr klug. In der Schule bekommt er in vielen Fächern — wie Deutsch, Englisch, Geschichte, Chemie und Biologie — oft° eine Eins.

Jürgen hat ein Moped°. Es ist neu. Er hat es sehr gern. Er fährt oft zu Oliver, Jürgens Freund. Oliver ist sechzehn und wohnt in Biburg, ungefähr fünf Kilometer von Jürgen. Es dauert° nur zehn Minuten zu Olivers Haus.

Jürgen:	Hallo, Oliver. Was machst du denn?
Oliver:	Ich muß dieses Buch lesen.
Jürgen:	Muß? Warum?
Oliver:	Für Englisch. Verstehst du das hier?
Jürgen:	Ja, das ist doch ganz leicht.
Oliver:	Das sagst du. Du bist eben klug.
Jürgen:	Komm, gehen wir zu Rolf. Renate und Silvia sind bestimmt dort.
Oliver:	Ja, und?
Jürgen:	Die bringen immer neue Hits.
Oliver:	Dann mal los!

(*oft* often; *das Moped* moped; *dauern* to take)

10. *Das ist falsch.* **The following statements which are based on the text above are incorrect. Can you provide the correct statements?** *Auf deutsch, bitte!*

1. Oliver hat ein Moped.
2. Jürgen wohnt in Biburg.
3. Jürgen und Oliver gehen zu Renate.
4. Oliver ist siebzehn.
5. Englisch ist für Oliver leicht.
6. Jürgen wohnt zehn Kilometer von Oliver.

7. Oliver bringt neue Hits zu Rolf.
8. Das Moped ist alt.
9. Neustadt ist groß.
10. Jürgen bekommt in Chemie eine Drei.

11. Supply the correct form of *sein*.

1. Um wieviel Uhr _____ Sie in der Stadt, Herr Walter?
2. _____ ihr heute pünktlich?
3. Birgit und Rainer _____ klug.
4. Ich _____ fünfzehn Jahre alt.
5. Frau Lehmann _____ morgen zu Hause.
6. _____ du sportlich?
7. Was _____ dein Lieblingsfach?
8. Wir _____ um zehn Uhr in der Stadt.

12. Provide the correct form of *haben*.

1. _____ Anna Zeit?
2. Was für Fächer _____ du?
3. Wir _____ Deutsch gern.
4. _____ Sie ein Telefon?
5. _____ ihr ein Lieblingsfach?
6. Ich _____ eine Freundin.

13. Write the numeral that identifies each of the following important historical dates. Do you know what happened that year?

1. neunzehnhundert(und)fünfundvierzig
2. vierzehnhundert(und)zweiundneunzig
3. siebzehnhundert(und)sechsundsiebzig
4. achtzehnhundert(und)einundsechzig
5. neunzehnhundert(und)vierzehn
6. achtzehnhundert(und)fünfundsechzig
7. Write the year you were born. Be sure to spell it out.

14. *Dürfen, können, mögen (möchten), müssen, sollen* oder *wollen*? Complete each sentence by using the proper form of the modal auxiliary indicated.

1. Ich _____ heute nicht mitkommen. (können)
2. _____ du den Film nicht sehen? (möchten)
3. Ja, aber Christa und ich _____ erst die Aufgaben machen. (müssen)
4. Das _____ ihr auch tun. (sollen)
5. Ich _____ gern später ins Kino gehen. (wollen)
6. Gut, wir _____ dann auch noch zum Eiscafé Roma. (können)
7. Ja, die _____ dort immer gutes italienisches Eis haben. (sollen)

8. Das _____ ich sehr gern. (mögen)
9. _____ ich um halb sieben zu dir kommen? (sollen)
10. Ja, das _____ du. (dürfen)

Nützliche Ausdrücke

Here is a summary of some phrases that you may find useful to
know when starting a conversation in German:

Sprechen Sie Englisch?	Do you speak English?
Verstehen Sie mich?	Do you understand me?
Ich spreche nur wenig Deutsch.	I speak only a little German.
Bitte, sprechen Sie etwas langsamer.	Please, speak a little more slowly.
Wiederholen Sie bitte!	Please repeat.
Ich verstehe Sie sehr gut.	I understand you very well.
Ich bin Amerikaner.	I am an American (male).
Ich bin Amerikanerin.	I am an American (female).
Woher kommen Sie?	Where are you from?
Ich komme aus...	I come from...
Ich bin seit zwei Wochen in Deutschland.	I have been in Germany for two weeks.
Mein Name ist... (Ich heiße...)	My name is...

Ich komme aus Fulda.

Woher kommst du?

Cultural Notes

Greetings

Hallo!
(Hi!)

is frequently used among children and young adults.

Guten Tag!
(Hello!)

is the most commonly used greeting throughout the day. *Tag!* is more commonly heard in conversations.

Grüß Gott!
(Hello!)

is used by people in southern Germany and Austria when greeting each other.

Grüß dich!
(Hello!)

is frequently heard among young adults in southern Germany.

Tag!

Hallo!

Grüß dich!

Servus! *(Hello!)*	is used occasionally by young people in southern Germany and Austria. Sometimes *Servus!* is used to say "Hello!" and "Good-bye!"
Grüezi! *(Hello!)*	is heard primarily in the northern part of Switzerland. It means the same as *Grüß dich!*
Guten Morgen! *(Good morning!)*	is used during the morning hours. *Morgen!* is more casual and heard quite frequently.
Guten Abend! *(Good evening!)*	is used during the evening hours until midnight. Many Germans, however, will simply say *'n Abend!*
Auf Wiedersehen! *(Good-bye!)*	is the most commonly used good-bye phrase. More informally, Germans will simply say *Wiedersehen!*
Auf Wiederhören! *(Good-bye!)*	is used when ending a telephone conversation. It means "hope to hear you again." More casually, a person will say *Wiederhören!*
Tschüs! *(Good-bye!)*	is the most common good-bye phrase in northern Germany. It is very casual, however, and only used among good friends and relatives. *Tschüs* originated from the French *adieu*.
Pfüat di! *(Good-bye!)*	is an informal good-bye in Bavaria and Austria and means *Behüt dich Gott!*

Germans have a reputation as great handshakers. They are used to shaking hands not only when being introduced but also as a normal part of everyday greetings, meaning little more than saying hello.

Nowadays, more and more Germans shake hands only when meeting strangers, when seeing friends or relatives after a prolonged absence or when congratulating someone. The practice now varies so much in all regions and population groups that it is impossible to state a general rule for all occasions. When in doubt whether a handshake is appropriate it's best to wait for the German to make the first move.

At a small German party, everybody will greet everybody else he or she knows with a handshake, beginning with the host and hostess. A stranger normally waits until the host or hostess makes the introductions.

When meeting acquaintances in the street, in shops or elsewhere in public, Germans usually shake hands only if they intend to stop and have a little chat. When people are invited for coffee or a meal, it is quite customary to bring along a little bouquet of flowers for the hostess and some candy for the children.

Die Gäste bringen Blumen mit.

Money

There are eight different coins in the German monetary system, based upon the *DM (Deutsche Mark)*. They are:

  1 Pfennig
  2 Pfennig
  5 Pfennig
10 Pfennig (called *Groschen*)
50 Pfennig
  1 Mark (100 Pfennig)
  2 Mark
  5 Mark

There are seven different banknotes used in the *Bundesrepublik*. They are:

    5 DM
  10 DM
  20 DM
  50 DM
 100 DM
 500 DM
1,000 DM

The coins are made of copper, brass or silvery metal; the banknotes have different colors and increase in size with the value. This makes it easier to distinguish between them.

Since 1990, Germany is slowly phasing out all banknotes over a period of several years replacing them with new ones, some of which are shown on this page. Both old and new banknotes will be in circulation for many years to come.

Austria's currency is called the *österreichische Schilling* (öS) — 1 öS = 100 *Groschen* — and the currency of Switzerland is the *Schweizer Franken* (SF) — 1 SF = 100 *Rappen*.

Popular English Words in the German Language

Germans borrow many words from English. Here are some of the English words with their corresponding articles. The pronunciation of these words in German is usually as close to English as possible, depending on the speaker's familiarity with English.

die Band	die Party	der Diskjockey	das Popcorn
die City	die Jeans	das T-Shirt	der Computer
der Job	das Hobby	der Teenager	der Manager
die Disco	das Makeup	das Feature	die Snackbar
das Poster	der Ski	der Basketball	der Trend

der Computer

Was kann man da kaufen?

181

182

Familie

6

Communicative Functions

- talking about a birthday
- identifying and talking about family relationships
- naming rooms of a house or apartment
- talking about a day's activities

183

Wer hat Geburtstag?

Mittwoch in zwei Wochen ist ein besonderer Tag für Sabine. An diesem Tag hat sie Geburtstag. Sabine wird fünfzehn Jahre alt. Zum Geburtstag möchte sie ein paar Freunde und Freundinnen einladen. Sie schreibt heute die Einladungen. Uschi, Sabines beste Freundin, bekommt die Einladung am nächsten Tag. Sie wird bestimmt kommen.

Endlich ist der Tag da. Sabines Oma bäckt schon am Morgen einen Kuchen. Sie dekoriert ihn auch schön. Dann deckt sie den Tisch und stellt den Kuchen auf den Tisch im Wohnzimmer. Um vier Uhr kommen die Gäste.

Was paßt hier?

1. Sabine schreibt
2. Die Oma deckt
3. Uschi bekommt
4. Die Gäste kommen
5. Heute ist
6. Sabine ist
7. Sabines Oma bäckt
8. Sabine möchte

a. ein paar Freunde und Freundinnen einladen
b. eine Einladung
c. fünfzehn Jahre alt
d. einen Kuchen
e. den Tisch
f. Einladungen
g. um vier
h. Mittwoch

Was stellt Sabines Oma auf den Tisch?

Was machen die Jugendlichen nach dem Essen?

184

Uschi:	Herzlichen Glückwunsch zum Geburtstag, Sabine!
Anne:	Endlich bist du fünfzehn.
Uschi:	Hier, ein Geschenk für dich.
Sabine:	Vielen Dank.
Anne:	Hoffentlich gefällt dir mein Geschenk.
Sabine:	Bestimmt. Kommt, essen wir! Wir können uns hier hinsetzen.
Anne:	Mmmh, dieser Kuchen schmeckt lecker.
Uschi:	Prost! Diese Limo ist gut für den Durst.
Sabine:	Auf dem Tisch dort ist ein kaltes Büfett. Ihr könnt nehmen, was ihr wollt.
Anne:	Deine Oma bäckt immer so gut.
Sabine:	Du, Uschi, komm schnell her. Sonst ist alles weg.
Uschi:	Keine Angst! Ich bekomme schon etwas.

Wer sagt das?

1. Du bist endlich fünfzehn.
2. Dort ist ein kaltes Büfett.
3. Der Kuchen schmeckt gut.
4. Essen wir jetzt!
5. Ich bekomme bestimmt etwas zu essen.
6. Das ist für dich.
7. Deine Oma kann gut backen.
8. Beeil dich!

Nach dem Essen sitzen sie im Wohnzimmer. Anne spielt Gitarre und die Jugendlichen singen ein paar Volkslieder. Später spielen sie Karten. Es macht viel Spaß. Gegen sieben Uhr verlassen alle das Haus. Einige fahren mit dem Fahrrad, andere gehen zu Fuß nach Hause. Sabine dankt ihren Freunden und Freundinnen für die Geschenke. Was für ein schöner Geburtstag!

Was fehlt hier?

1. Die Jugendlichen spielen _____.
2. Sie singen ein paar _____.
3. Alle sitzen im _____.
4. Sabine dankt den Freunden und Freundinnen für die _____.
5. Um sieben gehen sie nach _____.
6. Anne spielt _____.

Fragen

1. Warum ist Mittwoch für Sabine ein besonderer Tag?
2. Wer kommt zum Geburtstag?
3. Wann bekommt Uschi Sabines Einladung?
4. Wer bäckt einen Kuchen?
5. Wohin stellt sie den Kuchen?
6. Wie schmeckt der Kuchen?
7. Was trinken sie?
8. Wo sitzen die Jugendlichen nach dem Essen?
9. Wer spielt Gitarre?
10. Was singen alle?
11. Was spielen sie später?
12. Um wieviel Uhr gehen die Gäste nach Hause?

Für dich

Herzlichen Glückwunsch zum Geburtstag! is the most accepted and popular form of congratulating a German on his or her birthday. The first two words, *Herzlichen Glückwunsch*, or the plural, *Herzliche Glückwünsche*, will fit almost any occasion if you wish to congratulate someone in German, be it a birthday *(Geburtstag)*, a name-day *(Namenstag)*, a wedding *(Hochzeit)* or an anniversary *(Jubiläum)*.

When writing invitations or congratulations, it is customary to add some personal comments before signing the card.

Uschi bekommt eine Einladung.

Was trinken sie?

Es schmeckt lecker.

Gegen sieben Uhr verlassen sie das Haus.

Kombiniere...

Wie viele Sätze kannst du bilden?

Die Oma	trinken	heute	in der Schule
Alle	essen	etwas	einen Kuchen
Wer	bäckt	gleich	Geburtstag
Die Mädchen	tanzen	am Freitag	Erdbeereis
Die Gäste	hat	gern	Limo

I ützliche Ausdrücke

Ich komme am Mittwoch in zwei Wochen.

Herzlichen Glückwunsch zum Geburtstag!

Wie gefällt dir das?

Setzt euch hin!

Nehmt, was ihr wollt!

Komm her!

Es macht Spaß.

Sie dankt ihnen.

I'll come two weeks from Wednesday.

Happy Birthday!

How do you like this?

Sit down.

Take what you like.

Come here.

It's fun.

She thanks them.

Was paßt hier?

1. Singen wir jetzt?
2. Was macht ihr im Wohnzimmer?
3. Gefällt dir der Hit?
4. Warum dankst du Holger?
5. Ich bin heute sechzehn.
6. Können wir etwas essen?
7. Setzt euch bitte hin!

a. Ja. Nehmt, was ihr wollt.
b. Er leiht mir zwanzig Mark.
c. Wir stehen gern.
d. Wir spielen Karten da.
e. Nein, er ist zu langsam.
f. Ja, das macht Spaß.
g. Herzlichen Glückwunsch zum Geburtstag!

Ergänzung

Herr Uwe Schmidt ist Ralfs und Julias Vater.
Frau Renate Schmidt ist Ralfs und Julias Mutter.
Herr und Frau Schmidt sind Ralfs und Julias Eltern.
Ralf ist Julias Bruder.
Julia ist Ralfs Schwester.
Ralf und Julia sind Geschwister.

Ralf ist der Sohn von Herrn und Frau Schmidt.
Julia ist die Tochter von Herrn und Frau Schmidt.
Ralf ist der Enkel von Herrn und Frau Neumann.
Julia ist die Enkelin von Herrn und Frau Neumann.

Herr Walter Neumann ist Ralfs und Julias Großvater (Opa).
Frau Gerda Neumann ist Ralfs und Julias Großmutter (Oma).
Herr und Frau Neumann sind Ralfs und Julias Großeltern.

Der Bruder von Herrn Uwe Schmidt ist Ralfs und Julias Onkel.
Die Schwester von Frau Renate Schmidt ist Ralfs und Julias Tante.

1. *Wann haben sie Geburtstag?* **Find out when these people have their birthday.** *Folge dem Beispiel!*

   ❏ Wolfgang / 5. Juli
   Wolfgang hat am fünften Juli Geburtstag.

   1. Günter / 23. Dezember
   2. Monika / 8. März
   3. Susanne und Dieter / 3. Juni
   4. Herr Tobler / 12. September
   5. dein Vater / 15. Februar
   6. Tinas Mutter / 30. Mai

2. *Wie sind sie verwandt?* **(How are they related?) Based on the information presented, indicate with a complete sentence how these people are related.**

   ❏ Ralf / Herr Neumann
   Ralf ist der Enkel von Herrn Neumann.

   1. Julia / Herr Schmidt
   2. Julia / Ralf
   3. Frau Neumann / Julia
   4. Herr Schmidt / Ralf
   5. Julia / Herr Neumann
   6. Herr und Frau Schmidt / Ralf

Sag's mal!

Was möchtest du zum Geburtstag? Ich möchte...

einen Fotoapparat

eine Uhr   ein Moped   Schmuck

einen Computer   Geld   einen Fernseher

einen Kassettenrekorder   Platten

Bücher   ein Paar Schuhe   Kleidung

Aussprache

/sch/		
schreiben	**s**pannend	**S**traße
Schule	**s**pät	**s**timmen
schnell	**s**pielen	**S**tunde
Schweiz	**S**port	**s**tehen
schön	**s**pitze	**S**taat
Ge**sch**ichte	**s**prechen	be**s**timmt
Deut**sch**	**S**panien	ver**s**tehen

Übungen

Personal Pronouns

Nominative (Third Person Singular)

In German, as you have learned in previous lessons, there are three personal pronouns *er*, *sie* and *es*, which can be replaced with *der*, *die* and *das* respectively.

Der Junge ist neu hier.	*Er* ist neu hier. (he)
Der Sommer ist heiß.	*Er* ist heiß. (it)
Die Verkäuferin steht da drüben.	*Sie* steht da drüben.
Die Karte ist ganz billig.	*Sie* ist ganz billig.
Das Mädchen ist sehr klug.	*Es* ist sehr klug.
Das Land ist groß.	*Es* ist groß.

Accusative (Third Person Singular)

The accusative case for the personal pronouns *er*, *sie* and *es* is *ihn*, *sie* and *es*. Notice that only the masculine pronoun, i.e. *er* changes to *ihn*. The other pronouns *sie* and *es* have the same forms in the nominative as well as in the accusative case.

Ich frage *den Lehrer*.	Ich frage *ihn*.
Singt er *den Hit*?	Singt er *ihn*?
Dieter kauft *einen Kuli*.	Dieter kauft *ihn*.

Kennst du *die Mutter*?   Kennst du *sie*?
Wir bringen *die Kassette*.   Wir bringen *sie*.
Heike bekommt *eine Karte*.   Heike bekommt *sie*.

Frag *das Mädchen*!   Frag *es*!
Lest ihr *das Buch*?   Lest ihr *es*?
Wir haben *das Geld*.   Wir haben *es*.

	masculine	feminine	neuter
nominative	er	sie	es
accusative	ihn	sie	es

3. *Was möchtest du?* **Several people ask you questions which you answer positively.**

❑ Möchtest du ein Fahrrad?
    Ja, ich möchte es.

    1. Möchtest du das Eis?
    2. Möchtest du einen Kuli?
    3. Möchtest du ein Glas Limo?
    4. Möchtest du die Schlagsahne?
    5. Möchtest du den Radiergummi?
    6. Möchtest du eine Karte?

4. **Your classmates are telling you several things which you seem to doubt.**

❑ Ich kaufe ein Fahrrad.
    Kaufst du es wirklich?

    1. Ich mag den Film.
    2. Ich schreibe eine Einladung.
    3. Ich lerne die Aufgabe.
    4. Ich habe das Mädchen gern.
    5. Ich verstehe die Lehrerin gut.
    6. Ich kenne den Hit.
    7. Ich kaufe ein Buch.
    8. Ich fotografiere die Band.

5. *Er tut es auch.* Everything Heiko does or wants to do, his little brother Jens claims he wants to do as well.

❏ Ich mache die Tür auf.
Ich mache sie auch auf.

1. Ich muß das Geld finden.
2. Ich kenne den Diskjockey.
3. Ich höre die Musik gern.
4. Ich lese die Seite.
5. Ich bringe das Fahrrad mit.
6. Ich schreibe die Arbeit.

Additional Personal Pronouns

In addition to the third person singular, of course, there are other personal pronouns. These, as well as the previously mentioned pronouns, are included in the table below.

Singular		Plural	
nominative	accusative	nominative	accusative
ich	mich (me)	wir	uns (us)
du	dich (you)	ihr	euch (you)
er	ihn (him, it)	sie	sie (them)
sie	sie (her, it)	Sie (sg. & pl.)	Sie (you)
es	es (it)		

6. Complete each sentence. *Folge dem Beispiel!*

❏ Susanne kennt _____. (Rainer)
Susanne kennt ihn.

Ich kann _____ nicht finden. (die Karten)
Ich kann sie nicht finden.

1. Sabine schreibt _____. (die Einladungen)
2. Die Jugendlichen verstehen _____. (die Sängerin)
3. Wir essen _____. (das Vanilleeis)
4. Sie trinken _____. (die Cola)
5. Ich kenne _____. (den Verkäufer)
6. Er fragt _____. (die Jugendlichen)

7. *Wen kennt er?* Tell whom he knows.

❑ er
Er kennt ihn.

die Mädchen
Er kennt sie.

1. die Freunde
2. du
3. deine Freundin
4. das Fach
5. die Bücher
6. den Kellner
7. wir
8. ihr

Er kennt sie.

8. Provide the pronouns for the nouns indicated in parentheses.

❑ Frau Hoffmann kauft (Karte) _____.
Frau Hoffmann kauft sie.

1. Werdet ihr (Film) _____ sehen?
2. Hast du (Mark) _____?
3. Ich möchte (Freund) _____ einladen.
4. Wir verstehen (Arbeit) _____ nicht.
5. Sie mögen (Eis) _____ nicht.
6. Die Schüler haben (Fach) _____ gern.
7. Frag (Verkäuferin) _____ doch!
8. Willst du (Eiscafé) _____ finden?
9. Warum seht ihr (Show) _____ nicht?
10. Wir trinken (Apfelsaft) _____ gern.

9. Supply the proper personal pronouns in German for those in parentheses.

1. Kann ich (you) _____ etwas fragen, Herr Peters?
2. Wir werden (her) _____ zum Geburtstag einladen.
3. Kennt ihr (him) _____ nicht?
4. Warum könnt ihr (me) _____ nicht verstehen?
5. Fragen Sie (us) _____ bitte!
6. Ich werde (you) _____ schon finden, Jörg.
7. Sie schreibt _____ (you) bald, Petra und Andrea.

Verbs with Stem Vowel Change

A number of verbs in German do not follow the regular pattern of conjugation but undergo a change in the second and third person singular (*du* and *er, sie, es* forms). You will become familiar with two such groups of verbs, one changing from *a* to *ä*, the other from *e* to *i* (or *ie*).

Stem vowel change *a* to *ä*

Here are the verbs with vowel changes that you already know.

	du	er, sie, es
backen	bäckst	bäckt
fahren	fährst	fährt
gefallen	gefällst	gefällt
laufen	läufst	läuft
verlassen	verläßt	verläßt

When forming commands, the familiar singular command form does not have a vowel change. For example: *Fahr nach Hause! Lauf schnell!*

Stem vowel change *e* to *i* and *e* to *ie*

Here are the verbs with vowel changes that you already know.

	du	er, sie, es
essen	ißt	ißt
geben	gibst	gibt
lesen	liest	liest
nehmen	nimmst	nimmt
sehen	siehst	sieht
sprechen	sprichst	spricht

10. *Nicht alle machen das.* Your uncle asks you if your friends are doing specific things, but you point out that only certain friends are involved. *Folge dem Beispiel!*

❏ Verlassen die Mädchen die Schule? (Claudia)
Nein, nur Claudia verläßt die Schule.

1. Lesen die Schüler das Buch? (Rainer)
2. Essen Uschi und Tanja ein Eis? (Jens)
3. Fahren viele in die Stadt? (Anne)
4. Laufen alle Jungen nach Hause? (Joachim)
5. Nehmen alle den Bleistift? (Boris)
6. Backen die Eltern einen Kuchen? (der Vater)
7. Sehen Holger und Maria diesen Film? (Maria)
8. Sprechen alle Verkäufer gut Deutsch? (Herr Schulz)
9. Geben die zwei eine Party? (Dieter)

11. *Wohin fahren sie alle?* **Tell where everybody is going.**

❑ Susanne / zum Park
Susanne fährt zum Park.

1. Erich / ins Kino
2. die Gäste / zu Sabine
3. wir / zu Bettinas Haus
4. mein Freund / nach München
5. die Verkäuferinnen / nach Hause
6. der Herr / um die Ecke

12. *Wer liest viel oder wenig?* **Indicate how much everyone is reading.**

❑ Kerstin und Anita / nicht viel
Kerstin und Anita lesen nicht viel.

1. Jörg / sehr wenig
2. meine Freundin / viel
3. Jürgen und Lars / nicht viel
4. Christa / wenig
5. Mein Lehrer / sehr viel
6. wir / viel

Was lesen die Schüler?

Was essen sie?

Wer bäckt Kuchen zum Geburtstag?

13. ***Wer bäckt den Kuchen zum Geburtstag?*** **You're inviting several people to your birthday party. Several classmates are asking you who will be baking the cake. As you aren't quite sure, you answer as follows.**

❐   meine Mutter
Ich glaube, meine Mutter bäckt ihn.

1. meine Oma
2. Julia und Bärbel
3. mein Onkel
4. Martinas Eltern
5. Boris
6. die Mädchen

14. ***Wann essen sie?*** **Indicate at what time everybody is eating.**

❐   Gisela / um drei
Gisela ißt um drei.

1. wir / um halb zwölf
2. Ralf / etwas später
3. die Jungen und Mädchen / bald
4. ihr / heute früh
5. meine Schwester / jetzt
6. du / um sechs

15. **Complete each sentence by providing the appropriate verb form as indicated in parentheses.**

1. Um wieviel Uhr (leave) _____ er das Haus?
2. Möchtest du diese Quizshow (see) _____?
3. Ich (read) _____ Bücher sehr gern.
4. (speak) _____ der Kellner Deutsch?
5. Wer (have) _____ am Sonnabend eine Party?
6. Olivers Oma (bake) _____ zwei Kuchen.
7. Der Film (run) _____ schon acht Wochen.
8. Viele Jugendliche (drive) _____ zur Konzerthalle.
9. Heidi (take) _____, was sie will.

16. *Ergänze diese Sätze!* (Complete these sentences.) Use the most appropriate verb listed and insert its proper form.

backen   fahren   gefallen   laufen   verlassen
essen   geben   lesen   sehen   sprechen

1. Der Herr _____ nicht gut Englisch.
2. Wie _____ dir das Geschenk?
3. _____ ihr diesen Kuchen gern?
4. Wir _____ zu Carstens Haus.
5. Kurt _____ mit dem Fahrrad zum Kino.
6. _____ Sie das kalte Büfett?
7. Was _____ deine Mutter in der Küche?
8. Ich _____ Anita ein schönes Geschenk.
9. Sie müssen zwanzig Seiten _____.
10. Um wieviel Uhr _____ du die Schule?

Die Jugendlichen fahren in die Stadt.

Was kann man hier kaufen?

Geben Sie mir bitte eine Karte.

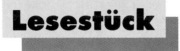

Wo geht Frau Huber einkaufen?

Was für ein Hobby hat Boris?

Bei Familie Huber

Hubers wohnen in Hohenschönhausen, einem Vorort° von Berlin. Hier sind die Mietshäuser° ganz neu. Herr und Frau Huber und ihr Sohn Boris wohnen erst zwei Jahre° in einer Wohnung.

suburb
apartment buildings
years

Jeden Tag (Montag bis Freitag) verlassen alle drei um halb acht das Haus. Herr Huber weiß nicht immer, wann er am Abend° nach Hause kommt. Heute hat er nicht viel im Büro° zu tun und wird bestimmt schon um Viertel nach fünf zu Hause sein. Er fährt immer mit dem Auto° zum Büro.

in the evening
office
car

Frau Huber arbeitet° in einem Kaufhaus° in der Stadt. Sie muß mit der Straßenbahn zum Kaufhaus fahren. Boris kann zu Fuß zur Schule gehen. Sie ist nicht weit. Boris geht auf ein Gymnasium. Er ist in der zehnten Klasse°.

works/ department store
class

Um Viertel nach eins kommt Boris aus der Schule. Zu Hause geht er gleich in die Küche, ißt dort ein Stück Brot° und trinkt ein Glas Milch. Fast jeden Tag hat er etwas auf, besonders in Mathe. Mit dem Taschenrechner° geht alles schneller.

piece of bread
pocket calculator

Boris hat ein Hobby — Briefmarken sammeln. Er hat schon viele Briefmarken von Deutschland und von anderen Ländern in einem Buch. Sein Freund Achim sammelt auch Briefmarken. Von Achim kann Boris immer ein paar neue bekommen.

Auf dem Weg nach Hause geht Frau Huber einkaufen°. *shopping* Es gibt einen Supermarkt gleich um die Ecke, wo sie wohnt. Dort kann sie kaufen, was sie für die Familie braucht°. In der Küche bereitet sie das Abendbrot zu°. *needs/prepares the supper* Heute gibt es Kalte Platte°. Die schmeckt immer gut. *cold cuts* Hubers sprechen viel über den Tag.

Nach dem Abendbrot geht Herr Huber in die Küche und spült das Geschirr°. Seine Frau sitzt im Wohnzimmer *washes dishes* und liest die Zeitung°. Später kommt auch Herr Huber *newspaper* ins Wohnzimmer, setzt sich hin und sieht mit seiner Frau fern°. Im Fernsehen gibt es oft° interessante Pro- *watches TV/often* gramme°. *interesting programs*

Boris holt° sein Fahrrad. Er fährt mit dem Fahrrad nur *fetches* ein paar Minuten. In Hohenschönhausen gibt es einen Jugendklub. Er fährt gern zu diesem Klub. Da ist immer viel los.

Wer...? Indicate who is involved in the following based on the *Lesestück*.

☐ im Kaufhaus arbeiten
   Frau Hubert arbeitet im Kaufhaus.

1. um halb acht das Haus verlassen |
2. mit dem Auto fahren
3. auf ein Gymnasium gehen
4. mit der Straßenbahn fahren
5. in Hohenschönhausen wohnen
6. um Viertel nach fünf zu Hause sein
7. um Viertel nach eins nach Hause kommen
8. Briefmarken sammeln
9. ein Glas Milch trinken
10. einkaufen gehen
11. einen Taschenrechner haben
12. das Geschirr spülen
13. über den Tag sprechen
14. die Zeitung lesen
15. fernsehen
16. das Fahrrad holen

Fragen

1. Wohnt Boris in einer Stadt?
2. Wie lange wohnen Hubers in dem Mietshaus?
3. Was weiß Herr Huber nicht immer?
4. Um wieviel Uhr kommt er heute nach Hause?
5. Wie kommt Herr Huber zum Büro?
6. Wo arbeitet Frau Huber?
7. Geht sie zu Fuß in die Stadt?
8. Wie alt ist Boris ungefähr? Wie weißt du das?
9. Wann kommt Boris aus der Schule?
10. Was macht er dann?
11. Warum kann er die Matheaufgaben schnell machen?
12. Was macht Boris gern?
13. Was macht Frau Huber auf dem Weg nach Hause?
14. Wo ist der Supermarkt?
15. Was macht sie in der Küche?
16. Was essen sie heute?
17. Wer spült das Geschirr?
18. Was machen Hubers später?
19. Wie kommt Boris zum Jugendklub?
20. Warum fährt er zum Jugendklub?

Übung macht den Meister!

1. *Was machen wir zum Geburtstag?* You want to give your friend a surprise birthday party. You discuss this with one of your relatives (father, mother, brother or sister). Your conversation should include such details as: the age of your friend, the day and time you would like to have the party, whom to invite, what to have to eat and drink, what to do at the party, etc. Have one of your classmates be the relative and present the finished conversation to the rest of the class.

2. *Meine Familie.* Develop a short family tree using the vocabulary from the lesson. Some additional names for relatives you may wish to use are: *der Urgroßvater und die Urgroßmutter* (the great-grandfather and the great-grandmother), *der Vetter* (the male cousin), *die Kusine* (the female cousin), *der Neffe* (the nephew), *die Nichte* (the niece).

3. *Was machst du während des Tages?* (What do you do during the day?) Prepare a number of questions. Some of the questions could be as follows: *Um wieviel Uhr gehst du zur Schule?*, *Welche Fächer hast du?*, *Wann kommst du nach Hause?*, *Was machst du dann?*, etc.

4. *Beschreibe deine Wohnung oder dein Haus!* (Describe your apartment or your house!) Your description may make reference to these questions: *Wie viele Zimmer gibt es?*, *Gefällt dir ein Zimmer besonders? Warum? (Es ist neu, schön, groß.).*

Was machen sie heute?

Wo wohnen sie?

Sie gehen zu Fuß. (Nürnberg)

Erweiterung

17. Ergänze diese Sätze!

1. Herbert hat einen Bruder und _____.
2. Wir essen in der _____.
3. Möchtest du im _____ sitzen und fernsehen?
4. Brittas _____ ist morgen. Sie wird vierzehn.
5. Ich schreibe heute _____.
6. Trinkst du gern _____?
7. Meine Mutter bäckt _____.
8. Sammelst du gern _____?
9. Abends geht sie oft zum _____.
10. Frau Müller muß _____ spülen.

18. *Was machst du heute?* Today is Saturday. You've got plenty of time. Your friend inquires what you're planning to do. Develop a conversation accordingly.

Was machst du heute?

_____

Komm doch mit zu Katrin!

_____

Sie hat eine Geburtstagsparty.

_____

Christian, Anita und viele andere.

_____

So gegen sieben.

_____

Die Straßenbahn fährt oft. (Frankfurt)

Warum kommen so viele gern zum Park? (Mainau)

19. *Was paßt hier?* Use the items below to complete each sentence.

gehe	Wohnzimmer	dekoriert	Brot
kommt	Fahrrad	trinke	Gäste
gibt	Büro	wollt	Straßenbahn

1. Meine Mutter bäckt das _____.
2. Wann fährt die _____?
3. Ich _____ Eistee.
4. Heute _____ es Kalte Platte.
5. Arbeiten Sie in einem _____?
6. Sie sehen im _____ fern.
7. Die _____ kommen schon früh.
8. Nehmt, was ihr _____!
9. Ich _____ auf ein Gymnasium.
10. Die Oma _____ den Kuchen.
11. Boris holt das _____.
12. Warum _____ ihr nicht zum Klub?

20. Group the following words into these four categories: *Familie, Geschenk, Haus* and *Fach.*

1. Küche
2. Erdkunde
3. Tante
4. Gitarre
5. Geschwister
6. Bad
7. Taschenrechner
8. Chemie
9. Oma
10. Eßzimmer
11. Onkel
12. Karten

Sprachspiegel

21. *Was ist heute los?* The following words when put in sequence describe what Rüdiger is up to today. Can you put them in the right order to figure out what is going on?

1. Sonntag / ist / heute
2. möchte / ein paar Freunde einladen / ich
3. kommen / wer / soll / Party / zur
4. Doris / Jana / bestimmt / kommen / und / wollen
5. Mutter / vielleicht / kann / Kuchen / einen / backen / meine

6. schnell / ich / schreiben / muß / Einladungen / die
7. nicht/ weiß / ich / wo / wohnt / Doris
8. fragen / Jana / ich / werde

22. *Wie sagt man's?* **From the list below, select the appropriate words to complete the various short conversational exchanges.**

beginnt	alt	Stunde	Küche
Tisch	fährt	acht	hast
Gitarre	lesen	singen	schön
trinken	Buch	Gäste	Programm

1. Wie gefällt dir die _____?
   Sie ist ganz toll.
   Jetzt können wir alle _____.
2. Deck bitte den _____.
   Warum so früh?
   Früh? Die _____ kommen bald.
3. Wann _____ du Geburtstag?
   Heute.
   Wie _____ bist du denn?
   Siebzehn.
4. Dieses Geschenk ist sehr _____.
   Was ist es denn?
   Ein _____ aus Deutschland.
   Kannst du es denn _____?

5. Im Fernsehen gibt es ein tolles _____.
   Um wieviel Uhr _____ es?
   Ich glaube, um _____.
   Oh, dann habe ich keine Zeit.
6. Uwe, komm bitte in die _____!
   Ich komme gleich.
   Möchtest du Limo _____?
   Nein, Milch bitte.
7. Wann _____ Rolf mit der Straßenbahn?
   In einer halben _____.
   Dann warte ich.

23. *Schreibe einen Dialog oder ein Lesestück!* Write a dialog or a narrative using the following details. Call your friend. Tell him or her that you have a present and would like to bring it. He or she wants to know why you have a present. Give a reason. Ask him or her if he or she would like to see it. Your friend does. Finally, you determine a time to get together.

24. **Beantworte diese Fragen!**

   1. Wann hast du Geburtstag?
   2. Wie alt bist du?
   3. Siehst du gern fern?
   4. Wie sind die Programme?
   5. Hast du ein Hobby?
   6. Was machst du abends?
   7. Hat dein Freund oder deine Freundin eine Schwester?
   8. Wohnst du in einem Haus oder einer Wohnung?
   9. Was schmeckt gut?
   10. Wer spült das Geschirr?

25. **Wie heißt das auf deutsch?**

   1. What would you like to eat?
   2. The cake tastes very good.
   3. I can play guitar.
   4. They leave the house at ten o'clock.
   5. I have to write invitations.
   6. We are collecting stamps.
   7. Where are you working?
   8. What is she eating?

Sie decken den Tisch.

Was kann man hier kaufen? (Nürnberg)

Rückblick

I. Convert these sentences into commands.

❐   Ihr seht das Programm.
     Seht das Programm!

1. Sie fragen den Verkäufer.
2. Du hast keine Angst.
3. Ihr backt das Brot.
4. Du bist heute pünktlich.
5. Sie kommen zum Geburtstag.
6. Ihr kauft die Karten.
7. Sie decken den Tisch.
8. Du arbeitest nicht so viel.

II. Provide the proper forms of *dürfen, können, mögen (möchten), müssen, sollen* or *wollen.*

1. (müssen) Ich _____ schon um sechs da sein.
2. (möchten) Was _____ ihr jetzt trinken?
3. (dürfen) _____ du später zur Party?
4. (können) Heike _____ die Aufgaben nicht machen.
5. (sollen) _____ Rudi das Geschenk bringen?
6. (mögen) Ich _____ das Zitroneneis nicht.
7. (wollen) Wann _____ ihr die Einladung schreiben?

III. *Was möchtest du heute machen?* Answer this question using the information provided. *Folge dem Beispiel!*

❏ eine Stunde warten (drei)
Ich möchte drei Stunden warten.

1. ein Glas Milch trinken (zwei)
2. eine Karte kaufen (viele)
3. einen Freund einladen (ein paar)
4. ein Geschenk bekommen (viele)
5. einen Kuchen backen (drei)
6. einen Film sehen (keine)

IV. *Was werden sie morgen machen?* Tell what everyone will do tomorrow.

❏ im Büro arbeiten (Jochen)
Jochen wird morgen im Büro arbeiten.

1. schon um zwölf aus der Schule kommen (wir)
2. viele Briefmarken kaufen (ich)
3. ein paar Freunde einladen (Helga)
4. zu Christa gehen (alle)
5. die Arbeit schreiben (du)
6. mit dem Auto nach Köln fahren (Dieter)

V. *viel* oder *viele?*

1. Ich habe nicht _____ Geld.
2. Wie _____ Bücher kaufst du denn?
3. Hast du heute _____ Zeit?
4. Uwe muß _____ arbeiten.
5. Tina kann nicht _____ Karten für das Konzert bekommen.
6. In der Klasse sind _____ Schüler.

Zungenbrecher

Sieben Schneeschaufler schaufeln sieben Schaufeln Schnee.

(Seven snow shovelers shovel seven shovels of snow.)

Kulturecke

Occupations

The Federal Republic of Germany is one of the major industrial countries. In terms of overall economic performance it comes fourth in the world; in world trade it even ranks second. Its economy relies primarily on heavy industry, such as coal mining and the steel industries, most of which are located in the Northrhine Westphalia region. The Federal Republic of Germany is the third largest automobile producer in the world, following the U.S. and Japan.

Germany is not only highly industrialized, its agricultural products take care of about 80 percent of its food requirements. In order to be more competitive, most farms have been consolidated and are part of cooperatives. Many farms are specialized and grow only certain crops such as vegetables or grapes for wine, which grow along the Rhine and Mosel rivers. About a quarter of the Federal Republic's land is forest. The law demands that forest areas be properly managed. Land laws require forest owners to replant harvested areas or replace dead trees with new ones. Areas like Lower Saxony, Schleswig Holstein and Bavaria are extensively involved in raising cattle and producing dairy products.

The computer industry is ever-changing. It requires specially trained personnel that is willing and able to keep up with the most recent computer technology. Specialists in the computer field are sought after by many companies. The importance of computer technology is highly noticeable in the medical profession. There the computer is used in various specialized areas. In Germany, there are about 154,000 physicians; that is one doctor for every 400 inhabitants. This makes the Federal Republic one of the best equipped countries in the world medically. Another health care occupation is the dentist or the dental technician. Pharmaceutical products tested by specialists are sold in pharmacies.

Major emphasis is placed on the importance of education. For many years, an acute shortage of teachers meant that every applicant who passed the proper examinations was accepted with open arms. For the past 10 years, however, many teachers have been without jobs, which poses a difficult problem for the country.

Every sixth person is employed by the federal, state or local government, providing services for the communities. For example, there are occupations concerned with public security and order, such as the police. The German Federal Post Office (*Deutsche Bundespost*) constitutes Europe's largest enterprise. Early in the morning, the mail is delivered to businesses and private homes.

The German monetary system, based on the mark, has become an important factor in international trade. Financial institutions such as banks employ specialists in the different areas of the complex financial business world. The stock exchange in Frankfurt, for example, keeps a careful eye on the constantly fluctuating stocks on the national and international scene. Managers in small and large companies provide the guidance and administration necessary to run their companies effectively.

Tourism has become an important economic opportunity for Germans. Therefore, it is not surprising to find an abundance of travel agents who plan tours and vacations for groups and individuals. There are about 1.5 million jobs dependent on tourism, either directly or indirectly. Some of these jobs, such as air traffic controllers, require extensive and specialized training. Lufthansa, the German airline, requires its cabin attendants to speak at least one or two foreign languages. It is no longer rare to see women in jobs that were once considered to be typically male occupations. Every second woman is now employed outside of the home.

Although many Germans go shopping in the local supermarkets today, individual shops are still extremely popular. The store owner and clerks know the individual customers, therefore providing a more personalized atmosphere. Many of these smaller stores, like the local butcher shop, are family-owned. The butcher takes special pride in offering homemade sausages and preparing the meats to the customers' special requests. Two-thirds of Germans go shopping once or twice a week at the local markets. Here clerks offer fresh fruits and vegetables, much preferred over packaged products.

Germans love flowers; therefore it's not surprising to find out that the professional florist and gardener hold important positions in the German work force.

The success of any restaurant business depends to a large extent on the skill of the cook. In Germany, there is an abundance of various types of eating establishments, ranging from the very elegant and expensive to the simple and reasonably priced. Waiters and waitresses can be seen serving in indoor and outdoor restaurants. Many waiters or waitresses are also employed in cafés. Germans love to sit in these cafés, relax and have coffee and delicious German cake.

Upon entering a town, particularly in southern Germany, the visitor will see a tall pole that is colorfully decorated with figures designating the trades of the town. This traditional pole dates back to the Middle Ages, a time when many apprentices and journeymen would go from town to town searching for jobs. However, today's apprentices are those who have chosen to enter the world of work after tenth grade.

Both folk arts and the formal arts flourish throughout Germany. Handicrafts are traditional, particularly in smaller towns and villages. For example, the visitor will find a number of potters who create unique pottery for sale. Other artists, particularly in the Bavarian town of Mittenwald, create handmade violins that are well-respected and recognized throughout the world. In southern Germany, the art of woodcarving is still practiced today and evidenced by the smaller woodcarving shops frequented by many local people and tourists alike.

Was weißt du?

one-fourth of one percent	17 percent	automobiles
southern Germany	tourism	tenth grade
Mittenwald	a job	80 percent
Northrhine Westphalia	Lufthansa	trades
the German Federal Post Office	Frankfurt	25 percent

1. The coal and steel industries are located primarily in _____.
2. About _____ of all Germans are employed by the federal, state or local government.
3. Many teachers today are without _____.
4. A colorfully decorated pole often designates the _____ offered by the town.
5. The city of _____ is a financial center.
6. Violins are made in _____.
7. There are only two other countries ahead of Germany in producing _____.
8. The official German airline is called _____.
9. One and a half million jobs depend on _____.
10. A young person usually starts an apprenticeship after _____.
11. German farms produce _____ of the country's food consumption.
12. _____ of all Germans are doctors.
13. About _____ of the land in the Federal Republic is forest.
14. The largest enterprise in Europe is _____.
15. Woodcarving is especially popular in _____.

Vokabeln

der **Abend,-e** evening
   am Abend in the evening
das **Abendbrot** supper
arbeiten to work
das **Auto,-s** car
backen to bake
das **Bad,-̈er** bathroom
best- best
brauchen to need
das **Brot,-e** bread
der **Bruder,-̈** brother
das **Büfett,-s** buffet
das **Büro,-s** office
der **Dank** thanks
   Vielen Dank. Many thanks.
decken to cover
   den Tisch decken to set the table
dekorieren to decorate
einkaufen to shop
   einkaufen gehen to go shopping
einladen to invite
die **Einladung,-en** invitation
endlich finally
der **Enkel,-** grandson
die **Enkelin,-nen** granddaughter
das **Essen** meal, food
das **Eßzimmer,-** dining room
die **Familie,-n** family
fernsehen to watch TV
der **Gast,-̈e** guest
der **Geburtstag,-e** birthday

gefallen to like
   Wie gefällt dir...? How do you like...?
das **Geschenk,-e** present, gift
das **Geschirr** dishes
die **Geschwister (pl.)** siblings
die **Gitarre,-n** guitar
die **Großeltern (pl.)** grandparents
die **Großmutter,-̈** grandmother
der **Großvater,-̈** grandfather
herkommen to come here
herzlich sincere, cordial
   Herzlichen Glückwunsch zum Geburtstag! Happy Birthday!
sich **hinsetzen** to sit down
holen to fetch, get
interessant interesting
das **Jahr,-e** year
die **Karte,-n** card
das **Kaufhaus,-̈er** department store
die **Klasse,-n** class
die **Küche,-n** kitchen
der **Kuchen,-** cake
lecker delicious
das **Mietshaus,-̈er** apartment building
die **Mutter,-̈** mother
der **Morgen-** morning
nehmen to take
die **Oma,-s** grandma

der **Onkel,-** uncle
der **Opa,-s** grandpa
die **Platte,-n** platter, plate
   die Kalte Platte cold-cut platter
das **Programm,-e** program
das **Schlafzimmer,-** bedroom
die **Schwester,-n** sister
der **Sohn,-̈e** son
sonst otherwise
der **Spaß** fun
   Es macht Spaß. It's fun.
spülen to wash, rinse
   Geschirr spülen to wash dishes
stellen to place, put
das **Stück,-e** piece
der **Supermarkt,-̈e** supermarket
die **Tante,-n** aunt
der **Taschenrechner,-** pocket calculator
die **Tochter,-̈** daughter
der **Vater,-̈** father
verlassen to leave
der **Vorort,-e** suburb
wegsein to be gone
die **Wohnung,-en** apartment
das **Wohnzimmer,-** living-room
die **Zeitung,-en** newspaper
das **Zimmer,-** room
zubereiten to prepare (a meal)

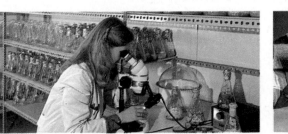

Reisen 7

Communicative Functions

- talking about traveling by train
- saying where you want to go
- naming various means of transportation
- giving directions
- naming important places in a city
- telling about an excursion or a trip

Auf dem Bahnhof

(vor dem Bahnhof)

Manfred: Es ist fast elf Uhr.

Willi: Das stimmt nicht ganz. Sieh auf die Uhr dort. Es ist schon drei nach elf.

Manfred: Meine Uhr geht mal wieder nach.

Willi: Komm, sehen wir uns den Fahrplan an.

Manfred: Hier steht's. Von Bremen nach Freiburg. Der Zug fährt um 11 Uhr 14 ab.

Willi: Den schaffen wir nicht. Fahren wir mit dem Intercity um 12 Uhr 11. Wir steigen in Hannover um und kommen um 19 Uhr in Freiburg an.

Was paßt hier?

1. Es ist	a. in Hannover um
2. Manfred und Willi lesen	b. nicht schaffen
3. Sie steigen	c. 19 Uhr an
4. Der Intercity wird um	d. 11 Uhr 3
5. Der Zug kommt um	e. nach
6. Manfreds Uhr geht	f. den Fahrplan
7. Sie können den Zug um 11 Uhr 14	g. 12 Uhr 11 abfahren

(im Bahnhof)

Willi: Da ist die Reiseauskunft.

Manfred: Gehen wir hinein!

Willi: Auf dem Bildschirm hier steht, ob die Züge pünktlich abfahren.

Manfred: Ja, der Intercity fährt pünktlich ab.

Willi: Wieviel müssen wir für die Karten ausgeben?

Manfred: Ich weiß nicht genau. Fragen wir doch. Zwei Karten nach Freiburg, bitte.

Beamtin: Hin und zurück?

Willi: Einfach und zweiter Klasse, bitte.

Falsch! The following statements are incorrect. Provide correct statements in German.

1. Die Reiseauskunft ist auf der Straße.
2. Auf dem Poster steht, ob die Züge pünktlich abfahren.
3. Manfred weiß, wieviel die Karten kosten.
4. Manfred kauft vier Karten.
5. Sie kaufen Karten erster Klasse.

Da ist die Reiseauskunft.

Was steht auf dem Bildschirm?

(beim Zeitungskiosk)

Manfred:	Die Reise dauert fast sieben Stunden.
Willi:	Ich kaufe eine Zeitung.
Manfred:	Ja, gut und ich kaufe eine Zeitschrift. Ich bezahle das.
Verkäuferin:	Bitte?
Manfred:	Diese Zeitung und die Zeitschrift.
Verkäuferin:	Das macht sieben Mark fünfzig.
Manfred:	Hier sind acht Mark.
Verkäuferin:	Und fünfzig Pfennig zurück.

Wer sagt das?

1. Das kostet DM 7,50.
2. Ich kaufe eine Zeitschrift.
3. Ich gebe Ihnen fünfzig Pfennig zurück.
4. Ich kaufe eine Zeitung.
5. Ich habe DM 8,00.

Was macht das?

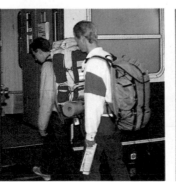

Sie steigen ein.

Jetzt geht's endlich los.

(auf dem Bahnsteig)

Willi:	Da steht der Zug schon.
Manfred:	Steigen wir doch ein!

Willi:	Dennis und Klaus kommen erst in drei Tagen nach Freiburg.
Manfred:	Ja, aber sie kommen mit dem Auto. Dann fahren wir zusammen zurück.
Willi:	Du, der Beamte gibt schon das Signal.
Manfred:	Jetzt geht's endlich los.

Ergänze jeden Satz. (Complete each sentence.)

1. Der Beamte gibt ein _____.
2. Manfreds und Willis Freunde kommen in drei _____ nach Freiburg.
3. Jetzt _____ wir endlich ab.
4. Der _____ ist schon da.
5. Klaus und Dennis haben ein _____.
6. Alle vier fahren später nach Bremen _____.

Fragen

1. Wo wohnen Manfred und Willi?
2. Wohin fahren sie?
3. Wo müssen sie umsteigen?
4. Um wieviel Uhr fährt der Zug ab?
5. Wann kommen sie in Freiburg an?
6. Was steht auf dem Bildschirm?
7. Wissen Willi und Manfred, wieviel die Karten kosten?
8. Wie viele Karten kaufen sie?
9. Fahren sie erster Klasse?
10. Was kaufen Willi und Manfred?
11. Wieviel kostet das alles?
12. Wann kommen Dennis und Klaus nach Freiburg?
13. Fahren sie auch mit dem Zug?
14. Wer gibt ein Signal?

Für dich

There are several columns on the *Abfahrt* (departure) schedule, with such headings as: *Zeit* (time of departure), *Zug Nr* (train number), *Nach* (meaning "to" or destination), *Gleis* (track) or *Bahnsteig* (platform).

Over 200 Intercity trains, which have both first and second class compartments, link all major German cities all over the country at one-hour intervals between 7 A.M. and 11 P.M.

You can buy train tickets at any window marked *Fahrkarten — Inland* when traveling within Germany; otherwise you must go to a window marked *Fahrkarten — Ausland*.

There are two classes of trains, first and second (*erste und zweite Klasse*). The first class is quite plush and costs about 50 percent more than a ticket for second class.

Kombiniere...

Wie viele Sätze kannst du bilden?

Der Zug	gehen	nicht	ab
Die Jugendlichen	kommen	um drei Uhr	mit dem Intercity
Alex	fährt	am Abend	nach Berlin
Meine Eltern	fahren	später	zum Bahnhof

Nützliche Ausdrücke

Meine Uhr geht nach.	My watch is slow.
Sehen wir uns den Fahrplan an.	Let's look at the (departure) schedule.
Wann fährt der Zug ab?	When does the train depart?
Um wieviel Uhr kommst du an?	What time do you arrive?
Wir schaffen das nicht.	We won't make it.
Hin und zurück?	Round trip?
Einfach, bitte.	One-way, please.
Eine Karte, zweiter Klasse.	One ticket, second class.
Wie lange dauert es?	How long does it take?
Ich bezahle das.	I'll pay (for) that.
Steigen wir ein!	Let's get in. Let's board.
Jetzt geht's los.	Now, we'll start. Here we go.

Was paßt hier? **Which of the words listed below are similar in meaning to the italicized words on the left.**

hineingehen   falsch sein   kosten
müssen...fahren   verlassen   beginnen

1. Das *macht* zwanzig Mark.
2. Der Zug *fährt* von der Stadt *ab*.
3. Wann *geht's los*?
4. Wie lange *dauert* die Reise?
5. *Steigt* doch schnell *ein*!
6. Das *stimmt* nicht.

Ergänzung

1. *Wie komme ich dorthin?* Imagine that you are a tour guide in Germany and you need to give directions to various people.

❐ Wie komme ich zur Bank? (hier nach links)
   Gehen Sie hier nach links.

   1. Wie komme ich zur Post?
      (geradeaus)
   2. Wie komme ich zum Museum?
      (zwei Ecken, dann nach rechts)
   3. Wie komme ich zum Rathaus?
      (auf dieser Straße bis zum Bahnhof)
   4. Wie komme ich zum Kino?
      (eine Ecke, dann links)
   5. Wie komme ich zum Hotel?
      (immer geradeaus bis zur Kantstraße)

2. **Wie kommst du in die Stadt?**

❐ mit dem Fahrrad
   Ich fahre mit dem Fahrrad.

   1. mit der Straßenbahn
   2. mit dem Moped
   3. mit dem Bus
   4. mit dem Zug
   5. mit dem Motorrad

Sag's mal!

Wo ist das Rathaus? Wie komme ich hin?

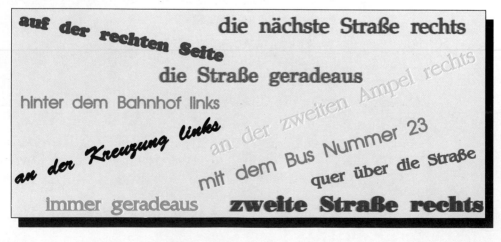

auf der rechten Seite

die nächste Straße rechts

die Straße geradeaus

hinter dem Bahnhof links

an der zweiten Ampel rechts

an der Kreuzung links

mit dem Bus Nummer 23

quer über die Straße

immer geradeaus

zweite Straße rechts

Aussprache

short /ü/	long /ü/
fünf	Tür
müssen	Süden
Küche	für
dürft	Bücher
Flüsse	Füße
Büfett	kühl
Büro	drüben
zurück	Brüder
Jürgen	Frühling

Übungen

Verbs with Separable Prefixes

You can combine verbs with prefixes and thus change their meaning. In most cases such prefixes are prepositions, just as in English (to take — to undertake).

Beispiele: (ankommen) *Der Zug kommt bald an.* The train is arriving soon.
(einsteigen) *Sie steigt in den Bus ein.* She is getting on the bus.

The prefixes, which you can add or eliminate, are called *separable*. The prefixes are separated from their verbs and placed at the end of the sentence.

Beispiele: (abfahren) Wann *fährt* die Straßenbahn *ab*?
(umsteigen) Manfred und Willi *steigen* in Hannover *um*.
(fernsehen) Wir *sehen* am Abend *fern*.

These are the verbs with separable prefixes you have learned so far:

abfahren	einladen	hineingehen	vorhaben
ankommen	fernsehen	mitbringen	zubereiten
ausgeben	herkommen	mitkommen	zurückfahren
einkaufen			

The accent is always on the separable prefix (*ab*fahren, *ein*laden).

3. *Was machen die Jungen?* Tell what the boys are doing. *Folge dem Beispiel!*

❑ ins Kino mitkommen
Die Jungen kommen ins Kino mit.

1. spät zu Hause ankommen
2. im Wohnzimmer fernsehen
3. in Köln umsteigen
4. viel Geld ausgeben
5. die Mädchen einladen
6. nichts vorhaben
7. das Abendbrot zubereiten

4. **Beantworte diese Fragen!**

❑ Um wieviel Uhr fährt Peter zurück? (um zehn Uhr)
Er fährt um zehn Uhr zurück.

1. Wo kauft die Oma ein?
(in der Stadt)
2. Wann kommt der Onkel an?
(am Freitag)
3. Wen bringt Rolf zur Party mit?
(Ingrid)
4. Wen laden die Großeltern ein?
(die Enkel)
5. Um wieviel Uhr fährt der Zug ab?
(um halb neun)
6. Wer geht in den Klub hinein?
(viele Jugendliche)

5. *Ergänze diese Sätze!* **Complete the sentences using the words provided.**

1. (vorhaben) Was _____ ihr denn _____?
2. (einladen) Wir _____ ein paar Jugendliche zu Annes Geburtstag _____.
3. (mitkommen) _____ du zur Party _____?
4. (mitbringen) Wen _____ du denn _____?
5. (fernsehen) Vielleicht _____ wir _____.
6. (zubereiten) Wer _____ denn das Essen _____?
7. (hineingehen) Ich _____ in dieses Kaufhaus _____.
8. (ausgeben) _____ du viel Geld _____?

Verbs with Inseparable Prefixes

There are a number of inseparable prefixes in German that remain with the verb, most frequently *ver-*, *be-*, *er-*, and *ent-*.

Beispiele: Christa bekommt eine Gitarre zum Geburtstag.
Verstehst du ihn?

As you can see from these examples, the verbs containing inseparable prefixes are treated the same way as those without prefixes.

Here is a list of verbs with inseparable prefixes that you have been exposed to up to this point:

beginnen   bekommen   besuchen   bezahlen   verlassen   verstehen

Sie besuchen ihre Freunde.

The accent is never on the inseparable prefix, but always on the stem of the verb (be*kommen*, er*zählen*).

6. *Was passiert hier alles? Uschi und ihre Freundin Andrea gehen zu einem Rockkonzert.* **Select the appropriate verb with its proper verb form to complete the dialog.**

verlassen   bezahlen   beginnen   verstehen   bekommen

1. Du, Andrea! Wann _____ denn das Konzert?
2. Um acht. Ich _____ für die Karten.
3. Vielen Dank. Ich bin froh, ich kann noch zwei Karten _____.
4. Sieh mal, ein paar Fans _____ schon die Show.
5. Das _____ ich nicht.

7. Bilde Sätze!

1. Ralf und Heiko / bekommen / viele / Geschenk
2. wann / verlassen / Tina / Schule
3. Party / beginnen / sehr früh
4. besuchen / ihr / Lehrer
5. warum / verstehen / du / alle / Aufgabe / so gut
6. wollen / du / das / bezahlen

Accusative Prepositions

The accusative case always follows these prepositions:

durch	through
für	for
gegen	against
ohne	without
um	around

Beispiele: Wir fahren durch die Stadt.
Hast du ein Geschenk für ihn?
Sie läuft gegen das Fahrrad.
Ich komme ohne das Buch.
Gehst du um den Bahnhof?

Contractions

These accusative prepositions and articles are contracted as long as there is no special emphasis on the article.

durch	+	das	=	durchs
für	+	das	=	fürs
um	+	das	=	ums

Beispiele: Bezahlst du fürs Konzert?
Ich bezahle viel Geld für das Auto.

8. ***Wohin geht ihr denn?*** **Tell where everyone is going.** *Folge dem Beispiel!*

❏ die Jungen / Schule
Die Jungen gehen durch die Schule.

1. wir / Bahnhof
2. die Gäste / Haus
3. ich / Museum
4. viele / Bank
5. die Jugendlichen / Stadt
6. mein Vater / Rathaus

9. *Nein, das mache ich nicht.* You don't agree with what you are being asked. Respond accordingly, using the cues provided.

❑ Gehst du ums Haus? (Schule)
Nein, ich gehe um die Schule.

1. Fährst du ums Haus?
(Ecke)
2. Läufst du ums Museum?
(Kino)
3. Gehst du um die Post?
(Bank)
4. Gehst du um den Vorort zu
Fuß? (Stadt)
5. Fährst du ums Rathaus?
(Bahnhof)

10. *Wieviel bezahlst du für...?* Indicate what you are paying for the different items.

❑ Moped / eintausend Mark
Ich bezahle eintausend Mark für das Moped.

1. Buch / dreißig Mark
2. Geschenk / nicht viel
3. Kuli / ein paar Mark
4. Auto / viel Geld
5. Gitarre / zweihundert Mark
6. Karte / fünfzehn Mark

11. *Bringst du das mit?* Daniela is getting together with several friends to study for a test. She is asking her classmates if they are bringing certain items, to which they reply as follows. *Folge dem Beispiel!*

❑ Bringst du die Kassette mit?
Nein, ich komme ohne die Kassette.

1. Bringst du das Buch mit?
2. Bringst du die Gitarre mit?
3. Bringst du den Taschenrechner mit?
4. Bringst du die Schultasche mit?
5. Bringst du das Geschenk mit?

12. *Wohin stellt ihr das Fahrrad?* Beantworte diese Frage! Folge dem Beispiel!

☐ Haus
Wir stellen das Fahrrad gegen das Haus.

1. Auto
2. Moped
3. Mietshaus
4. Tür
5. Boot

13. Replace the italicized words with those listed in parentheses.

1. Viele Gäste kommen durch *die Stadt.*
(Museum, Straße, Mietshaus, Rathaus,
2. Er fährt mit dem Auto gegen *das Haus.*
(Fahrrad, Moped, Bus, Straßenbahn, Zug)
3. Gehen wir schnell um *das Kaufhaus.*
(Mietshaus, Park, Bahnhof, Schule, Café)
4. Hat er ein Geschenk für *uns?*
(du, ihr, wir, Mädchen, Freund)
5. Ohne *dich* gehe ich nicht hinein.
(er, ihr, Lehrerin, Schultasche, Buch)

14. *Beende diese Sätze!* Some sentences may require more than one word.

1. Ist dieses Buch für _____?
2. Ich möchte nicht gern gegen _____.
3. Sein Büro ist gleich um _____.
4. Kannst du ohne _____?
5. Haben Sie etwas gegen _____?
6. Sie kaufen die Geschenke für _____.
7. Ohne Geld kann ich _____.
8. Sie fahren durch _____.

Expression of Quantity: *Wieviel?* (How much?) — *Wie viele?* (How many?)

Generally speaking, *wieviel?* is used when expressing a mass or a sum.

Beispiele: Wieviel Uhr ist es?
Wieviel kostet das Moped?

On the other hand, *wie viele?* is used when referring to items that can be counted.

Beispiele: Wie viele Karten brauchen wir?
Wie viele Freunde hast du?

15. Ask questions about the italicized words, using *wieviel* and *wie viele*.

❑ Wir kaufen *ein paar* Karten.
Wie viele Karten kaufen wir?

1. Die Klasse beginnt um *acht* Uhr.
2. Ich habe *etwas* Geld.
3. *Zwölf* Gäste kommen zum Geburtstag.
4. Meine Mutter kauft *drei* Brote.
5. Er hat *keine* Zeit.
6. Herr Gerber hat *zwei* Autos.

16. *Wieviel?* oder *Wie viele?*

1. _____ kostet die Reise?
2. _____ Wochen seid ihr in Europa?
3. _____ Bleistifte müßt ihr kaufen?
4. _____ ist elf und sieben?
5. _____ Schüler sind in der Klasse?
6. _____ Geld brauchst du denn?
7. _____ Zeit hast du morgen?
8. _____ Städte werden Sie besuchen?

Wie viele Zeitschriften kaufen sie?

Wieviel kostet der Kuchen?

Ein Ausflug nach Speyer

Brigitte besucht Margit in Mannheim. Beide sind gute Freundinnen. Brigitte wohnt in Köln. Sie will ein paar Tage in Mannheim bleiben°. Heute haben sie vor, einen Ausflug nach Speyer und Umgebung zu machen°.

stay

einen Ausflug machen go on an excursion

Margits Vater leiht Margit sein Auto. Mannheim ist nur 40 Kilometer von Speyer entfernt. Das dauert nur eine halbe Stunde. Schon aus der Entfernung sehen sie den Dom° von Speyer. Er ist sehr bekannt. Sie parken° das Auto ganz in der Nähe vom Dom und gehen dann zu Fuß. Margit erzählt° Brigitte wie alt der Dom ist. Auf einem Schild° können sie es genau lesen: „Erbaut° von 1030 bis 1061." Sie gehen in den Dom hinein. Dort bestaunen° sie ihn.

cathedral/park

tells

sign/built

marvel at

Margit:	Wenn° Gäste uns besuchen, kommen wir oft her.
Brigitte:	Das glaube ich. Der Dom ist wirklich interessant.
Margit:	Alle wollen immer die Kaisergruft° sehen.
Brigitte:	Was ist denn die Kaisergruft?
Margit:	Komm mit! Siehst du? Das sind die Kaisergräber°.
Brigitte:	Unglaublich°! Fast alle sind mehr als 800 Jahre alt.

when

emperors' tomb

emperors' graves

unbelievable

Vor dem Dom kaufen Margit und Brigitte ein paar Ansichtskarten°. Dann gehen sie zum Rhein°. Er ist nicht weit vom Dom. Sie sitzen dort auf einer Bank° und schreiben die Karten.

picture postcards/ Rhine River

bench

Brigitte:	Ich schicke° eine Karte nach Hause.
Margit:	Du wirst schneller zu Hause sein als die Karte.
Brigitte:	Das macht nichts. Der Rhein ist hier nicht so breit wie° in Köln.
Margit:	Das stimmt. Viele Touristen fahren schon von Basel auf dem Rhein. Dann kommen sie hier in Speyer an und fahren weiter° nach Köln.

I'm sending

not as wide as

continue on

Brigitte und Margit gehen zum Auto zurück. Beide sehen auf eine Landkarte. Margit will wissen, wie sie von Speyer nach Bad Dürkheim fahren muß. Diese Stadt liegt nordwestlich von Speyer. Dann steigen sie ein und fahren auf einer Bundesstraße° nach Bad Dürkheim. In 45 Minuten sind sie da. Margit fährt auch gleich zur Sehenswürdigkeit° der Stadt: das Riesenfaß°.

Federal Highway

sight/gigantic barrel

Brigitte fotografiert das Riesenfaß. Sie fotografiert auch Margit vor dem Riesenfaß. Sie will Margit das Foto später schicken.

Margit:	Sehen wir uns die Andenken° an.
Brigitte:	Die Auswahl ist groß. Ich kaufe zwei Ansichtskarten.
Margit:	Schreibst du schon wieder nach Hause?
Brigitte:	Nein, die sammle ich nur. Was ist denn in dem Riesenfaß?
Margit:	Ein Restaurant. Da kann man gut essen.
Brigitte:	Möchtest du etwas essen?
Margit:	Ja, ich habe Hunger°.
Brigitte:	Gut, gehen wir hinein!

souvenirs

I'm hungry.

Was haben sie heute vor?

Was ist in der Kaisergruft?

Welche Wörter fehlen in diesen Sätzen? (Which words are missing in these sentences?) Use the verbs listed below and complete each sentence by using an appropriate verb form.

schicken   liegen   fotografieren   essen
kaufen   haben   bleiben   sein
sehen   parken   stehen   wohnen
dauern   gehen

1. Brigitte _____ in Köln.
2. Sie _____ ein paar Tage in Mannheim.
3. Die Reise von Mannheim nach Speyer _____ ungefähr dreißig Minuten.
4. Die Mädchen _____ das Auto nicht weit vom Dom.
5. Auf einem Schild _____:„Erbaut von 1030 bis 1061."
6. Margit und Brigitte _____ in den Dom hinein.
7. Margits Gäste wollen oft die Kaisergräber _____.
8. Brigitte und Margit _____ Ansichtskarten.
9. Brigitte _____ eine Karte nach Hause.
10. Der Rhein _____ in Speyer nicht sehr breit.
11. Bad Dürkheim _____ nicht weit von Speyer.
12. Brigitte _____ das Riesenfaß.
13. Im Riesenfaß kann man _____.
14. Margit _____ Hunger.

Fragen

1. Wo wohnt Brigitte?
2. Was wollen Margit und Brigitte heute machen?
3. Wie weit ist Speyer von Mannheim entfernt?
4. Wo parken sie das Auto?
5. Wie alt ist der Dom?
6. Was ist in der Kaisergruft?
7. Was kaufen Margit und Brigitte vor dem Dom?
8. Ist der Rhein in Speyer so breit wie in Köln?
9. Wie weiß Margit den Weg nach Bad Dürkheim?
10. Wo liegt diese Stadt?
11. Wie lange fahren sie nach Bad Dürkheim?
12. Was ist in Bad Dürkheim besonders interessant?
13. Wen fotografiert Brigitte?
14. Was sammelt Brigitte?
15. Was ist in dem Riesenfaß?
16. Warum gehen sie hinein?

Welcher Fluß fließt durch Speyer?

Wie ist die Auswahl?

Übung macht den Meister!

1. *Wir fahren mit dem Zug.* Create your own dialog by using the following information as a guideline. Be as creative as possible.

   You and your friend have arrived at the railroad station one hour before your train is leaving. You have plenty of time. You suggest to your friend that you check the departure time on the monitor or telescreen. It shows that the train will depart ten minutes late. Both of you go to the ticket window to buy your tickets. You'll tell the official that you're buying two second class round-trip tickets to Hamburg. He tells you the cost. Since you have plenty of time, you suggest to your friend that you go and have some ice cream.

2. Imagine yourself in the center of a German city giving directions to travelers who need your assistance. Can you come up with different directions for these questions?

   1. Können Sie mir bitte sagen, wie ich zum Bahnhof komme?
   2. Wo ist das Hansa Hotel?
   3. Wie komme ich von hier zum Rathaus?
   4. Ist die Post hier in der Nähe?
   5. Wie weit ist die nächste Bank von hier entfernt?

3. *Sie machen einen Ausflug.* Develop a short narrative or dialog including the following details.

   Your parents are planning a trip. Find out if they are going by car or train...when they are leaving...where they are going...how far it is...what they will see there...when they will come back.

4. *Können Sie das lesen?* Imagine that while studying the train schedule an elderly gentleman comes up to you and asks for your help, as he has difficulties reading the small print on the *Ankunft* (arrival) schedule. Can you help him out? Here are some of the questions you may have to respond to.

   Mann: Können Sie das lesen?
   Du: _____
   Mann: Meine Enkelin kommt heute aus Münster hier an.
   Du: _____
   Mann: Nein, sie muß in Düsseldorf umsteigen.
   Du: _____
   Mann: Ich glaube, der Zug kommt etwas später. Es ist vielleicht der nächste.
   Du: _____
   Mann: Ja, das stimmt. Es ist ein Intercity.
   Du: _____
   Mann: Vielen Dank.
   Du: _____

5. *Wie gefällt Ihnen meine Stadt?* Pretend to show a visitor your town. Indicate some main points of interest. Have one of your classmates be the visitor and you the guide.

Wir machen einen Ausflug nach Augsburg.

Wohin fahren die Züge? (Frankfurt)

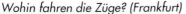

234

Wohin fährt die Straßenbahn? (Dresden)

Erweiterung

17. *Was paßt hier?* **Complete this short conversation using the words below to make each sentence meaningful. You will not need all the words listed.**

fahren	gehen	bezahlt	lange
zurück	einfach	viel	glaube
erster	entfernt	zweiter	an

1. Um wieviel Uhr kommen wir _____?
2. Ich weiß nicht. Die Stadt ist weit _____.
3. Wie _____ dauert diese Reise?
4. Ich _____ vier Stunden.
5. Fahren wir _____ Klasse?
6. Kostet das nicht zu _____?
7. Ja, aber mein Onkel _____ für die Reise.
8. Wohin möchten Sie _____?
9. Nach Augsburg, hin und _____,
10. Erster oder _____ Klasse?

18. Beantworte diese Fragen!

1. Wohin fährt die Straßenbahn?
2. Wie kommst du zum Stadtzentrum?
3. Warum kaufst du eine Zeitung?
4. Warum gehst du in die Reiseauskunft?
5. Wie lange dauert der Ausflug?
6. Was macht der Beamte?
7. Fährst du mit dem Bus?
8. Um wieviel Uhr fährst du ab?

19. *Was ist logisch?* (What's logical?) From the list below, select the verbs that best complete the phrases.

schreiben	fotografieren	lesen	essen	lernen
spielen	gehen	fahren	singen	einladen

1. in der Schule
2. mit dem Moped
3. zu Fuß
4. Freunde zum Geburtstag
5. die Zeitung
6. das alte Rathaus
7. den beliebten Hit
8. die Gitarre
9. eine Arbeit
10. das Abendbrot

20. Du willst im Sommer deine Tante besuchen. Dein Freund oder deine Freundin stellt dir Fragen (asks you questions). Kannst du sie beantworten?

Was machst du im Sommer?

_____

Wo wohnt sie denn?

_____

Wie weit ist das von hier?

_____

Wie lange bleibst du dort?

_____

Wirst du eine Karte schicken?

_____

Sprachspiegel

21. Pretend to be an official at a railroad station answering questions for tourists who are not familiar with the station or the German train system.

1. Wo ist der Zug nach Bonn, bitte?
2. Haben Sie einen Fahrplan?
3. Wie lange dauert die Reise nach Bremen?
4. Um wieviel Uhr kommt der Zug aus Österreich an?
5. Wo ist die Reiseauskunft?
6. Was ist die Entfernung von hier nach Regensburg?
7. Wann fährt der Zug nach Berlin ab?
8. Wissen Sie, wieviel Uhr es ist?

22. *Wie sagt man's?* From the list below, select the appropriate words to complete the various conversational exchanges.

Auto   hin   weit   zwanzig   Straßenbahn
Mark   billig   drüben   Museum   geradeaus
Ecke   zu   habe   Karte   Uhr

1. Wann kommt der Zug?
   In _____ Minuten.
   Gut, dann _____ ich noch Zeit.
   Nein, es ist schon vier _____.

2. Bitte sehr?
   Eine _____ nach München, bitte.
   Einfach?
   Nein, _____ und zurück.

3. Wo kommt die _____ an?
   Dort drüben an der _____.
   Vielen Dank.

4. Gehst du _____ Fuß?
   Nein, das ist zu _____.
   Ich habe ein _____.
   Toll!

5. Wie komme ich zum _____?
   Gehen Sie _____!
   Und wo ist das Rathaus?
   Dort _____.

6. Diese Zeitschrift ist sehr _____.
   Dann kaufe sie doch.
   Hast du drei _____?
   Ja, hier bitte.

23. *Fragen und Antworten.* Match the questions on the left with the appropriate answers on the right.

1. Wann willst du sie besuchen?
2. Weißt du, wie alt der Dom ist?
3. Warum siehst du auf eine Landkarte?
4. Willst du nicht einsteigen?
5. Kaufst du Ansichtskarten?
6. Sollen wir in das Restaurant gehen?
7. Wer sitzt dort auf einer Bank?
8. Dauert der Ausflug lange?

a. Nein, das Essen ist da nicht sehr billig.
b. Nein, ich gehe zu Fuß.
c. Vielleicht eine Stunde.
d. Die Sabine? Im Sommer.
e. Mein Freund Thomas.
f. Ja, ich will Anita schreiben.
g. Ungefähr dreihundert Jahre.
h. Ich weiß nicht, wo wir sind.

24. Wie heißt das auf deutsch?

1. When does the train depart?
2. We'll have to transfer in Freiburg.
3. They are arriving too late.
4. Can you pay for the car?
5. How much money is he spending?
6. Do we want to drive back?

Rückblick

I. Complete the sentences using the information given plus the infinitive form of a verb of your choice where needed.

❏ (müssen) _____ du ein Geschenk _____?
Mußt du ein Geschenk kaufen?

1. (sollen) Wir _____ mit dem Zug nach Ulm _____.
2. (dürfen) _____ ihr dort _____?
3. (werden) _____ du nach Hause _____?
4. (können) Er _____ gut Gitarre _____.
5. (mögen) _____ du das nicht?
6. (müssen) Die Schüler _____ die Aufgaben _____.
7. (wollen) Ich _____ ein Moped _____.

II. Put each verb into the present and then into the future tense.

❏ du / nach Bonn fahren
Du fährst nach Bonn.
Du wirst nach Bonn fahren.

1. ich / später fernsehen
2. Uwe / das Buch lesen
3. die Lehrerin / laut sprechen
4. du / das Haus verlassen
5. wir / das Abendbrot essen

III. Substitute an appropriate singular or plural pronoun for the italicized words.

❏ Kennst du *die Tante?*
Kennst du sie?

1. Möchtest du *das Motorrad* kaufen?
2. Ich will *Erika und Dieter* fragen.
3. Trinkt ihr *ein Glas Limo?*
4. Wir besuchen *den Dom.*
5. Warum fotografierst du *das Rathaus?*
6. Mußt du *die zehn Seiten* lesen?
7. Schreib doch *die Einladung!*
8. Ich kann *die Züge* schon sehen.

IV. Beende diese Sätze!

1. Frag doch _____!
2. Kannst du ihn _____?
3. Warum kommt _____?
4. Was macht ihr _____?
5. Die Jungen spielen _____.
6. Wir schreiben _____.
7. Weißt du, wie _____?
8. Der Zug fährt _____.

V. Change these sentences from the singular to the plural.

❏ Der Gast bringt ein Geschenk. (drei)
Die Gäste bringen drei Geschenke.

1. Ich habe einen Freund. (ein paar)
2. Hast du ein Auto? (zwei)
3. Er kauft ein Glas. (viele)
4. Der Junge kauft eine Zeitung. (fünf)
5. Ich brauche einen Kuli. (nicht viele)
6. Siehst du einen Film? (vier)

Land und Leute

Die Schweiz

Die Schweiz ist ein sehr beliebtes Land. Jedes Jahr kommen viele Besucher° in die Schweiz. Dieses kleine Land paßt ungefähr 190 mal in die Vereinigten Staaten (ohne Alaska und Hawaii). Die Schweiz ist halb so groß wie der Staat South Carolina. — *visitors*

Die Schweiz hat fünf Nachbarländer: Frankreich, Italien, Österreich, Liechtenstein und die Bundesrepublik Deutschland. Mehr als sechs Millionen Menschen° wohnen in diesem Land. 65% sprechen Deutsch, 18% Französisch, 12% Italienisch und 5% andere Sprachen°. Die Nationalfahne ist rot und hat ein weißes Kreuz° in der Mitte. — *people / languages / cross*

Der größte Teil der Schweiz liegt in den Bergen. Die Alpen erreichen° eine Höhe° von über 4 600 m (Monte Rosa). Der Rhein ist der längste Fluß in der Schweiz. Er fließt 376 Kilometer durch das Land und dann weiter° durch die Bundesrepublik Deutschland und die Niederlande zur Nordsee°. — *reach/height / further / North Sea*

Viele Touristen fahren gern in die Schweiz.

240

Der Rhein ist der längste Fluß in der Schweiz. (Rheinfall/Schaffhausen)

Die Nationalfahne ist rot und hat ein
weißes Kreuz in der Mitte.

Wann besuchen viele Touristen die Schweiz? (St. Moritz)

Die größte° Stadt der Schweiz ist Zürich. Diese Stadt liegt am Zürichsee. Die zweitgrößte Stadt ist Basel. Wie Zürich liegt auch Basel im Norden der Schweiz. Der Rhein fließt durch Basel. Genf ist eine andere große Stadt. Diese Stadt liegt im Süden am Genfer See, direkt an der Grenze° zu Frankreich. Bern, die Hauptstadt der Schweiz, ist die viertgrößte Stadt und liegt im Westen. Dann kommt Luzern. Diese Stadt liegt in der Mitte der Schweiz.

largest

border

Während der Sommermonate besuchen die Touristen die Schweiz sehr gern. Hier können sie viel in den Bergen wandern°. Warum kommen auch viele Besucher im Winter in die Schweiz? Während dieser Jahreszeit ist die Schweiz ein Paradies. Tausende von Wintersportlern kommen in die Schweiz und laufen dort Ski.

hike

Brienz, eine kleine Stadt in der Schweiz

Zürich, die größte Stadt in der Schweiz

Bern, die Hauptstadt der Schweiz

Was paßt hier?

1. Der längste Fluß ist
2. Die Nationalfahne hat
3. Die zweitgrößte Stadt ist
4. Der höchste Berg ist
5. Ungefähr vier Millionen sprechen
6. Genf liegt
7. Im Winter kann man in der Schweiz
8. Der Rhein fließt
9. Die Schweiz ist
10. Bern ist

a. halb so groß wie der Staat South Carolina
b. Basel
c. zur Nordsee
d. Deutsch
e. Ski laufen
f. die Hauptstadt
g. ein Kreuz in der Mitte
h. an der Grenze zu Frankreich
i. der Monta Rosa
j. der Rhein

Wohin geht es hier?

Ist das Land flach?

Beantworte diese Fragen!

1. Besuchen viele Touristen die Schweiz?
2. Wie groß ist die Schweiz?
3. Wie viele Nachbarländer hat die Schweiz?
4. Wie heißen sie?
5. Sprechen alle Deutsch?
6. Ist das Land flach?
7. Wohin fließt der Rhein von der Schweiz weiter?
8. Wie heißt die Hauptstadt der Schweiz?
9. Wo liegt Luzern?
10. Kommen Besucher nur im Sommer in die Schweiz?

Ein krummer Krebs kroch über eine krumme Klammer.

(A crooked crab crawled over a crooked paper clip.)

Kulturecke

Traveling by Train

Traveling by train in Germany can be rewarding or frustrating for the foreign traveler. If you're well prepared, however, you won't have any problems coping with this new and exciting adventure. When traveling between major cities, look for the main railroad station (*Hauptbahnhof*), usually located in the heart of the city. Should you depart from a small town, simply ask for the *Bahnhof*.

Sie steigen in den Zug ein. (Hamburg)

Der Intercity-Zug

Zweite Klasse

Wo ist der Bahnhof?

Upon entering a main station, become familiar with the facilities. If you need information about a certain train, look for the schedules usually posted in a prominent location behind a glass window. There are normally two such schedules. One is marked *"Abfahrt"* (departure), the other *"Ankunft"* (arrival). The first schedule gives destinations, times of departure and other valuable information. In case you want to study these details in more privacy and at leisure, you should look for the information office, marked either *"Reiseauskunft"* or *"Information."*

The major stations have begun to install large overhead departure schedules that indicate the departure time, type of train, destination and other information such as possible transfers. If you are in a hurry or need speedy personal attention, look for an official wearing a uniform. Sometimes there is a small information stand which is easily recognized. The official usually has a detailed train schedule and will have an answer to your questions at his fingertips.

The facilities at train stations are generally well marked. Know the German names and you'll have no difficulty finding your way around. Buy your ticket at any window marked *"Fahrkarten."* Let's assume you want to travel to Frankfurt. To ask for a ticket, simply say to the clerk, *"Nach Frankfurt, bitte."* If your ticket is to be one-way, add the word *"einfach,"* which means literally "simple." If you want a round-trip ticket, say *"hin und zurück,"* which means "there and back."

After you have purchased your ticket, you may decide to check your luggage instead of taking it directly to the train. Look for a sign marked *"Reisegepäck-Annahme."* Most travelers, however, prefer to take their luggage with them on the train. To check your luggage temporarily until departure, you should look for coin-operated lockers marked *"Schließfächer."*

Every station, large or small, usually has some eating facilities. In major stations you may find the words *"Cafeteria," "Imbiß,"* which is a snack bar, and *"Restaurant."* If you don't want to sit down at a table, try to locate a snack bar that offers hot dogs, cold sandwiches and beverages. Those who would like to take some of the delicious German chocolates or candies on their trip can buy these goodies at specialty stands. Would you like to read some newspapers, magazines or books? Look for a stand marked *"Zeitungen-Bücher."* Germans rarely go to visit friends or relatives in other towns without taking a small gift along, such as candies or more typically flowers. It is quite common to find flower shops at the station.

If you have little luggage to carry, you won't have any problems taking it directly to the train. However, if you have more luggage than you can carry easily, look for a luggage cart marked *"Koffer-Kuli."* You can place your luggage on the cart and wheel it right to the train. In most cities, there is no charge for the use of these carts. Be sure to give yourself plenty of time to get to the train. The trains of the German Rail (*Deutsche Bundesbahn*) are punctual and won't wait for you.

If you have a reserved seat, you can look at a chart located at your designated track or platform (*Gleis* or *Bahnsteig*) to determine exactly where your train car will stop. This assures you that you won't have to walk any farther once the train arrives and you're ready to get on.

Most Germans travel second class (*Zweite Klasse*). Second class usually has vinyl seats; it's not luxurious but fairly comfortable. First class seats (*Erste Klasse*) are more plush and rather expensive. These accommodations are recommended only if you want to assure yourself of a seat during the rush period if you did not reserve a seat in advance. If you're not sure, you can purchase a second class ticket and pay the difference after you have boarded the train. Check also to determine whether your car is a *Raucher* (smoker) or a *Nichtraucher* (non-smoker). Most trains have specially designated cars.

Wo fährt der Zug nach Köln ab? (Hamburg)

Was kann man hier kaufen? (München)

246

Der Lufthansa Airport Express fährt von Köln nach Frankfurt.

Shortly before departure there will be the final call over the loudspeaker and a warning to step back and close the doors. Once the train has left the station, you can relax and examine your surroundings. You will find the compartment and the other facilities quite comfortable. Remember, most Germans travel by train and not by plane as in the U.S. Therefore, special care is taken to ensure a pleasant environment on trains. If you don't want to bring your own sandwiches, you can have a warm or cold meal in the train car labeled *"Restaurant."* Don't be surprised if someone else sits down at your table after asking you *"Ist hier noch frei?"* This is quite common here and in most German restaurants.

If you want to take a nap, some of the second class seats may be adjustable. They are always adjustable in first class. On a longer trip, you can reserve sleeping quarters in the *Schlafwagen* (sleeper) or in a *Liegewagen* (couchette) for an additional fee.

Some of the long-distance trains have very modern facilities such as a conference room, a playroom for small children and even a party car called *Gesellschaftswagen* in which social functions such as dancing can be arranged.

Wohin fährt dieser Zug?

Auf dem Hauptbahnhof in München ist viel los.

There are several types of trains, differing in distance and speed of their runs. Most foreigners want to cover distances quickly. Therefore, you may prefer to travel in a *D-Zug* or in a *FD-Zug*. A *D-Zug* or *FD-Zug* makes fewer stops and connects more than 70 German cities. A faster train, however, is the *Intercity* which links all major German cities and runs at one-hour intervals between 7 A.M. and 11 P.M. Intercity trains that travel beyond the border of the Federal Republic are called *Euro-City*. The various stops are usually posted on some of the cars outside. These Intercity trains never stop in small towns. And, finally, should you fly in or out of Frankfurt — coming from or going to the area of Köln — Lufthansa, the German airlines, will transport you in their Airport Express to your final destination.

Was weißt du? Match the items on the left with those on the right.

1. Imbiß	a. departure
2. Raucher	b. luggage cart
3. Koffer-Kuli	c. arrival
4. Reisegepäck-Annahme	d. track
5. Hauptbahnhof	e. snack bar
6. Gleis	f. sleeper
7. Schließfächer	g. smoker
8. Abfahrt	h. main station
9. Schlafwagen	i. luggage checking
10. Ankunft	j. lockers

Wieviel kannst du verstehen? Auf deutsch, bitte!

1. Der _____ fährt zwischen 7 und 23 Uhr.
2. In großen Städten gibt es einen _____.
3. Auf dem _____ Poster steht, wann die Züge abfahren.
4. Ich weiß nicht, um wieviel Uhr der Zug fährt.
   Ich frage in der _____.
5. Wenn man mit dem Zug fahren will, braucht man eine _____.
6. Der Zug ist schon da. Er steht auf _____ 3.
7. Ich habe nicht genug Geld. Ich fahre zweite _____.
8. Wenn man essen will, gibt es in vielen Zügen ein _____.

Vokabeln

Friday

abbiegen to turn (to)
abfahren to depart, leave
das Andenken,- souvenir
ankommen to arrive
sich ansehen to look at
die Ansichtskarte,-n picture postcard
der Ausflug,-̈e excursion
einen Ausflug machen to go on an excursion
ausgeben to spend
das Auto,-s car
der Bahnhof,-̈e (train) station
der Bahnsteig,-e platform
die Bank,-en bank
die Bank,-̈e bench
der Beamte,-n official (male)
die Beamtin,-nen official (female)
bestaunen to marvel at
bezahlen to pay
bleiben to stay, remain
das Boot,-e boat
breit wide
der Bus,-se bus
das Café,-s café
dafür for it
dauern to last, take (time)
der Dom,-e cathedral
durch through

einfach simple, one-way (ticket)
einsteigen to get in, board
entfernt away, distant
erbauen to build, construct
erbaut built, constructed
erzählen to tell
der Fahrplan,-̈e schedule
das Flugzeug,-e airplane
gegen against
geradeaus straight ahead
hin und zurück round trip
das Hotel,-s hotel
der Hunger hunger
Hunger haben to be hungry
links left
nach links to the left
das Motorrad,-̈er motorcycle
das Museum,-seen museum
nachgehen to be slow (watch)
die Nähe nearness, proximity
in der Nähe nearby
ob if, whether
ohne without
parken to park

die Post post office
das Rathaus,-̈er city hall
rechts right
nach rechts to the right
die Reise,-n trip
das Restaurant,-s restaurant
schaffen to manage (it), make (it)
schicken to send
das Schiff,-e ship, boat
sehen auf to look at
die Sehenswürdigkeit,-en sight(s)
das Signal,-e signal
so...wie as...as
um around
umsteigen to transfer
unglaublich unbelievable
das Verkehrsmittel,- means of transportation
weiterfahren to continue on, drive on
wenn when
die Zeitschrift,-en magazine
der Zeitungskiosk,-e newspaper stand
der Zug,-̈e train
zurückfahren to drive back
zurückgehen to go back

Auf der Tafel steht, wann die Züge abfahren. (Hamburg)

Für wen ist dieser Wagen?

Einkaufen

8

Communicative Functions

- talking about shopping for clothes
- naming items of clothing and their colors
- asking about prices
- describing what people are wearing
- telling about a shopping experience
- paying the bill

251

Im Kaufhaus

(vor dem Kaufhaus)

Tanja: Der Pulli da ist schick.
Britta: Hast du nicht schon viele?
Tanja: Die Farben sind aber zu dunkel.
Karin: Ich brauche auch einen Pulli.
Tanja: Vielleicht ist die Auswahl im Kaufhaus gut.
Britta: Stehen wir doch nicht hier beim Eingang!
Karin: Stimmt. Gehen wir hinein!

Fragen

1. Wie ist der Pulli?
2. Hat Tanja Pullis zu Hause?
3. Wer will auch einen Pulli kaufen?
4. Wo stehen die drei Mädchen?
5. Was machen sie endlich?

Der Pulli da ist schick.　　　Tanja　　　Gehen wir ins Kaufhaus hinein!

(im Kaufhaus)

Tanja: Dieser Pulli steht dir gut, Karin.
Karin: Nein, er ist viel zu groß.
Britta: Und wie findest du den Pulli hier?
Karin: Nicht schlecht.
Tanja: Der weiße Pulli da gefällt mir.
Britta: Ganz preiswert.
Tanja: Und er paßt mir auch.
Britta: Na, dann ist die Entscheidung einfach.

Die Auswahl hier ist gut.

Wie findest du den Pulli?

Fragen

1. Wie ist der Pulli für Karin?
2. Welche Farbe hat Tanja gern?
3. Kostet der weiße Pulli viel?
4. Paßt der Pulli Tanja?

Tanja:	Gehen wir zur Kasse!
Karin:	Du hast mal wieder Glück. Ich kann nie etwas finden.
Tanja:	Du bist eben zu wählerisch.
Verkäuferin:	Ein schöner Pulli. So, das macht achtzehn Mark.
Tanja:	Bitte sehr.
Verkäuferin:	Und zwei Mark zurück.
Britta:	Jetzt schnell aus dem Kaufhaus.
Karin:	Hast du Angst, ich kaufe doch noch etwas?
Britta:	Nein, ich muß zum Café. Meine Eltern warten dort.

Das macht achtzehn Mark.

Bitte sehr.

Fragen

1. Warum gehen sie zur Kasse?
2. Findet Karin einen Pulli?
3. Warum nicht?
4. Wieviel kostet der Pulli?
5. Warum will Britta schnell aus dem Kaufhaus?

Von wem spricht man hier? (Tanja, Britta, Karin, die Verkäuferin)
Indicate who the following statements refer to.

1. Sie glaubt, die Auswahl im Kaufhaus ist gut.
2. Der weiße Pulli gefällt ihr.
3. Sie will auch einen Pulli kaufen.
4. Sie sagt, wieviel der Pulli kostet.
5. Ihre Eltern warten im Café.
6. Sie meint, der Pulli kostet nicht viel.
7. Sie sollen nicht vor dem Kaufhaus stehen.
8. Sie hat Glück.
9. Sie kann keinen Pulli finden.
10. Sie bekommt achtzehn Mark.

Für dich

A pullover, called *Pullover,* is often referred to as *Pulli* for short. When buying clothing items in Germany, you should be aware that sizes are different. For example, a U.S. size 8 for a dress would be size 36 in Germany, and U.S. size 8 for a pair of shoes is size 39 in Germany.

Sales throughout the year, which are quite common in this country, are not known in Germany. Generally, there are two sales during the year, each lasting two weeks. One is called *Sommerschlußverkauf* (end of summer sale) and the other *Winterschlußverkauf* (end of winter sale) which takes place in late January. Each sale starts officially on the last Monday in July and the last Monday in January, respectively. Many shops have started with *Ausverkauf* (seasonal sale, bargain sale) much earlier than on the fixed dates, offering certain items at reduced prices as *Sonderangebote* (special offers).

Die Größen der Kleider in Deutschland sind anders als hier.

Was kann man in diesem Laden kaufen?

Kombiniere...

Wie viele Sätze kannst du bilden?

Die Pullis	sind	ganz	schick
Die Kasse	ist	da	Geld
Das Kaufhaus	braucht	heute	um die Ecke
Tanja		nicht	im Kaufhaus
Der Eingang			einen Pulli

Nützliche Ausdrücke

Es ist schick.	It's chic.
Der Pulli steht dir gut.	The sweater looks good on you.
Wie findest du diesen Pulli?	What do you think of this sweater?
Es paßt mir.	It fits me.
Die Entscheidung ist einfach.	The decision is simple (easy).
Gehen wir zur Kasse!	Let's go to the cash register.
Du bist zu wählerisch.	You're too choosy.

Was paßt hier?

1. Wie findest du das Sweatshirt?
2. Was ist deine Entscheidung?
3. Wo muß ich bezahlen?
4. Ist der Pulli zu groß?
5. Warum bist du so wählerisch?
6. Wie ist die Farbe?

a. Es kostet viel Geld.
b. Nein, er paßt dir.
c. Etwas zu dunkel.
d. An der Kasse.
e. Es steht dir gut.
f. Ich werde zum Kaufhaus gehen.

der Mantel

das T-Shirt

die Hose

der Strumpf
(das Paar
Strümpfe)

der Handschuh
(das Paar Handschuhe)

Welche Farbe hat
die Hose?
Sie ist dunkelbraun.
Und das T-Shirt?
Es ist hellblau.

257

1. *Was hat er/sie an?* Describe what various people are wearing.

❑ Paul
Er hat einen Anzug an.

1. Heike

2. die Lehrerin

Rolf

3. Rolf

4. Tanja

5. Ingrid

6. Holger

2. *Welche Farbe ist...?* Explain the colors of the various clothing items indicated.

❑ T-Shirt / weiß
Das T-Shirt ist weiß.

1. Paar Handschuhe / braun
2. Hose / dunkelblau
3. Krawatte / bunt
4. Pulli / rot
5. Jeans / blau
6. Bluse / hellgrau
7. Paar Strümpfe / dunkel
8. Schuhe / schwarz

Sag's mal!

Wie findest du diesen Pulli? Er ist...

schrecklich mein Stil überhaupt nicht schick schön zu klein modisch nicht so gut schick nicht mein Geschmack zu bunt eintönig nett toll elegant nicht schlecht

Aussprache

short /ö/	long /ö/	short /ä/	long /ä/
könnt	mögen	März	Nähe
Köln	schön	Länder	spät
möchte	Österreich	Fläche	Fahrräder
Töchter	größte	Mäntel	Väter
Röcke	hören	gefällt	wählerisch
zwölf	Söhne	Städte	Gläser

Übungen

Dative

Indirect Object

In the sentence *Ich kaufe ein Buch*, you know that *Ich* is the subject, *kaufe* is the verb and *ein Buch* is the direct object or accusative.

Now, consider this sentence: *Ich kaufe dem Freund eine Karte.* In this sentence *dem Freund* is called the indirect object or dative. Whereas *eine Karte* is directly connected with the action of the verb, *dem Freund* is indirectly connected with the verb and therefore called the indirect object. The easiest way to identify the indirect object is to determine if "to" or "for" can be put before the noun. In the above example, it would be "I am buying a ticket *for* the friend." (Or: I am buying the friend a ticket.)

	Singular			Plural
	masculine	feminine	neuter	
nominative	der	die	das	die
	ein	eine	ein	
accusative	den	die	das	die
	einen	eine	ein	
dative	dem	der	dem	den
	einem	einer	einem	

The following nouns you have learned up to now add an -*n* in the dative singular: *der Herr, der Junge, der Beamte.*

Beispiel: Gib dem Herrn einen Fahrplan!

To form the dative plural noun an -*n* or -*en* is added to the plural, unless the plural noun already ends in -*n* or -*s*. In the plural, the dative article is always *den*, regardless of the gender of the noun.

You are already familiar with the question word *wer?* (who), which refers to the subject (person), and the question word *wen?* (whom), which refers to the direct object (person). The question word *wem?* (to whom or for whom) refers to the dative case (person).

Beispiele: Sie geben *dem* Lehrer die Hefte. *Wem* geben sie die Hefte?
Wir kaufen *der* Tante eine Bluse. *Wem* kaufen wir eine Bluse?

3. ***Wem gibst du die Karte?* Tell whom you want to give the ticket to.**

   ❐   Onkel
   Ich gebe einem Onkel die Karte.

   1. Lehrer
   2. Mädchen

3. Verkäuferin
4. Herr
5. Freundin
6. Gast

4. *Wem soll ich das denn schicken?* **You have several items which you are supposed to send off. Can you take care of it?**

❑ Freund / Brief
Schick doch dem Freund einen Brief!

1. Schüler / Buch
2. Onkel / Hemd
3. Frau / Ansichtskarte
4. Lehrer / Briefmarke
5. Tochter / Kassette
6. Junge / Pulli

5. *Was willst du ihnen nicht leihen?* **(What don't you want to lend them?) Indicate that you don't want to lend the following.**

❑ die Gäste / das Fahrrad
Ich will den Gästen das Fahrrad nicht leihen.

1. die Jungen / die Gitarre
2. die Eltern / das Buch
3. die Mädchen / der Taschenrechner
4. die Freundinnen / der Fahrplan
5. die Frauen / die Landkarte

Verbs Followed by the Dative Case

There are a number of verbs in German that require the dative case. Some of these verbs are *antworten* (to answer), *glauben* (to believe), *gefallen* (to like, please), *helfen* (to help), *passen* (to fit, suit), *stehen* (to suit).

Beispiele: Antworte dem Lehrer!
Das Sweatshirt paßt dem Mädchen.
Kannst du dem Herrn helfen?

6. *Glaubst du ihnen?* **Rainer is asking his friend Christian whether or not he believes these people. Take the part of Christian to respond to Rainer.**

❑ Glaubst du der Beamtin? (Nein,...)
Nein, ich glaube der Beamtin nicht.

1. Glaubst du dem Lehrer? Nein,...
2. Glaubst du der Verkäuferin? Ja,...
3. Glaubst du dem Beamten? Nein,...
4. Glaubst du der Frau? Ja,...
5. Glaubst du dem Jungen? Nein,...

7. *Der Mantel paßt dieser Person nicht.* Imagine you're working in a department store selling coats. Several people are trying on different coats but none of them seems to fit.

❐ Vater
Der Mantel paßt dem Vater nicht.

1. Herr
2. Mädchen
3. Frau
4. Verkäuferin
5. Junge

8. **Construct meaningful sentences using the cue words given.**

1. Wir / geben / Kellner / Geld
2. Können / du / Herr / Zeit / sagen
3. Warum / antworten / Sie / Beamter / nicht
4. Hose / passen / Junge / sehr gut
5. Kaufen / du / Mädchen / Paar Handschuhe
6. Stehen / Tante / Kleid
7. Ich / sollen / Frau / helfen
8. Peter / holen / Lehrer / Buch

Dative Prepositions

The dative case always follows these prepositions:

aus	out of, from
außer	besides, except
bei	with, near, at
mit	with
nach	after
seit	since
von	from, of
zu	to, at

Beispiele: Sie kommt aus der Schule.
Ich habe außer dem Bruder auch eine Schwester.

Herr Schulz wohnt beim Bahnhof.
Kommst du mit einer Freundin?
Wohin gehen wir nach dem Film?
Seit einem Jahr wohne ich hier.
Ich komme vom Kino.
Sie fahren zum Bahnhof.

Contractions

These dative prepositions and articles are contracted as long as there is no special emphasis on the article.

bei	+	dem	=	beim
von	+	dem	=	vom
zu	+	dem	=	zum
zu	+	der	=	zur

9. *Wo warten die Jugendlichen?* **Indicate where these youth groups are waiting.**

❑ Rathaus
Sie warten beim Rathaus.

1. Kino
2. Kasse
3. Café
4. Schule
5. Park
6. Eingang

10. *Alle wollen zwei Kleidungsstücke kaufen.* **Ask what else everyone wants to purchase besides what they have selected.**

❑ Was kaufst du außer dem T-Shirt?

1.   2.   3.   4.   5.   6.

11. *Was wollen wir später machen?* Find out what your friends want to do after certain activities.

❑ Was wollen wir nach der Schule machen? (Kaufhaus)
Gehen wir doch zum Kaufhaus!

1. Was wollen wir nach dem Kino machen? (Park)
2. Was wollen wir nach dem Konzert machen? (Stadt)
3. Was wollen wir nach der Party machen? (Café)
4. Was wollen wir nach dem Essen machen? (Jugendklub)
5. Was wollen wir nach der Arbeit machen? (Tante)

12. *Woher kommen alle?* It's five o'clock. Downtown München is very crowded. People are heading home. Where is everyone coming from?

❑ Café
Viele kommen aus dem Café.

1. Bank
2. Museum
3. Post
4. Rathaus
5. Bahnhof
6. Büro

13. Provide the proper preposition and the correct form of the definite article. Use these dative prepositions: *aus, außer, bei, mit, nach, seit, von, zu.* There may be more than one possible preposition in some sentences.

1. Parken Sie das Auto _____ Museum.
2. Warum kommt ihr so spät _____ Schule?
3. Ich werde eine Karte _____ Verkäuferin bekommen.
4. Monika geht _____ Freundin ins Kino.
5. Herr Schmidt ist _____ Monat Juni nicht mehr zu Hause.
6. Wohnst du weit _____ Bahnhof?
7. _____ Jungen kommt auch noch ein Mädchen.
8. Sie stehen direkt _____ Tür.
9. Was macht ihr _____ Geburtstag?
10. Gehen wir _____ Rathaus zu Fuß!

Was wollen wir nach dem Kino machen?

Wo stehen sie?

14. Beende diese Sätze!

1. Um wieviel Uhr kommen Sie aus _____?
2. Was macht ihr nach _____?
3. Der Mantel paßt _____ gut.
4. Die Schuhe gefallen _____.
5. Die Schüler gehen zum _____.
6. Sie werden beim _____ warten.
7. Ich glaube _____ nicht.
8. Wir fahren mit _____.

15. Change the following sentences from the singular to the plural.

❏ Der Gast kommt aus dem Zimmer.
Die Gäste kommen aus den Zimmern.

1. Der Schüler geht zum Zug.
2. Hilfst du der Frau nicht?
3. Der Kellner kommt aus dem Restaurant.
4. Der Beamte antwortet dem Jugendlichen.
5. Das Kleid steht der Dame gut.
6. Er parkt das Fahrrad beim Mietshaus.
7. Der Lehrer kommt von der Stadt.

Dative

Personal Pronouns

As you have already learned, the direct object (accusative) is the result of the action (verb) of the sentence, whereas the indirect object receives the action indirectly through the direct object.

		direct object
Beispiele: Ich kaufe		eine Karte

	indirect object	**direct object**
Ich kaufe	dem Gast	eine Karte

Now substitute a personal pronoun for the indirect object in the last sentence.

	indirect object	**direct object**
Ich kaufe	ihm	eine Karte

Notice that there is no change in word order but simply a substitution of an indirect object pronoun. For review, the pronouns you have already learned are also included in the table following.

Singular			Plural		
nominative	accusative	dative	nominative	accusative	dative
ich	mich	mir	wir	uns	uns
du	dich	dir	ihr	euch	euch
er	ihn	ihm	sie	sie	ihnen
sie	sie	ihr			
es	es	ihm	Sie (sg. & pl.)	Sie	Ihnen

16. *Was bringst du ihnen?* Tell what you are bringing to each of the people indicated.

❏ Was bringst du dem Jungen? (eine Gitarre)
Ich bringe ihm eine Gitarre.

1. Was bringst du dem Gast? (einen Kuchen)
2. Was bringst du dem Jugendlichen? (eine Mark)
3. Was bringst du der Tante? (ein Geschenk)
4. Was bringst du dem Bruder? (eine Zeitung)
5. Was bringst du dem Herrn? (einen Fahrplan)

17. *Wem kauft ihr ein Geschenk?* Indicate for whom you are buying a present.

❏ du
Wir kaufen dir ein Geschenk.

Herr Hoffmann
Wir kaufen ihm ein Geschenk.

1. er
2. die Lehrerin
3. Herr und Frau Tobler
4. die Oma
5. ihr
6. Rudi

18. *Wie geht es ihnen?* Find out how the various people are. Use the information provided in your response.

❏ Wie geht es dem Peter? (sehr gut)
Es geht ihm sehr gut.

1. Wie geht es Tina? (schlecht)
2. Wie geht es Frau Schell? (gut)

3. Wie geht es dem Alex? (super)
4. Wie geht es der Lehrerin? (nicht besonders)
5. Wie geht es den Gästen? (nicht schlecht)

19. **Change the italicized nouns with their corresponding articles into pronouns.**

◻ Ich spreche oft mit *den Jugendlichen*.
Ich spreche oft mit *ihnen*.

1. Wann fahren wir wieder zu *der Tante*?
2. Außer *den Jungen* kommen noch viele Mädchen.
3. Er wird *dem Diskjockey* eine Kassette geben.
4. Antworte *dem Lehrer* doch!
5. Christine wohnt schon zwei Wochen bei *Müllers*.
6. Die Kleidungsstücke gefallen *den Mädchen*.
7. Wir gehen mit *der Mutter* ins Museum.
8. Petra kauft *der Freundin* eine Bluse.

20. **Ergänze diese Sätze!**

1. Wir möchten es (them) _____ sagen.
2. Er kann (you) _____ das Buch nicht kaufen, Uwe.
3. Die Großmutter wohnt bei (us) _____.
4. Die Schüler antworten (him) _____ nicht.
5. Ich hole (you) _____ die Schuhe, Herr Holz.
6. Der Kellner wird mit (you) _____ sprechen, Jan und Heiko.
7. Geben Sie (me) _____ eine Mark, bitte!
8. Glaubst du (her) _____ denn?
9. Darf ich (you) _____ helfen, Frau Tauke?
10. Wirst du (him) _____ den Taschenrechner geben?

21. **Beantworte diese Fragen!**

1. Mit wem gehst du in die Stadt?
2. Gefällt dir die Hose?
3. Was gibst du dem Freund?
4. Wer kommt außer dir noch mit?
5. Fahrt ihr zu Frau Schmidt?
6. Sprichst du von dem Sänger?
7. Kannst du Herrn Meier zwei Karten kaufen?
8. Wem mußt du das Essen bezahlen?

Johann und Astrid gehen in die Stadt

Johann Seiler besucht seine Freundin Astrid Baumann gern. Beide wohnen in Thalwil, einem Vorort von Zürich. Heute haben sie viel vor. Astrid muß zum Optiker°. Sie braucht eine neue Brille°. Johann will eine Jacke kaufen. In einer Zeitschrift sehen sie, was heute Mode° ist. Astrid hat einen guten Geschmack°. Sie wird Johann helfen°, eine schicke Jacke zu finden.

optician
glasses

fashion
taste
help

Von Astrids Haus sind es nur fünf Minuten zum Optiker. Herr Haas, der Optiker, begrüßt° beide.

greets

Astrid:	Ich brauche eine Brille. Auf dem Rezept° hier stehen die Einzelheiten°.
Optiker:	Na, gut. Wir haben eine große Auswahl. Wie gefallen Ihnen diese Brillen?
Astrid:	Kann ich eine Brille aufsetzen°?
Optiker:	Natürlich°.
Astrid:	Ja, sie paßt mir gut. Wie findest du diese Brille?

prescription
details

put on
of course

Herr Haas begrüßt sie.

Wo wohnen Johann und Astrid?

Johann und Astrid stehen vor dem Modehaus Zahn.

Astrid bestellt eine Brille.

Johann:	Super. Die steht dir gut.	
Astrid:	Dann ist meine Entscheidung leicht. Ich bestelle° sie. Setz diese Brille einmal auf.	*I'll order*
Johann:	Ich kann fast nichts sehen.	
Astrid:	Du siehst ja wirklich komisch aus°.	siehst... komisch aus *look funny*

Sie verlassen den Laden°. Vom Optiker gehen sie über die Straße° und stehen auch bald vor dem Modehaus Zahn. Sie gehen hinein. Die Verkäuferin zeigt° ihnen, wo die Jacken sind. Johann probiert eine weiße Jacke an°.

store
across the street

shows

probiert...an *tries on*

Johann:	Die weiße Jacke gefällt mir gut.	
Astrid:	Sie ist aber viel zu klein.	
Verkäuferin:	Die steht Ihnen wirklich nicht. Hier ist eine andere. Gute Qualität und nicht teuer°.	*expensive*

Astrid:	Probier sie doch an!
Johann:	Es ist die richtige Größe. Was meinst du?
Astrid:	Ja, sie steht dir gut.
Johann:	Bitte sehr. Ich kaufe sie.
Verkäuferin:	Diese Jacke können Sie bestimmt lange tragen°. Bezahlen Sie bar° oder mit Kreditkarte? *wear/pay cash*
Johann:	Ich bezahle bar.
Verkäuferin:	So, bitte sehr. Und kommen Sie bald wieder.
Astrid:	Heute haben wir beide Glück. Ich bekomme eine Brille und du hast eine neue Jacke.
Johann:	Wir haben aber fast kein Geld mehr.
Astrid:	Komm, wir müssen noch zum Kaufhaus.

Es ist die richtige Größe.

Was kauft Johann?

Astrid will noch schnell zum Kaufhaus.

Bezahlt Johann mit einer Kreditkarte?

Was paßt hier?

1. Astrid muß
2. Johann probiert
3. Der Optiker heißt
4. Johann und Astrid gehen
5. Astrid bestellt
6. Johann bezahlt
7. Modehaus Zahn ist
8. Johann kauft
9. Johann setzt
10. Die Verkäuferin ist

a. nicht weit vom Optiker
b. sehr nett
c. Herr Haas
d. bar
e. zum Optiker gehen
f. die weiße Jacke nicht
g. eine Jacke an
h. eine Brille
i. auch eine Brille auf
j. später zum Kaufhaus

Fragen

1. Wohin gehen Johann und Astrid?
2. Wo wohnen sie?
3. Warum muß Astrid zum Optiker?
4. Wer ist der Optiker?
5. Wo stehen die Einzelheiten?
6. Wie steht Astrid die Brille?
7. Bekommt sie die Brille sofort?
8. Wohin gehen beide dann?
9. Warum kauft Johann die weiße Jacke nicht?
10. Wie bezahlt Johann für die Jacke?

Übung macht den Meister!

1. *Wir gehen einkaufen.* You are planning to go shopping. Make a list of clothing or other items you intend to buy. Ask one of your classmates to do the same. After both of you have finished your shopping list, ask each other questions. You may want to ask such questions as: *Wohin gehst du einkaufen?, Wo ist der Laden?, Was kann man da alles kaufen?, Was kaufst du dort?, Für wen?, Wieviel Geld wirst du ausgeben?,* etc.

2. *Bitte?* Pretend that you are standing in front of a counter in a big department store and the salesperson is ready to help you. You are looking for a specific clothing item. Ask him or her about the cost, the color you want and any suggestions for purchasing your desired item. Be as creative as possible. Some useful expressions might be: *Wieviel kostet...?, Welche Farbe?, Möchten Sie...?* Either create a complete conversation or have one of your classmates take the part of the *Verkäufer* or *Verkäuferin.*

3. *Was hat er/sie heute an?* Select three of your classmates and describe what they are wearing, including the colors.

4. *Was möchtest du zum Geburtstag?* Develop a short narrative of what you would like to have for a birthday present. Your wish list may include the names of several items, description and what you would like to do with these.

Erweiterung

22. **Which word from the list best matches each statement?**

| Geld | Optiker | Jugendklub | Kasse | Bahnhof |
| Bank | Mietshaus | Wohnzimmer | Museum | Schule |

1. Ein Zug kommt dort pünktlich an.
2. Viele wohnen da.
3. Die Schüler lernen dort.
4. Wir bestellen die Brillen dort.
5. Ich bezahle da.

6. Dort tanzen die Jugendlichen oft.
7. Man kann dort Geld bekommen.
8. Ich brauche es. Dann kann ich ein Fahrrad kaufen.
9. Die Touristen gehen gern dort hinein.
10. Wir sitzen dort und sehen fern.

23. *Beschreibe jedes Wort. (Describe each word.) Schreibe einen Satz über jedes Wort.*

❏ Kino
Dort läuft ein Film.

1. Buch
2. Haus
3. Schuhe
4. Büro
5. Stadt
6. Bahnhof
7. Optiker
8. Eßzimmer

24. *Was ist logisch?* **From the list below, find the words that best complete the phrases.**

anprobieren   bezahlen   bekommen   haben   verlassen
aufsetzen   essen   gehen   helfen   sein

1. eine Brille
2. Glück
3. eine Jacke
4. zur Kasse
5. den Laden
6. mit Kreditkarte
7. dem Mädchen
8. Mode
9. ein Geschenk
10. Abendbrot

Soll sie den Pulli anprobieren?

25. Beantworte diese Fragen!

1. Was kaufst du im Kaufhaus?
2. Wieviel willst du ausgeben?
3. Welche Farbe gefällt dir?
4. Wie ist die Auswahl im Kaufhaus?
5. Was hast du heute an?
6. Brauchst du eine Brille? Warum? Warum nicht?

Sprachspiegel

26. Imagine that you are employed in a department store and have to assist customers. Complete the following two dialogs with meaningful sentences.

Du: ____
Herr: Ich möchte ein Hemd.
Du: ____
Herr: Blau oder grau.
Du: ____
Herr: Ja. Wieviel kostet es?
Du: ____
Herr: Das ist preiswert. Ich kaufe es.
Du: ____
Herr: Wo ist die Kasse?
Du: ____

Frau: Wo sind die Blusen?
Du: ____
Frau: Oh, die Auswahl ist groß.
Du: ____
Frau: Wieviel kostet diese Bluse?
Du: ____
Frau: Das ist nicht teuer.
Du: ____
Frau: Ja, ich kaufe sie.
Du: ____
Frau: Nein, mit Kreditkarte.

27. *Wie sagt man's?* **From the list below, select the appropriate words to complete the various short conversational exchanges.**

aufsetzen	Jacke	preiswert	Kaufhaus
Bahnhof	Fuß	Krawatte	Seite
finde	teuer	Farbe	Anzug
auch	weit	gut	kalt

1. Welche _____ hast du gern?
   Grün oder braun.
   Ich _____.
2. Ich _____ dieses Kleid sehr schick.
   Es ist aber sehr _____.
   Ich kaufe es ja nicht.
3. Wo ist das nächste _____?
   In der Stadt, beim _____.
   Kann man zu _____ gehen?
   Nein, das ist zu _____.
4. Der _____ steht dir gut.
   Ja, ich kaufe ihn. Er ist ganz _____.
   Jetzt brauchst du noch ein Hemd und eine _____.
5. Kannst du die _____ hier lesen?
   Nicht sehr _____.
   Ich glaube, du mußt deine Brille _____.
6. Heute ist es sehr _____.
   Ohne eine _____ kannst du nicht in die Stadt gehen.

28. *Beantworte diese Fragen!* **Provide as much detail as possible.**

1. Du hast 200 Mark. Was möchtest du kaufen?
2. Was hast du heute an? Welche Farben haben die Kleidungsstücke?
3. Wo gehst du gern einkaufen? Warum?
4. Probierst du gern Kleidungsstücke an? Warum? Warum nicht?
5. Dein Freund oder Freundin hat bald Geburtstag. Was willst du ihm oder ihr kaufen?

29. Wie heißt das auf deutsch?

1. Which color do you like?
2. Can't you find a shirt?
3. The pair of shoes is very expensive.
4. The jacket is dark blue.
5. I'm paying cash.
6. Which size do you have?

Rückblick

I. *Beende diese Sätze!* Complete each sentence with one of the prefixes listed below. You will use some prefixes more than once.

ab   an   aus   ein   hin   hinein   vor

❏   Setz doch deine Brille _____!
    Setz doch deine Brille auf!

1. Die Touristen steigen in den Zug _____.
2. Christa hat einen schicken Mantel _____.
3. Die Besucher gehen ins Museum _____.
4. Setzen Sie sich hier bitte _____!
5. Wen ladet ihr zur Party _____?
6. Was hast du am Sonnabend _____?
7. Kauft deine Mutter heute _____?
8. Ich probiere diese Jacke _____.
9. Wieviel gibst du für das Essen _____?
10. Wann fährt der Bus _____?
11. Du siehst ganz komisch _____.
12. Die Gäste kommen nächste Woche hier _____.

II. Complete the following sentences by using an appropriate article and noun.

1. Wieviel willst du für _____ bezahlen?
2. Ich kann ohne _____ nicht lesen.
3. Die Touristen fahren durch _____.
4. Gehen Sie um _____?
5. Ich stelle das Moped gegen _____.
6. Ohne _____ können wir nicht ins Kino.
7. Habt ihr ein Geschenk für _____?
8. Ich will nicht zu Fuß um _____ laufen.

III. Form complete sentences by using the cues given.

1. Ich / bestellen / Buch
2. Abfahren / Zug / pünktlich
3. Wir / zurückfahren / mit / Bus
4. Können / du / Kellner / verstehen
5. Rudi / müssen / Frankfurt / umsteigen
6. Frau Lehmann / zubereiten / Essen
7. Bekommen / heute / Karte
8. Heike / mitbringen / Buch / zu / Schule

IV. Rewrite the following sentences incorporating the words indicated in parentheses.

❑ Ich probiere die Jacke an. (wollen)
Ich will die Jacke anprobieren.

1. Gehst du morgen ins Büro? (müssen)
2. Wir kaufen ein paar T-Shirts. (möchten)
3. Kommt ihr ohne Mädchen zur Party? (wollen)
4. Ich bezahle das Fahrrad nicht. (sollen)
5. Boris sieht spät am Abend fern. (dürfen)
6. Tanzen die Jugendlichen im Jugendklub? (werden)

V. Beende diese Sätze!

1. Wir bestellen beim Kellner _____
2. Ich brauche _____.
3. Steht ihr _____?
4. Die Gäste kommen _____.
5. Wie gefällt dir _____?
6. Zeig ihm doch _____!
7. Diese Farbe ist _____.
8. Der Mantel paßt _____

Zungenbrecher

Hinter Hermann Hannes' Haus hängen hundert Hemden 'raus.
(Behind Hermann Hannes' house a hundred shirts are hanging.)

Kulturecke

Shopping

When shopping in Germany, you should become familiar with the German monetary system. There are seven different bills: 5 marks, 10 marks, 20 marks, 50 marks, 100 marks, 500 marks and 1,000 marks. The 5-mark bill is rarely in circulation today. The denominations are easily recognized — the larger the size of the bill, the greater the value. There are eight different coins: 1 pfennig, 2 pfennigs, 5 pfennigs, 10 pfennigs, 50 pfennigs, 1 mark, 2 marks and 5 marks.

German shops are not open as many hours as American stores. Although stores are open Monday through Friday from about 8:00 or 9:00 A.M. until 6:00 P.M., they close on Saturday at 2:00 P.M., except on the first Saturday of each month and the four Saturdays before Christmas. Banks, post offices and small stores usually close for a two-hour break at noon. Banks are not open on Saturdays.

Most Germans go shopping several times a week to take care of their daily needs. Signs posted outside the shops indicate what kind of commodity is being sold. Germans usually buy their breads and rolls fresh at the local bakery (*Bäckerei*). There are some 200 different kinds of bread (*Brot*), 30 kinds of rolls (*Brötchen* or *Semmeln*) and no less then 1,200 different kinds of pastries. Wherever there is a bakery, the butcher shop (*Metzgerei*)

Horten ist ein großes Kaufhaus. (Heilbronn)

Was kauft man hier?

ein bekanntes Einkaufszentrum in Stuttgart

Sie gehen schon früh am Morgen ins Kaufhaus. (Heilbronn)

is not far away. There are many different types of butcher shops, most of which highlight their own homemade sausages. There are more than 1,500 different kinds of German sausages — raw, boiled, smoked, seasoned in various ways and shaped in all kinds of forms.

Two-thirds of all Germans like to do some of their shopping at the local market (*Markt*), which is usually in the vicinity of the main shopping area of the town or city. Market day (*Markttag*) is held once or twice a week. Germans prefer to buy their fresh vegetables and fruits at the market. And they love flowers; therefore it is not surprising to see colorful flower stands at every market. Most of the shopping, however, is done in the supermarket (*Supermarkt*) found throughout the country. At these chain-operated stores, the shopper can purchase all items necessary for daily living.

The big, American-style department store (*Kaufhaus*) also plays an important role, particularly in the larger towns and cities. Besides offering

Lektion 8

279

all the items as in our stores, the German department store includes an extensive grocery store usually located on the lower level. Some of the big cities like Hamburg offer additional shopping opportunities in an inside shopping mall (*Einkaufszentrum*). American influence is readily noticed in stores throughout Germany.

There are still differences, however. A *Drogerie* is not the same as an American drugstore. A *Drogerie* will sell toiletries, household cleaners, baby food, camera supplies, wallpapers, paints and even seeds. However, it does not fill prescriptions. An *Apotheke* (pharmacy) sells both prescription and non-prescription medicines.

To buy clothes and shoes, you will have to study the German measurement system carefully. The measurements are considerably different and can easily create problems, unless there is some reference to the American system. In cities, you will find a great variety of shoe stores (*Schuhgeschäfte*) and clothing stores (*Kleidergeschäfte*). American-made jeans are still very popular among Germans. Every average-sized town and city has specialty jeans shops. The American influence on dry-cleaning stores becomes quite apparent as well. More and more Germans take their clothes to a dry-cleaner (*Reinigung*).

Germans are quite health conscious. Every city caters to the needs of that part of the population. Germans will buy their health foods in a store called *Reformhaus*. It sells special foods, teas and vitamins, always with an eye toward health. Of course, there are numerous specialty stores catering to the sweet tooth, ranging from a variety of candies to the most elaborate chocolates.

eine Metzgerei (Schwäbisch-Hall)

Viele Deutsche gehen gern auf den Markt.

die Verkäuferin ein Fotogeschäft

Leisure time is enjoyed in Germany more than ever. Therefore, the visitor will find numerous stores related to leisure-time activities. A store marked *Spiel und Freizeit* attracts that group of people. German parents buy many toys for their children. Many toy stores (*Spielwaren*) will attest to that fact. And for the traveler and photo buff, German cameras have long been known for their superior quality. Camera equipment and film can be bought at camera shops (*Fotogeschäfte*) found everywhere. A special attraction is always a store that offers souvenirs and specialty items from all over Germany. Just look for a store labeled with the words *Geschenke* and *Andenken*.

Reading is an important pastime. There are many newspaper stands where local, national and sometimes international newspapers and magazines, as well as postcards and stamps are sold. Many bookstores (*Buchhandlungen*) display their books outside of the shop so that people can browse and decide which book they want to buy. You can buy writing utensils and stationery at a *Schreibwarengeschäft*. Record shops (*Schallplattengeschäfte*) sell many recordings of current German and American hits. These stores sell audio and video cassettes, records and compact discs.

In jeder deutschen Stadt kann man gut einkaufen. (Hameln)

Regardless of what your shopping needs are, you won't be disappointed when searching for any item of your choice. Germans cater to many different tastes and will be ready for your demands.

Was weißt du? Was kann man hier kaufen? Match the items on the left with those on the right.

1. Apotheke	a. *Schuhe*
2. Reformhaus	b. toys
3. Bäckerei	c. camera supplies and wallpaper
4. Kleidergeschäft	d. *Kassetten*
5. Schreibwarengeschäft	e. *Wurst*
6. Markt	f. *Papier*
7. Schallplattengeschäft	g. health food products
8. Metzgerei	h. camera equipment
9. Supermarkt	i. *Semmeln*
10. Fotogeschäft	j. *Kleidungsstücke, Bücher und Musikinstrumente*
11. Schuhgeschäft	k. *Mäntel*
12. Kaufhaus	l. prescriptions
13. Drogerie	m. *Milch und Brot*
14. Spielwarengeschäft	n. flowers
15. Buchhandlung	o. *Bücher*

Vokabeln

anhaben to have on, wear
anprobieren to try on
antworten to answer
der **Anzug,-̈e** suit
aufsetzen to put on
aussehen to look, appear
außer besides, except
bar: bar bezahlen to pay cash
begrüßen to greet
bestellen to order
blau blue
die **Bluse,-n** blouse
braun brown
die **Brille,-n** glasses
bunt colorful
dunkel dark
    dunkelbraun dark brown
der **Eingang,-̈e** entrance
die **Einzelheit,-en** detail
die **Entscheidung,-en** decision
die **Farbe,-n** color
finden to find, think
    Wie findest du...? What do you think of...?

gelb yellow
der **Geschmack** taste
grau gray
die **Größe,-n** size
grün green
der **Handschuh,-e** glove
helfen to help
hell light
    hellblau light blue
das **Hemd,-en** shirt
die **Hose,-n** pants, slacks
die **Jacke,-n** jacket
die **Jeans** (pl.) jeans
die **Kasse,-n** cash register
das **Kleid,-er** dress
das **Kleidungsstück,-e** clothing item
komisch comical, funny
die **Krawatte,-n** tie
die **Kreditkarte,-n** credit card
der **Laden,-̈** store
der **Mantel,-̈** coat
die **Mode,-n** fashion
natürlich naturally, of course
der **Optiker,-** optician
orange orange
das **Paar,-e** pair
preiswert reasonable

der **Pulli,-s** sweater, pullover
der **Pullover,-** sweater, pullover
die **Qualität,-en** quality
das **Rezept,-e** prescription
richtig correct, right
der **Rock,-̈e** skirt
rosa pink
der **Schuh,-e** shoe
schwarz black
seit since
die **Socke,-n** sock
der **Strumpf,-̈e** stocking
das **T-Shirt,-s** T-shirt
teuer expensive
tragen to wear
über across
    über die Straße gehen to cross the street
von of
wählerisch choosy, particular
wiederkommen to come again (back)
zeigen to show

der Markt

Was kann man in diesem Laden kaufen? (Frankfurt)

Sport

9

Communicative Functions

- talking about sports competition
- naming different kinds of sports
- asking about other person's interest
- identifying parts of the body
- talking about weekend activities

285

Beim Tischtennisturnier

Was ist heute in Leipzig los? In der Sporthalle findet ein Tischtennis-turnier statt. Die besten Spieler der Stadt sind zur Sporthalle gekommen. An sechzehn Platten zeigen alle, was sie können. Klaus und Sascha sind auch hergekommen.

Klaus: Sascha, hast du unsere Namen gehört?
Sascha: Ja, der Ansager hat gesagt, wir sollen zur Platte Nummer elf.
Klaus: Üben wir zuerst etwas.
Sascha: Stimmt. „Übung macht den Meister."
Klaus: Du bist mal wieder in Form.
Sascha: Aber doch nicht ganz so gut wie du. Na, dann mal los!

Falsch! Die folgenden Sätze sind falsch. **Kannst du die richtigen Sätze machen?**

1. Das Tischtennisturnier ist in Dresden.
2. Alle können beim Turnier spielen.
3. In der Sporthalle gibt es sechzig Platten.

Klaus und Sascha spielen ein Spiel. Klaus ist heute wirklich gut. Er gewinnt gegen Sascha. Sascha gratuliert Klaus. Dann geht Sascha zu einem kleinen Tisch und gibt den Richtern das Ergebnis bekannt.

Sascha: Wenn du so weiterspielst, hast du eine gute Chance.
Klaus: Heute ist nicht dein Tag gewesen.
Sascha: Da hast du recht. Das letzte Mal habe ich dich geschlagen.

Klaus spielt gegen Sascha.

Sie warten auf ihr nächstes Spiel.

Sascha gratuliert Klaus.

Die besten Spieler sind zur Sporthalle gekommen.

Klaus:	Leider haben wir in derselben Gruppe gespielt.
Sascha:	Du bist jetzt in der fünften Runde.
Klaus:	Es gibt noch acht Spieler bis zum Endspiel.
Sascha:	Ich glaube, du kannst es schaffen.
Klaus:	Hoffentlich.
Sascha:	Der Ansager hat deinen Namen aufgerufen. Viel Glück, Klaus!

Sascha, Klaus oder der Ansager? Determine who the following statements refer to.

1. Er kann es vielleicht schaffen.
2. Er hat heute keinen guten Tag gehabt.
3. Er gibt den Richtern das Ergebnis.
4. Er hat den Namen von Klaus aufgerufen.
5. Er gewinnt die vierte Runde.
6. Das letzte Mal hat er gewonnen.

Fragen

1. In welcher Stadt findet das Tischtennisturnier statt?
2. Wo spielen alle?
3. Wer sagt ihnen, wo sie spielen sollen?
4. Wie viele Spiele spielen Klaus und Sascha in der vierten Runde?
5. Wer gewinnt das Spiel?
6. Wer muß die Ergebnisse wissen?
7. Wie viele Spieler sind noch in der fünften Runde?
8. Wer ruft Klaus auf?

Für dich

Sports events are an important part of the daily life in Germany. Table tennis is one of the most popular sports in the country following soccer, fishing, gymnastics, bowling, track and field, team handball and volleyball.

Klaus and Sascha are participating in a single elimination tournament in which a participant who loses once is out of the tournament.

Fußball

Tischtennis

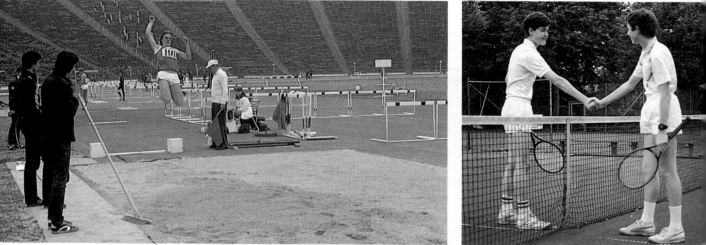

Weitsprung

Tennis

Handball

Kegeln und Bowlen

Kombiniere...

Wie viele Sätze kannst du bilden?

Der Spieler	hat	heute	das Ergebnis
Der Ansager	spielt	viel	Tischtennis
Klaus	zeigt	nicht	Glück
Das Mädchen		kein	

Nützliche Ausdrücke

Was findet dort statt?	What takes place there?
Er kann alles.	He can do everything.
Übung macht den Meister.	Practice makes perfect.
Bist du in Form?	Are you in form (shape)?
Du hast recht.	You're right.
Hast du ihn geschlagen?	Did you beat him?
Wer hat dich aufgerufen?	Who called (announced) you?

Was paßt hier?

1. Was ist da los?
2. Wen hat er aufgerufen?
3. In welcher Runde bist du?
4. Hörst du den Ansager?
5. Wann findet das statt?
6. Spielt sie gut?
7. Gewinnt er heute gegen ihn?
8. Wie viele Runden gibt es noch?

a. Ja, heute kann er alles.
b. Nein, es ist zu laut.
c. Ich glaube, nur noch drei.
d. Um drei.
e. Ein Turnier findet da statt.
f. Die Spieler.
g. Ja, sie ist in Form.
h. In der zweiten.

Ergänzung

die Sportarten

Welche Sportart treibst du?

Ich spiele Tischtennis.

Ich spiele Tennis.

Ich spiele Basketball.

Ich spiele Fußball.

Ich spiele Golf.

Ich spiele Eishockey.

Was machst du noch gern?

Ich laufe gern Ski.

Ich schwimme gern.

Ich wandere gern.

Ich fahre gern Rad.

Ich laufe gern Schlittschuh.

291

1. Beantworte diese Fragen!

1. Welche Sportart hast du gern?
2. Wo treibst du diesen Sport?
3. Wie viele Jahre machst du das schon?
4. Welche Körperteile brauchst du für diesen Sport?

2. Kannst du diese Sätze ergänzen?

1. Ich spreche mit dem _____.
2. Ich schreibe mit der _____.
3. Ich denke (think) mit dem _____.
4. Ich zeige mit dem _____ auf die Landkarte.
5. Ich höre mit dem _____.
6. Ich rieche (smell) mit der _____.
7. Ich habe _____ auf dem Kopf.
8. Ich kann mit dem _____ sehen.

Welche Sportart hat er gern?

Was spielen sie?

Tennis ist in Deutschland sehr beliebt.

Sag's mal!

Welcher Sport gefällt dir? Mir gefällt...

Aussprache

initial /r/	middle /r/	final /r/
rot	Karte	Sommer
Reise	fahren	hier
regnen	Jahre	Uhr
Rathaus	Arbeit	Nummer
Rockband	dürfen	mir
Rock	warten	vor
rosa	Norden	aber
richtig	Europa	für
Freund	während	Jahr
fragen	interessant	fährt
braun	morgen	Sport
groß	Norden	März
Straße	werden	dort
Krawatte	zurück	gern
drüben	sportlich	Berg
Frau	März	mehr

Sie haben gejubelt und geklatscht.

Gestern hat es geregnet.

Übungen

Present Perfect Tense

The present perfect is used more frequently in German conversation than in English. It is often called the "conversational past."

Regular verbs

> *haben* + (*ge* + third person singular)
> *Er hat gefragt.* (He has asked.)

In English, three forms (*He has asked, He was asking* or *He asked*) may be used. To simplify the presentation, only the present perfect form is used throughout.

The form *gefragt* (asked) is called the past participle, which in German is placed at the end of the sentence.

Beispiel: *Ich habe meine Freundin gefragt.*
           (I have asked my girlfriend.)

Some of the regular verbs you have learned so far are:

antworten (to answer)	machen (to do, make)
arbeiten (to work)	passen (to fit)
brauchen (to need)	regnen (to rain)
dauern (to last, take)	sagen (to say)
fragen (to ask)	sammeln (to collect)
glauben (to believe)	schicken (to send)
holen (to get, fetch)	schmecken (to taste)
hören (to hear)	spielen (to play)
jubeln (to cheer)	spülen (to wash, rinse)
kaufen (to buy)	tanzen (to dance)
klatschen (to clap, applaud)	warten (to wait)
lernen (to learn)	zeigen (to show)

The past participle of verbs with inseparable prefixes like *be-*, *ent-*, *er-* or *ver-* is simply the third person singular form of the present tense. This is also true of verbs ending in *-ieren*.

Beispiel: *Ich habe ihm das nicht erzählt.*
(I haven't told him that.)

Haben Sie die Familie fotografiert?
(Did you take pictures of the family?)

The few regular verbs with inseparable prefixes you have learned so far are:

begrüßen (to greet)
bestellen (to order)
besuchen (to visit)
bezahlen (to pay)
erzählen (to tell)

The past participle of verbs with separable prefixes has the prefix in front of the participle form.

Beispiel: *Er hat die Tür aufgemacht.*
(He opened the door.)

3. *Was hast du gestern gemacht?* **Explain what you did yesterday.**

❑   Tennis spielen
Ich habe Tennis gespielt.

1. ein paar Karten schicken
2. im Jugendklub tanzen
3. beim Kino warten
4. im Konzert jubeln
5. das Moped bezahlen
6. die Aufgaben lernen
7. die Gäste begrüßen

4. *Was paßt hier?* **Be sure to use the proper past participle.**

spülen	warten	klatschen	schmecken
dauern	passen	kaufen	regnen

1. Haben Sie die Jeans _____?
2. Wie hat das Abendbrot _____?
3. Das Kleid hat Monika nicht _____.
4. Habt ihr lange in der Schule _____?

5. Heute scheint die Sonne, aber gestern hat es _____.
6. Ich habe das Geschirr _____.
7. Das Konzert war toll. Alle haben viel _____.
8. Die Arbeit hat drei Stunden _____.

5. *Kannst du erzählen, was die Jugendlichen am Freitag gemacht haben?* **Use the information provided to describe what the various people did last Friday.**

❏ Peter / Anne / besuchen
Peter hat Anne besucht.

1. Rudi und Holger / Briefmarken sammeln
2. Petra und Tanja / Tennis spielen
3. Rita / mit Günter tanzen
4. wir / die Tante besuchen
5. meine Eltern / das Geschenk schicken
6. Hans und Rainer / zu Hause arbeiten

Present Perfect Tense

Irregular verbs

The irregular verbs, as the term suggests, do not follow the same pattern of forming the past participle of the regular verbs. Some of these verbs use *sein* instead of *haben*. Therefore, you must learn each present perfect form individually.

Beispiele: *Sie hat die Cola getrunken.*
(She has drunk the cola.)

Sie ist nach Hause gefahren.
(She has driven home.)

Verbs that use a form of *sein* must both (a) indicate motion or change of condition *and* (b) be intransitive, i.e., verbs that cannot have a direct object. This is true in cases like *gehen, laufen, kommen, fahren, schwimmen.*

Here are the irregular forms for most of the verbs you have learned so far:

Infinitive	Past Participle
backen (to bake)	gebacken
beginnen (to begin)	begonnen
bekommen (to receive, get)	bekommen
bleiben (to stay)	ist geblieben
bringen (to bring)	gebracht
essen (to eat)	gegessen
fahren (to drive)	ist gefahren
finden (to find)	gefunden
geben (to give)	gegeben
gefallen (to like)	gefallen
gehen (to go)	ist gegangen
gewinnen (to win)	gewonnen
haben (to have)	gehabt
helfen (to help)	geholfen
kennen (to know)	gekannt
kommen (to come)	ist gekommen
laufen (to run)	ist gelaufen
leihen (to loan, lend)	geliehen
lesen (to read)	gelesen
liegen (to lie, be located)	gelegen
schlagen (to beat)	geschlagen
schreiben (to write)	geschrieben
schwimmen (to swim)	ist geschwommen
sehen (to see)	gesehen
sein (to be)	ist gewesen
singen (to sing)	gesungen
sitzen (to sit)	gesessen
sprechen (to speak)	gesprochen
stehen (to stand)	gestanden
tragen (to wear, carry)	getragen
trinken (to drink)	getrunken
tun (to do)	getan
verlassen (to leave)	verlassen
verstehen (to understand)	verstanden
wissen (to know)	gewußt

Verbs with inseparable prefixes (*bekommen, verstehen*) do not have the *ge-* in the past participle.

Beispiele: Er hat meinen Brief bekommen.
Hast du sie verstanden?

Verbs with separable prefixes have the *ge-* as part of the participle.

Beispiele: Susi hat mich angerufen.
Der Ansager hat das Ergebnis bekanntgegeben.

The accent or emphasis is always on the separable prefix.

6. Was hast du an diesem Tag gemacht? Folge dem Beispiel!

❏ Was hast du am Montag gemacht? (in die Stadt fahren)
Ich bin in die Stadt gefahren.

1. Was hast du am Sonntag gemacht? (einen Kuchen backen)
2. Was hast du am Freitag gemacht? (Onkel Walter helfen)
3. Was hast du am Mittwoch gemacht? (eine Arbeit schreiben)
4. Was hast du am Donnerstag gemacht? (Zeitschriften lesen)
5. Was hast du am Dienstag gemacht? (keine Zeit haben)
6. Was hast du am Sonnabend gemacht? (nichts tun)

7. *Was ist denn hier alles passiert?* Tell what all happened here. *Folge dem Beispiel!*

❏ die Jugendlichen / Volkslieder singen
Die Jugendlichen haben Volkslieder gesungen.

1. Helga / eine Reise gewinnen
2. wir / viel Geld finden
3. die Gäste / keine Geschenke bringen
4. ich / meine Arbeit beginnen
5. Lisel / das Schokoeis essen
6. Frau Holz / mit den Eltern sprechen

8. Bilde Sätze!

❏ die Schüler / nach Hause gehen
Die Schüler sind nach Hause gegangen.

1. viele / zur Party kommen
2. die Familie / in Europa sein
3. Daniela / zu Hause bleiben
4. ich / im Büro sein
5. wir / zum Rathaus laufen

9. Imagine you are at a party and your friend is giving you a report of several events that took place while you were gone. Take your friend's part. *Folge dem Beispiel!*

❏ meine Arbeit beginnen
Ich habe meine Arbeit begonnen.

1. das Tennisspiel gewinnen
2. wenig Zeit haben
3. nach Deutschland fahren
4. zehn Kilometer laufen
5. im Jugendklub singen
6. im Kaufhaus sein

10. Provide the correct form of *haben* or *sein*.

1. Wann _____ ihr nach Hause gekommen?
2. Die Jugendlichen _____ Tischtennis gespielt.
3. Es _____ gestern viel geschneit.
4. Angelika _____ mir die Schultasche gebracht.
5. Die Gäste _____ im Wohnzimmer gewesen.
6. Mein Freund _____ lange vor dem Bahnhof gewartet.
7. Um wieviel Uhr _____ ihr Abendbrot gegessen?
8. _____ Sie mit dem Zug gefahren?
9. Was _____ du am Abend getrunken?
10. Wir _____ zur Bank gelaufen.

11. *Ich habe das gern gemacht. Und du?* **Everybody wants to know what everyone else has done over the weekend.** *Folge dem Beispiel!*

❐ Eishockey spielen
Ich habe Eishockey gespielt.

1. ein Buch lesen
2. in den Bergen wandern
3. zum Turnier gehen
4. Tina eine Karte schreiben
5. eine Reise machen
6. mit dem Auto fahren
7. nichts machen
8. in der Stadt sein

12. Change the following sentences from the present to the present perfect.

❐ Sie klatschen sehr laut.
Sie haben sehr laut geklatscht.

1. Wie schmeckt der Kuchen?
2. Ich habe viel Glück.
3. Wir laufen zehn Kilometer.
4. Die Sängerin singt bekannte Hits.
5. Die Mädchen gehen um acht Uhr ins Kino.
6. Sie hören die Musik.
7. Viele spielen Tischtennis.

8. Sprecht ihr Deutsch?
9. Er gibt das Signal.
10. Das weiß ich nicht.
11. Ich bin heute zu Hause.
12. Brauchst du einen Kuli?

Ist er heute zu Hause gewesen?

13. *Ergänze diese Sätze!* Use the proper form of *haben* or *sein* and one of the verbs from the below. Be sure to use the proper form of the conversational past (present perfect).

lesen   kommen   klatschen   kaufen
dauern   essen   sammeln   zeigen
sehen   fahren   singen   sein

1. Die Reise _____ acht Stunden _____.
2. _____ Sie schon Abendbrot _____?
3. _____ ihr gejubelt und _____?
4. Helga _____ nicht zum Geburtstag _____.
5. Jochen _____ Briefmarken _____.
6. Wir _____ Volkslieder _____.
7. Ich _____ ihr das Rathaus _____.
8. Die Touristen _____ Berlin _____.
9. _____ du die Zeitung _____?
10. Die Musik _____ ganz toll _____.
11. _____ ihr nach Hamburg _____?
12. Frau Schulz _____ ein Kleid _____.

14. *Beende diese Sätze!* Use a different verb (in the present perfect tense) each time.

1. Am Dienstag haben wir _____.
2. Mein Freund hat _____.
3. Bist du in der Stadt _____?
4. Haben die Schüler viel _____?
5. Wir haben Tennis _____.
6. Hast du etwas _____?
7. Uwe ist heute spät _____.
8. Habt ihr die Aufgaben _____?

Compound Nouns

The article of a compound noun is determined by the article of the last word in the compound.

Beispiele: der Nachbar, das Land = das Nachbarland
die Geburt, der Tag = der Geburtstag

15. *Welche Wörter passen zusammen?* (Which words match?) Form compound nouns by locating the appropriate nouns that match those on the left. Determine the new article as well.

der Klub   die Bahn   die Karte   der Teil   das Brot

das Stück   die Halle   der Schuh   die Tasche   die Zeit

1. die Straße
2. die Kleidung
3. der Abend
4. das Jahr
5. die Hand
6. die Jugend
7. der Körper
8. die Schule
9. das Land
10. das Konzert

Wer wird heute der beste sein?

Dirk und Michael spielen einmal die Woche Tennis.

302

Wie kommen sie zum Tennisklub?

Wer hat gewonnen?

Lesestück

Tennis macht Spaß

Dirk und Michael spielen einmal die Woche Tennis.
Jeden Donnerstag fährt Dirk mit dem Fahrrad zu
Michael. Er klingelt° an der Tür und wartet bis Michael
aus dem Haus kommt.

Dirk:	Wer wird heute der beste sein?	
Michael:	Das letzte Mal° hast du gewonnen.	*last time*
	Heute bin ich an der Reihe°.	*it's my turn*
Dirk:	Das glaube ich nicht.	
Michael:	Weißt du, ich habe einen anderen	
	Schläger° gekauft.	*racket*
Dirk:	Ist der teuer gewesen?	
Michael:	Nein, er ist nicht neu.	
Dirk:	Na, dann viel Glück!	

rings

Beide fahren jetzt mit den Fahrrädern zum Tennisklub.
Zuerst müssen sie eine Strecke° durch die Stadt fahren.
Da ist immer viel Verkehr, aber schon bald kommen sie
zum Fluß. Der Tennisklub ist ganz in der Nähe vom
Fluß. In diesem Tennisklub sind Michaels Eltern Mitglie-
der°. Deshalb° können Dirk und Michael hier oft
spielen. Auf einem Spielplan° notiert° Michael, wie
lange sie spielen werden. Meistens° spielen sie eine
Stunde.

stretch

members/therefore
game schedule/notes
mostly

Michael und Dirk ziehen sich schnell um°. Dann gehen *change clothes*
sie zum Tennisplatz°. *tennis court*

Michael:	Jetzt kann es losgehen.
Dirk:	Wer soll denn aufschlagen°? *serve (ball)*
Michael:	Du kannst zuerst aufschlagen. Ich muß
	meinen Schläger etwas ausprobieren°. *try out*
Dirk:	Also, dann mal los.
Michael:	Mein Schläger ist wirklich gut.
Dirk:	Ja, diesen Ball hast du gut geschlagen°. *hit*

Beide spielen zwei Sätze°. Dirk ist heute wirklich in *sets*
Form. Er bekommt fast jeden Ball. Nach dem Spiel
gratuliert Michael seinem Freund.

Michael:	Ich gratuliere. Du hast sehr gut gespielt.
Dirk:	Vielleicht habe ich auch etwas Glück ge-
	habt. Du mußt mit deinem Schläger noch
	etwas üben.
Michael:	Das nächste Mal werde ich bestimmt besser
	sein.
Dirk:	Hoffentlich.

Welche Wörter fehlen in diesen Sätzen?

notiert	spielen	Sätze	Fahrrad	klingelt
Donnerstag	gewonnen	wartet	ziehen	Eltern
Stadt	Fluß	Form	aufschlagen	gekauft

1. Dirk _____ an der Tür.
2. Sie spielen am _____ Tennis.
3. Vor dem Spiel _____ sie sich um.
4. Dirk und Michael spielen zwei _____.
5. Michael hat einen Schläger _____.
6. Dirk soll zuerst _____.
7. Beide fahren mit dem _____ zum Tennisklub.
8. Sie _____ oft eine Stunde.
9. Der Tennisklub ist nicht weit vom _____ entfernt.
10. Dirk _____, bis Michael aus dem Haus kommt.
11. Michaels _____ sind Mitglieder im Klub.
12. Dirk ist heute in guter _____.
13. Michael _____ etwas auf dem Spielplan.
14. Michael hat das letzte Mal nicht _____.
15. Von Michaels Haus fahren sie durch die _____.

Beantworte diese Fragen!

1. Was machen Michael und Dirk jede Woche?
2. Wie kommt Dirk zu Michael?
3. Wer hat das letzte Mal gewonnen?
4. Was hat Michael gekauft?
5. Wohin fahren sie von Michaels Haus?
6. Warum können sie dort spielen?
7. Wie lange spielen sie?
8. Wer schlägt zuerst auf?
9. Wie viele Sätze spielen sie?
10. Wer hat das Spiel gewonnen?

Übung macht den Meister!

1. *Ich werde in diesem Turnier spielen.* Select a sport you're interested in. Imagine you are participating in a scheduled tournament in this sport. Describe it. In your description you may want to include some of these details: location, date, number of players or participants (*der Teilnehmer*), length of tournament, how often it takes place and some specific items during this event.

2. *Was machst du gern?* Ask your classmates what they would like to do this weekend (*das Wochenende*). Here are some questions you may wish to use:

   Was machst du dieses Wochenende?
   Wo findet das statt?
   Wie viele werden kommen?
   Was ist da alles los?
   Wie lange dauert es?

3. *Was für Körperteile hat ein Mensch? Ein Mensch hat...* In your description, give such answers as: *Ein Mensch hat zwei Augen.* Furthermore, ask each other the question: *Wozu braucht man Augen?* (Answer: *Zum Sehen.*) Here are some additional useful words for your answers: *denken* (to think), *riechen* (to smell). Others that you already know are: *hören, sprechen, essen, schwimmen, Schlittschuh laufen, wandern,* etc.

Erweiterung

16. Ist das eine Sportart, ein Kleidungsstück, ein Körperteil oder ein Verkehrsmittel?

❏   Mantel
Das ist ein Kleidungsstück.

1. Anzug
2. Zug
3. Schwimmen
4. Schulter
5. Motorrad
6. Fußball
7. Rock
8. Handschuh
9. Flugzeug
10. Bein
11. Golf
12. Stirn

17. Beantworte diese Fragen!

1. Welche Sportart macht Spaß?
2. Warum hast du diesen Sport gern?
3. Welche Sportarten gibt es bei dir in der Schule?
4. Was hat der Ansager gesagt?

18. Beende diese Sätze!

1. In der Sporthalle gibt es _____.
2. Der Ansager hat _____.
3. Die Spieler zeigen, was _____.
4. Hast du ihn _____?
5. Das Turnier ist _____.
6. Er gibt den Richtern _____.
7. Sie spielen mit _____.
8. Er ist heute _____.

19. *Kannst du die Wörter finden?* From the list below, find the compound nouns that best complete the following sentences.

der Sport	die Stunde	der Nachbar	die Halle
das Mittel	der Verkehr	der Tag	die Marke
der Kredit	das Rad	die Geburt	die Karte
der Motor	das Land	der Brief	der Plan

1. Ich brauche eine _____ für diese Ansichtskarte.
2. Herzlichen Glückwunsch zum _____!
3. Die Straßenbahn ist ein gutes _____.
4. Ich bezahle bar. Ich habe keine _____.
5. Ich gehe nicht zu Fuß. Ich komme mit dem _____.
6. Belgien ist ein _____ von Deutschland.
7. In der _____ findet ein Turnier statt.
8. Auf dem _____ stehen viele Fächer.

Sprachspiegel

20. *Fahren wir mit dem Rad zum Fluß!* The following words when put in sequence describe what Daniela is planning to do on the weekend. Can you put the words for each sentence in the right order and read what will take place?

1. Daniela / am Sonntag / will / Ausflug / machen / einen
2. mitkommen / wird / Danielas Freundin / Heike
3. fahren / sie / wohin / sollen
4. meint / Heike / München nach
5. viel / immer / zu / sagt / Verkehr / Daniela / dort ist
6. eine / Daniela / Idee / hat
7. fahren / mit / Fluß / Rad / zum / dem / wir
8. drei / komme / um / zu / Uhr dir / ich

21. *Wie sagt man's?*

treibt	Sporthalle	Arme	schaffen
Hobbys	Nähe	Hemd	gehabt
Spieler	Fluß	wandern	Sommer
statt	toll	Schläger	schwitzt
Limo	Turnier	fragen	Tag
sportlich	weiß	gesehen	spielst

1. Wann findet das Fußballspiel _____?
   Ich _____ nicht genau.
   Kannst du Peter _____?
   Ja, das mache ich.
2. Gehst du zum _____?
   Ja, die besten _____ kommen.
   Das wird bestimmt _____ sein.
3. Wo _____ du Tennis?
   In der _____.
   Wo ist die denn?
   Oh, hier gleich in der _____.

4. Welchen Sport _____ Uwe denn?
   Er ist nicht _____.
   Was macht er denn den ganzen _____?
   Uwe hat ein paar _____.

5. Kannst du die 10 Kilometer _____?
   Hoffentlich.
   Du _____ sehr.
   Gib mir bitte eine _____.
6. Ist dein _____ neu?
   Nein, ich habe ihn schon lange _____.
   Komisch, ich habe ihn noch nie _____.
7. Wir _____ sehr gern.
   Wohin geht ihr denn immer?
   Meistens zum _____.
   Im _____ ist es dort besonders schön.
8. Dieses _____ paßt mir nicht.
   Das stimmt. Deine _____ sind zu lang.

22. *Was ist dein Lieblingssport?* Describe your favorite sport in one or two paragraphs. Your description might include such items as: When do you particpate (time of season)? Where do you do your sport? With whom do you play? How long have you participated in this sport?

23. Wie heißt das auf deutsch?

1. I played tennis yesterday.
2. Did you beat him?
3. No, he was (has been) very good.
4. Would you like to play with me?
5. Are you so bad?
6. No, but against you I have a chance.

Rückblick

I. *Ergänze diese Sätze!* Use the appropriate prefixes listed below.

ab   an   auf   aus   ein   mit   um   zurück

1. Welche Jeans probierst du _____?
2. Steigen Sie in Köln _____?
3. Bring doch deinen Freund _____!
4. Wir fahren heute nach Ulm und am Montag fahren wir wieder _____.
5. Ich lade sie gern _____
6. Der Bus fährt pünktlich _____.
7. Setz doch eine Brille _____!
8. Gebt doch nicht viel Geld _____!

II. **Provide the proper form of the verb provided in parentheses.**

1. (gefallen) Wie _____ dir dieser Hit?
2. (essen) Was _____ du zum Abendbrot, Rolf?
3. (sehen) Wir _____ viele Berge und Flüsse.
4. (sprechen) _____ Tanja gut Deutsch?
5. (fahren) Herr Schmidt _____ nach Bonn.
6. (lesen) Warum _____ ihr die Bücher nicht?
7. (laufen) Der Film _____ schon zwei Wochen.
8. (geben) Hans, _____ mir zehn Mark, bitte.

III. **Beende die folgenden Sätze!**

1. Nach _____ können wir zum Eiscafé gehen.
2. Wohnt er nicht bei _____?
3. Um wieviel Uhr kommt ihr aus _____?
4. Das Auto steht nicht weit von _____.
5. Sie fahren zu _____.
6. Außer _____ spielt auch der Vater Tennis.
7. Ich fahre mit _____ in die Stadt.
8. Die Touristen fahren von _____ zu _____.

IV. **Provide the proper personal pronouns (dative or accusative) for the italicized words.**

❏ Können Sie *den Zug* schon sehen?
Können Sie ihn schon sehen?

1. Wir werden *die Zeitschrift* bestimmt finden.
2. Was bekommst du von *der Mutter*?

3. Sprechen Sie doch mit *dem Herrn!*
4. Wie viele Wochen wohnst du bei *dem Onkel und der Tante?*
5. Fragen sie *den Beamten!*
6. Ich kann *die Verkäuferin* nicht verstehen.
7. Hast du *die Jugendlichen* gesehen?
8. Rainer geht mit *Holger* zur Schule.

V. **Complete the following sentences by using the prepositions and nouns listed in parentheses.** *Folge den Beispielen!* **Contract prepositions and articles, where possible.**

❏ Warum bist du so oft (um / Ecke) _____ gelaufen?
  Warum bist du so oft um die Ecke gelaufen?

  Ich habe schon lange nichts (von / du) _____ gehört.
  Ich habe schon lange nichts von dir gehört.

1. Sie fahren langsam (durch / Stadt) _____.
2. Ich bin lange (bei / er) _____ geblieben.
3. (Ohne / Karten) _____ können wir nicht ins Kino.
4. Dieter geht um drei Uhr (zu / Tennisplatz) _____.
5. Wir haben (für / Konzert) _____ kein Geld.
6. Fährst du (mit / Zug) nach Hamburg?
7. (Von / Rathaus) _____ ist es nicht weit zum Bahnhof.
8. Hast du (gegen / sie) _____ gespielt?
9. Klaus geht oft (um / Park) _____.
10. Um fünf Uhr kommen sie (aus / Büro) _____.

Der Rhein ist der längste Fluß.

Der höchste Berg ist die Zugspitze.

Land und Leute

Deutschland heute

Im Norden grenzt die Bundesrepublik an° die Nordsee. Direkt auf der anderen Seite°, in der Nähe von Kiel, beginnt die Ostsee°. Im Norden ist das Land flach, und im Süden findet man die Alpen. Die Bundesrepublik hat neun Nachbarländer — Dänemark, Holland (die Niederlande), Belgien, Luxemburg, Frankreich, die Schweiz, Österreich, die Tschechoslowakei und Polen. Wo liegen diese Länder — im Norden, Süden, Osten oder Westen?

grenzt...an borders on side
Baltic Sea

Der höchste Berg ist die Zugspitze (fast 3 000 m). Die Zugspitze liegt an der Grenze zu Österreich. Der zweit-höchste Berg ist der Watzmann (ungefähr 2 700 m). Dieser Berg liegt im Südosten.

Der Rhein ist der längste Fluß (867 km in der Bundesre-publik). Der Rhein entspringt° in der Schweiz, fließt durch den Bodensee°, dann durch die Bundesrepublik und die Niederlande bis in die Nordsee. Zwei andere große Flüsse sind die Elbe (793 km) und die Donau (647 km).

originates
Lake Constance

Die Donau fließt von Westen nach Osten.

Wo liegen die Alpen?

Der Bodensee ist der größte See. Nur ein Teil vom Bodensee liegt in der Bundesrepublik. Andere Teile liegen in Österreich und in der Schweiz. Es gibt aber viele kleine Seen°. Die meisten liegen im Süden, wie zum Beispiel° der Chiemsee und der Starnberger See.

Die größten Inseln° sind Rügen und Fehmarn. Diese Inseln liegen in der Ostsee. Die meisten Inseln liegen in der Nordsee. Helgoland zum Beispiel ist im Sommer ein beliebter Ausflugsort°.

lakes
as for example

islands

excursion area

Die Elbe ist der zweitgrößte Fluß in Deutschland.

Die Stadt Kiel liegt im Norden.

an der Ostsee

Helgoland ist ein beliebter Ausflugsort.

Wie ist das Land im Norden?

Was ist das (Fluß, Insel, Berg, Stadt, See)?

❏   Helgoland
     Helgoland ist eine Insel.

1. Rügen
2. die Zugspitze
3. Fehmarn
4. Polen
5. der Bodensee
6. Dänemark
7. der Rhein
8. der Watzmann
9. die Elbe
10. der Chiemsee

Beantworte diese Fragen!

1. Wie ist das Land im Norden Deutschlands?
2. Wie viele Nachbarländer hat Deutschlands?
3. Wo entspringt der Rhein?
4. Wo liegt Fehmarn?
5. Wann kommen viele Touristen nach Helgoland?
6. Welches Land grenzt im Süden an Dänemark?

Zungenbrecher
Hundert hurtige Hunde hetzen hinter hundert hurtigen Hasen her.
(A hundred speedy dogs are racing after a hundred speedy rabbits.)

Kulturecke

Sports

Germans are just as conscious about physical fitness as we are. There are numerous health and fitness clubs in Germany where members can work out and improve or maintain their physique. Running, jogging, hiking and walking are just some of the sports supported by the German Sports Federation (*DSB — Deutscher Sportbund*) for people of all ages. Throughout Germany, usually in a forest or park area, you can find designated exercise areas marked *"Trimm-Dich-Pfad"* (literally meaning "Slim Down Path"). To keep physically fit or to participate in organized sports, Germans join local sports clubs. Every third person in the Federal Republic is a member of a sports club.

Tennis kann man auch in den Bergen spielen.

Sie laufen gern Ski.

Soccer (*Fußball*) is by far the most popular sport. During the soccer season, from September to June, millions of people watch the games in the various stadiums around the country or on television at home. The 18 teams of the national league (*Bundesliga*) receive the most attention.

The sport with the longest tradition in Germany is gymnastics (*Turnen*), which became popular in the early nineteenth century and is today the second most popular sport with over three million Germans participating. For many decades, tennis (*Tennis*) in Germany was reserved only for the upper class. This is no longer true today. With the world-class champions Boris Becker and Steffi Graf, the sport of tennis has skyrocketed in popularity more than any other sport in Germany and now ranks third on the list. Typically, tennis courts have a clay surface and can be found in most small towns and all larger cities.

Germany has produced world-class athletes in track and field competition (*Leichtathletik*) as well. Meets between countries are scheduled continuously to compare athletic achievements with those in the rest of the world. The sport of handball (*Handball*) is not the same as we know it. The German handball is an indoor sport played with a ball slightly smaller than a soccer ball. Similar to soccer, the object is to get the ball between the goal posts.

Over a million Germans belong to rifle and pistol clubs (*Schützenvereine*). Many members enjoy the marksmanship training as well as hunting (*Jagen*) in areas that are leased to trained and licensed hunters. A less expensive sport is fishing (*Angeln*). Germans fish not only in the lakes but also in the various rivers.

Table tennis (*Tischtennis*) is among the top 10 most popular sports. Besides numerous clubs, many people play this sport in the schools, youth hostels or at home. The sport of golf (*Golf*) is very expensive and played by only a few Germans who belong to private clubs. There still are not many golf courses in Germany today.

Most cities have indoor or outdoor skating facilities. Here Germans practice and improve their skill. Germany has produced several world-class figure skaters (*Eiskunstläufer*) during the past three decades. Ice hockey (*Eishockey*) was relatively unknown 25 years ago. During the last two decades, however, Germany has done quite well in international competition.

During the winter months, many Germans head for the mountains in southern Germany, Austria or Switzerland to go skiing (*Ski laufen*). Those who master the skill after years of hard training can compete in local, national or even international competition. Endurance is tested not only in downhill skiing but also in cross-country skiing (*Skilanglauf*). Another winter sport is curling, seen mostly in the southern part of Germany.

Various types of horse races (*Pferderennen*) take place in major cities from early spring through late fall. Horseback riding (*Reiten*) has been popular for centuries. However, this sport is expensive and practiced by only a few. In horsemanship competition, German riders have done extremely well in international competition, winning many medals in the Olympics over the last three decades.

The water sports, such as sailing (*Segeln*), enjoy a tremendous popularity among Germans. The famous annual *Kieler Woche*, an international sailing regatta, has the best sailors compete for the grand prize. Others enjoy sailing more as a leisure-time sport. Sailing is particularly popular on the North Sea and Baltic Sea as well as in the few sailing lakes that Germany has to offer. During the past 10 years, surfing (*Surfen*) has been enthusiastically received by Germans. There are well over one million people who participate in this sport. Another popular sport is rowing (*Rudern*) in which athletes compete on rivers around the country. Those who enjoy more treacherous waters are involved in white water canoeing (*Wildwasserfahren*), which was officially introduced as an Olympic sport in the 1972 Olympic Games held in Munich.

Was für einen Sport treiben sie? *Reiten ist bei den Deutschen auch beliebt.*

Segeln

Im Sportklub

For those who enjoy participating in more challenging sports, Germany offers numerous opportunities. Gliding (*Segelfliegen*) is particularly popular in central and southern Germany. There the hills and mountains provide favorable air currents needed to stay in the air for a long time. Recently, hot-air ballooning (*Ballonfahren*) has been received enthusiastically by many Germans. The challenge is not only to go up and stay in the air, but also to come down in the original spot. Those who are most daring participate in a sport called hang-gliding (*Drachenfliegen*), in which these sporting people push themselves off cliffs or hills while being strapped to a kite-like sail and glide high through the air. Finally, the sport of mountaineering (*Bergsteigen*) is practiced in the mountainous regions of Germany. Those who become experts eventually climb the many challenging peaks found in the Alps.

Eishockey *Drachenfliegen*

Was weißt du? Match the items on the left with those on the right.

1. Pferderennen		a.	fishing
2. Leichtathletik		b.	soccer
3. Drachenfliegen		c.	hunting
4. Jagen		d.	hot-air ballooning
5. Skilanglauf		e.	hang-gliding
6. Segelfliegen		f.	handball
7. Fußball		g.	track and field
8. Bergsteigen		h.	white water canoeing
9. Handball		i.	table tennis
10. Wildwasserfahren		j.	gymnastics
11. Ballonfahren		k.	gliding
12. Angeln		l.	ice skating
13. Tischtennis		m.	horse racing
14. Eiskunstlauf		n.	mountaineering
15. Turnen		o.	cross-country skiing

Ergänze diese Sätze mit dem Namen einer Sportart. Auf deutsch, bitte!

1. _____ is the second most popular sport.
2. The mountains and hills of southern Germany provide the right conditions for _____.
3. The national soccer league is called the _____.
4. Germans go to other German-speaking countries for _____.
5. The mountain peaks of the Alps are popular for _____.
6. The _____ is an annual sailing regatta.
7. The sport of _____ was introduced in the 1972 Olympics.
8. People like to go jogging and doing exercises on a path called _____.
9. Germans who are interested in the sport of _____ have to lease the land.
10. In _____ the players use a ball slightly smaller than a soccer ball.

Vokabeln

der **Ansager,-** announcer
der **Arm,-e** arm
   aufrufen to announce
   aufschlagen to serve
   (tennis)
das **Auge,-n** eye
   ausprobieren to try (out)
der **Ball,-e** ball
der **Basketball,-e** basketball
das **Bein,-e** leg
das **Beispiel, -e** example
   zum Beispiel for
   example
   bekanntgeben to announce
die **Chance,-n** chance
   derselbe the same
   deshalb therefore
das **Eishockey** ice hockey
das **Endspiel,-e** final (game)
das **Ergebnis,-se** result, score
der **Finger,-** finger
die **Form,-en** form
der **Fußball,-e** soccer
   gewinnen to win
das **Golf** golf
   gratulieren to congratulate
die **Gruppe,-n** group
das **Haar,-e** hair
der **Hals,-e** neck
die **Hand,-e** hand

die **Insel,-n** island
das **Kinn,-e** chin
der **Körperteil,-e** part of body
   leider unfortunately
die **Lippe,-n** lip
das **Mal,-e** time(s)
   meistens mostly
das **Mitglied,-er** member
der **Mund,-er** mouth
   notieren to note
die **Nummer,-n** number
das **Ohr,-en** ear
die **Platte,-n** table (top)
das **Rad,-er** bike, bicycle
   recht right
   Du hast recht. You're
   right.
die **Reihe,-n** row
   Ich bin an der Reihe.
   It's my turn.
der **Richter,-** judge
die **Runde,-n** round
der **Satz,-e** set
   schlagen to beat, hit
der **Schläger,-** racket
   Schlittschuh laufen to
   skate
die **Schulter,-n** shoulder
   schwimmen to swim
das **Spiel,-e** game
der **Spieler,-** player

der **Spielplan,-e** game
   schedule
die **Sportart,-en** kind of sport
die **Sporthalle,-n** sports hall
   stattfinden to take place
die **Stirn,-e** forehead
die **Strecke,-n** stretch,
   distance
das **Tennis** tennis
der **Tennisklub,-s** tennis club
der **Tennisplatz,-e** tennis
   court
das **Tischtennis** table tennis
das **Tischtennisturnier,-e**
   table tennis tourna-
   ment
   treiben to do
   Sport treiben to participate in sports
   üben to practice
die **Übung,-en** exercise,
   practice
   **Übung macht den
   Meister!** Practice
   makes perfect.
   umziehen to change
   clothes
   weiterspielen to continue
   playing
   wenn if
der **Zahn,-e** tooth
   zuerst first

Wildwasserfahren

Surfen

Musik

10

Communicative Functions

- talking about musical interest
- naming musical instruments
- asking for a date
- talking about meeting somewhere
- describing how to prepare for a school dance

Machen wir Musik!

Sonja kommt gern zu Bärbel. Beide sind gute Freundinnen und in derselben Klasse in der Schule. Sonja klingelt an der Tür. Bärbel ist da und macht gleich die Tür auf.

Bärbel: Ach, du bist's. Ich habe schon Geige geübt.
Sonja: Ohne mich? Du brauchst doch meine Begleitung.
Bärbel: Trotzdem muß ich etwas alleine üben.
Sonja: Meinst du nicht, es geht besser zusammen?
Bärbel: Ich glaube schon. Komm rein. Hier draußen machen wir keine Musik.
Sonja: Na, da hast du recht. Spielen wir zusammen im Haus!

Fragen

1. Wer hat alleine geübt?
2. Wer kommt zu Bärbel?
3. Ist Bärbel zu Hause?
4. Was machen sie draußen nicht?

Beide gehen ins Wohnzimmer und sehen sich ein paar Musikbücher an. Bärbel hat schon viele Jahre Klavier gespielt. Deshalb hat sie auch eine große Auswahl an Büchern.

Sonja: Spielen wir dieses Stück!
Bärbel: Das ist zu kompliziert. Da muß ich erst üben.
Sonja: Du bist mal wieder viel zu wählerisch.
Bärbel: Hier, ein Stück von Mozart. Da kannst du mich gut begleiten.
Sonja: Versuchen wir es doch!
Bärbel: Setz dich bitte hin!

Bärbel begrüßt Sonja.

Spielen wir dieses Stück!

Was ist richtig und was ist falsch? Determine whether or not the following statements are correct or incorrect. If they are incorrect, provide the correct statement. *Auf deutsch, bitte.*

1. Bärbel hat schon lange Klavier gespielt.
2. Bärbel hat nur ein paar Musikbücher.
3. Sonja und Bärbel gehen in die Küche.
4. Sie sehen sich Zeitungen an.
5. Bärbel weiß nicht genau, was sie spielen will.

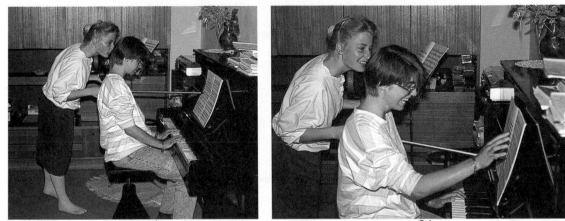

Fangen wir von hier an? *Jetzt Spaß beiseite.*

(am Klavier)

Bärbel: Fangen wir von hier an?
Sonja: In der Mitte? Wir verlieren dann ganz den Rhythmus.
Bärbel: Hast du denn einen?
Sonja: Jetzt Spaß beiseite.
Bärbel: Hier von dieser Stelle geht's bestimmt besser.
Sonja: Also, fangen wir jetzt an.

Fragen

1. Fangen sie in der Mitte an zu spielen?
2. Warum will Sonja nicht in der Mitte anfangen?
3. Was für Musikinstrumente spielen sie?

Wer hat das gesagt oder gefragt? Identify the speaker of the following sentences which reflect the content of the previous dialogs. Answer with *Bärbel/Sonja hat das gesagt* or *Bärbel/Sonja hat das gefragt.*

Beispiel: Dieses Stück ist zu kompliziert.
Bärbel hat das gesagt.

1. Setz dich hin!
2. Du kannst mich zu diesem Stück begleiten.
3. Glaubst du nicht, wir sollen zusammen üben?
4. Du bist sehr wählerisch.
5. Komm ins Haus!
6. Beginnen wir von dieser Stelle?
7. Vielleicht sollen wir dieses Stück versuchen.
8. Vor dem Haus können wir nicht spielen.
9. Du kannst doch nicht ohne mich spielen?
10. Spielen wir ein Stück von Mozart!

Für dich

Austria is famous for its music. One of the greatest Austrian composers was Wolfgang Amadeus Mozart (1756-91) who was born in Salzburg. Most of his music was composed for piano and violin.

Kombiniere...

Wie viele Sätze kannst du bilden?

Sonja und Bärbel	klingelt	gleich	im Wohnzimmer
Seine Schwester	spielen	am Abend	Klavier
Wer	übt	immer	Musik
Viele	stehen	nicht gern	an der Tür

Was machen sie?

Was für ein Musikinstrument spielt sie?

Sie machen Musik.

Nützliche Ausdrücke

Bist du in derselben Klasse?	Are you in the same class?
Machst du die Tür auf?	Are you opening the door?
Komm rein!	Come inside.
Machen wir Musik!	Let's make music.
Wir versuchen es.	We'll try it.
Setz dich hin!	Sit down.
Spaß beiseite.	Joking aside.
Fangt ihr an?	Are you starting?

Was paßt hier?

1. Warum macht sie die Tür auf?
2. Willst du alleine üben?
3. Setz dich bitte hin!
4. Fang von dieser Stelle an!
5. Bist du in derselben Klasse?
6. Kommen Sie bitte rein!
7. Versuch doch zu spielen!
8. Wann fangt ihr an?

a. So gegen acht.
b. Das ist ja viel zu schwer.
c. Nein, ich bin nicht so alt wie er.
d. Es hat geklingelt.
e. Hier an den Tisch?
f. Leider habe ich kein Klavier.
g. Vielen Dank.
h. Nein, ich brauche Begleitung.

Ergänzung

die Flöte

die Klarinette

die Geige

das Akkordeon

Was für ein Musikinstrument spielst du? Ich spiele...

1. *Frage deine Klassenkameraden (classmates)!*

1. Was für ein Musikinstrument spielst du?
2. Wo spielst du es?
3. Wie lange spielst du es schon?

WA2, WA3

4. Wer spielt in deiner Familie ein Musikinstrument?

Sag's mal!

Wie ist die Musik? Sie ist...

zu schnell   alt   rockig   ganz gut

modern   unmöglich   mittelmäßig

neu   angenehm

zu laut   romantisch   poppig   zu leise

langweilig   schlecht   schrill

schrecklich   prima   super   abartig

Aussprache

/ai/	/oi/	/au/
kl**ei**n	n**eu**	**au**f
w**ei**t	**eu**ch	**Au**to
M**ai**	t**eu**er	k**au**ft
ein	d**eu**tsch	bl**au**
bl**ei**bt	Kr**eu**z	Fr**au**
Kl**ei**d	n**eu**n	gl**au**ben
l**ei**cht	Fr**eu**nd	**Au**gust
s**ei**n	h**eu**te	br**au**chen

Übungen

Possessive Adjectives

A possessive adjective is a pronoun that is used as an adjective to indicate who owns the noun that follows it. It replaces the article in front of the noun and takes on the same endings as those of the indefinite article (*ein*-words).

	Nominative Singular			Plural
	masculine	**feminine**	**neuter**	
ich	mein	meine	mein	meine
du	dein	deine	dein	deine
er	sein	seine	sein	seine
sie	ihr	ihre	ihr	ihre
es	sein	seine	sein	seine
wir	unser	unsere*	unser	unsere*
ihr	euer	euere*	euer	euere*
sie	ihr	ihre	ihr	ihre
Sie	Ihr	Ihre	Ihr	Ihre

*The e in front of the r in *unser* and *euer* is often omitted if the ending begins with a vowel.

Beispiele: Meine Freundin heißt Angelika.
Wo ist unser Schläger?

	Accusative Singular			Plural
	masculine	**feminine**	**neuter**	
ich	meinen	meine	mein	meine
du	deinen	deine	dein	deine
er	seinen	seine	sein	seine
sie	ihren	ihre	ihr	ihre
es	seinen	seine	sein	seine
wir	unseren*	unsere*	unser	unsere*
ihr	eueren*	euere*	euer	euere*
sie	ihren	ihre	ihr	ihre
Sie	Ihren	Ihre	Ihr	Ihre

Beispiele: Kennst du seinen Bruder?
Ich kaufe ihr Buch.

	Dative Singular			Plural
	masculine	**feminine**	**neuter**	
ich	meinem	meiner	meinem	meinen
du	deinem	deiner	deinem	deinen
er	seinem	seiner	seinem	seinen
sie	ihrem	ihrer	ihrem	ihren
es	seinem	seiner	seinem	seinen
wir	unserem*	unserer*	unserem*	unseren*
ihr	euerem*	euerer*	euerem*	eueren*
sie	ihrem	ihrer	ihrem	ihren
Sie	Ihrem	Ihrer	Ihrem	Ihren

Beispiele: Kommt ihr zu unserer Party?
Der Mantel paßt ihrer Schwester.

2. *Wer ist da gewesen?* Andrea is telling her friend Gabriele who all has been at her party. Can you take Andrea's part, using the cues provided? *Folge dem Beispiel!*

❏ Freund
Mein Freund ist da gewesen.

1. Bruder
2. Tante
3. Freundin
4. Vater
5. Lehrerin

3. *Habt ihr...?* Imagine you're organizing a club function. You will need a number of items before your meeting. Ask the assembled club members if they have these items.

❏ die Gitarre
Habt ihr eure Gitarre?

1. die Kassette
2. der Taschenrechner
3. der Ball
4. das Buch
5. der Computer
6. das Fahrrad

4. *Wir machen einen Ausflug.* Your class is planning a field trip. Your teacher is asking your class who has specific things that will be needed. Several students are responding.

❐ Wer hat eine Uhr?
Ich kann meine Uhr mitbringen.

1. Wer hat eine Klarinette?
2. Wer hat einen Schläger?
3. Wer hat ein Paar Handschuhe?
4. Wer hat ein Heft?
5. Wer hat eine Landkarte?
6. Wer hat einen Pullover?

5. *Wen besuchen wir noch?* Tell who else we are visiting.

❐ Schwester / sein
Wir besuchen seine Schwester.

1. Oma / unser
2. Bruder / dein
3. Mutter / euer
4. Onkel / mein
5. Lehrerin / ihr

6. *Was brauchst du?* Several people ask you what items you need to go on a trip. Use the cues in your response.

❐ Handschuhe / mein
Ich brauche meine Handschuhe.

1. Zeitungen / sein
2. Fahrkarten / unser
3. Bücher / dein
4. Ansichtskarten / ihr
5. Bälle / euer

7. Beantworte diese Fragen! Folge dem Beispiel!

❐ Wen möchtest du fragen? (Freund / sein)
Seine Freunde.

1. Was mußt du haben? (Karte / mein)
2. Was willst du lesen? (Zeitschrift / ihr)
3. Wen möchtest du besuchen? (Großvater / unser)
4. Was wirst du brauchen? (Kassette / dein)
5. Wen holst du? (Freundin / sein)

8. *Wem paßt der Mantel nicht?* Several family members are trying on a coat that has been in the family for a long time. Whom doesn't it fit? *Folge dem Beispiel!*

❑ Onkel / sein
Der Mantel paßt seinem Onkel nicht.

1. Mutter / dein
2. Großmutter / unser
3. Onkel / ihr
4. Schwester / mein
5. Tante / sein

9. Complete each sentence by providing the missing endings where necessary.

1. Brauchst du mein _____ Computer?
2. Siehst du sein _____ Geschenke?
3. Wann ist dein _____ Geburtstag?
4. Ich gehe mit mein _____ Freundin ins Kino.
5. Mußt du zu unser _____ Haus fahren?
6. Verstehst du sein _____ Schwester?
7. Wir besuchen unser _____ Tante nächste Woche.
8. Lies doch dein _____ Buch!
9. Wo sind euer _____ Gitarren?
10. Glaubst du ihr _____ Freunden nicht?
11. Frag bitte mein _____ Vater!

10. Supply the German equivalent for the words given in parentheses.

1. Wo wohnt (your brother) _____, Herr Weise?
2. (Their father) _____ besucht (my uncle) _____.
3. Hast du (your sister) _____ bei der Arbeit geholfen, Tina?
4. (Our school) _____ ist nicht weit.
5. (My girlfriend) _____ holt (her cassette) _____.
6. Warum kaufst du (his tickets) _____?
7. Ich bin ohne (my books) _____ in die Schule gegangen.
8. Fährst du mit (your moped) _____ in die Stadt, Bernd?
9. Bringt doch (your ball) _____, Dieter und Heike!

11. Complete the following sentences, using a possessive adjective and a noun of your choice.

❑ Verstehst du _____?
Verstehst du seinen Freund?

1. Sie spielen mit _____.
2. Kannst du _____ anprobieren?
3. Ich wohne bei _____.
4. Bezahlst du für _____?
5. Bring doch _____ mit!
6. Wo sind _____?
7. _____ fährt sehr schnell.
8. Wir helfen _____.
9. Sie müssen _____ fragen.
10. Paul möchte _____ besuchen.
11. Ich bin um _____ Haus gelaufen.
12. Hast du etwas von _____ gehört?

Comparison of Adjectives

In adjectives of comparison there are two levels of comparing that are constructed from the basic form of the adjectives, i.e., the *comparative* and the *superlative*. The formation from the basic form, the *positive*, to the superlative is similar in both German and English. For instance, take the word *fast* (schnell). The comparative is *faster* (schneller) and the superlative is *fastest* (schnellst + ending).

Beispiele: das schnelle Auto   the fast car
              das schnellere Auto   the faster car
              das schnellste Auto   the fastest car

These examples are listed here merely to illustrate the comparison of adjectives. These adjectives (because they involve endings) will be treated specifically in later units. When the adjective is used as part of the verb, follow this example. Notice that *am* precedes the superlative and *-en* is added.

Peter ist pünktlich.   Peter is punctual.
Maria ist pünktlicher.   Maria is more punctual.
Holger ist am pünktlichsten.   Holger is most punctual.

Comparison of Adverbs

The comparison of adverbs is similar to the above. Whereas the adjective (see above) modifies the noun, the adverb (see next page) modifies the verb.

Beispiele: *Die Straßenbahn fährt*   The streetcar goes fast.
schnell.
Das Auto fährt schneller. The car goes faster.
Der Zug fährt   The train goes the fastest.
am schnellsten.

When the adjectives or adverbs end in *d, t, s, ß, sch, st, x* or *z,* the ending in the superlative has an additional *e.*

Beispiele: (am) interessantesten, heißesten

Most one-syllable adjectives or adverbs containing an *a,* o or *u* change to *ä, ö, ü* in the comparative and the superlative.

Beispiele: warm   wärmer   am wärmsten
              groß   größer   am größten
              klug   klüger   am klügsten

A few irregular forms are also listed here:

gut	besser	am besten
viel	mehr	am meisten
hoch	höher	am höchsten
nahe	näher	am nächsten
gern	lieber	am liebsten

In comparing two equal items, use *so...wie.*

Beispiel: *Der Morgen ist so kalt wie der Abend.* The morning is as cold as the evening.

When an unequal comparison is made, use the comparative form and the word *als* (meaning "than").

Beispiel: Uwe spielt besser als Hans. Uwe plays better than Hans.

12. You don't seem to agree with your classmates. *Folge dem Beispiel!*

❐   Das Auto fährt so schnell wie der Zug.
Nein, das Auto fährt schneller als der Zug.

1. Der Winter ist so kalt wie der Herbst.
2. Das Buch ist so toll wie der Film.
3. Susi liest so gut wie Dieter.
4. Michael kommt so spät wie Kerstin.
5. Der Abend ist so warm wie der Morgen.

13. *Das stimmt, aber...* You agree with what is being said. However, you add some additional information.

> ❐ Der Vorort ist groß. (die Stadt)
> Ja, aber die Stadt ist größer.

1. Am Montag ist es kühl. (Dienstag)
2. Jörg ist klug. (Monika)
3. Das Fahrrad ist schnell. (das Motorrad)
4. Das Konzert beginnt spät. (der Film)
5. Das Rathaus sieht schön aus. (das Museum)
6. Das Hemd ist billig. (die Bluse)

14. Provide the comparative and superlative forms. *Folge dem Beispiel!*

> ❐ Das Moped fährt schnell. (die Straßenbahn, der Zug)
> Die Straßenbahn fährt schneller.
> Der Zug fährt am schnellsten.

1. Köln ist groß.
   München
   Berlin
2. Sven ist klug.
   Petra
   Heike
3. Ich trinke gern Milch.
   Limo
   Apfelsaft
4. Herr Gruber kommt spät.
   Herr Hesse
   Frau Peters
5. Die Krawatte ist teuer.
   die Hose
   der Anzug

15. Give both comparative and superlative forms.

1. schlecht
2. alt
3. hoch
4. toll
5. billig
6. schön
7. heiß
8. gut
9. viel
10. groß

Auf zur Disko!

Olivers Hobby ist sein Computer. Er hat ihn von seinen Eltern zum Geburtstag bekommen. Jeden Tag, wie auch heute, sitzt er in seinem Zimmer und spielt mit dem Computer. Es macht viel Spaß. Manchmal° sitzt er auf dem Sofa, liest ein Buch und hört Kassetten. Heute ist er aber etwas unruhig°. Er möchte gern zur Disko gehen. Sie ist nicht weit von seinem Haus entfernt. Es ist sieben Uhr. Die Disko soll erst um acht aufmachen. Soll er Susanne anrufen°? Wird sie mitkommen? Er geht zu einem Telefon und wählt° Susannes Nummer.

sometimes

restless

call
dials

(am Telefon)

Oliver:	Tag, Susanne. Hier ist Oliver. Was machst du denn jetzt?
Susanne:	Wir haben eben Abendbrot gegessen. Jetzt muß ich noch auf der Klarinette üben.
Oliver:	Kannst du das nicht ein anderes Mal machen?
Susanne:	Nein, mein Musiklehrer kommt morgen.
Oliver:	Wie lange dauert das denn?
Susanne:	Vielleicht eine halbe Stunde.
Oliver:	Das klappt°. Die Disko macht um acht auf.
Susanne:	Da hast du mich wieder einmal überzeugt°.
Oliver:	Treffen wir uns° um acht bei der Disko. Tschüs.

That works out.

convinced

Let's meet...

Oliver ruft Susanne an.   Susanne möchte gern in die Disko gehen.

(später)

Oliver: Hallo, Susanne. Hast du schon lange gewartet?

Susanne: Nein, ich bin auch erst jetzt gekommen.

Oliver: Hast du gut geübt?

Susanne: Ich habe schon geübt. Wie gut, das ist eine andere Frage.

Oliver: Wie viele Jahre spielst du denn schon?

Susanne: Fast sechs Jahre.

Oliver: Dann kannst du ja heute in der Band spielen.

Susanne: Warum sagst du das? Willst du nicht mit mir tanzen?

Oliver: Ja, da hast du recht.

Oliver und Susanne treffen sich vor der Disko.

Beide gehen um die Ecke. Da begrüßen sie Susannes Freundinnen, Katrin und Renate. Sie warten schon ein paar Minuten.

Katrin: Es ist erst nach acht.

Susanne: Was heißt nach acht? Die Disko geht doch um acht los.

Renate: Das stimmt nicht. Die Musik beginnt um halb neun. Wir sind auch zu früh gekommen.

Oliver: Susanne, ich habe dich leider nicht richtig informiert°.   *informed*

Susanne: Dann habe ich Glück gehabt. Ich habe nur eine halbe Stunde geübt.

Renate: Wir müssen nicht hier draußen° stehen.   *outside*

Oliver: Gut, gehen wir hinein!

Welche Wörter fehlen in diesen Sätzen?

Freundinnen   mitkommen   Kassetten   gegessen
Zimmer   üben   ruft   Haus
gehen   Buch   Disko   Computer
Jahre   kommen   warten   spielt

1. Oliver sitzt in seinem _____.
2. Er mag seinen _____ sehr.
3. Oliver hört _____ und liest ein _____.
4. Die Disko ist in der Nähe von Olivers _____.
5. Oliver weiß nicht, ob Susanne _____ wird.
6. Er _____ Susanne an.
7. Susanne hat eben Abendbrot _____.
8. Sie muß noch auf der Klarinette _____.
9. Susannes Musiklehrer wird morgen _____.
10. Oliver und Susanne wollen gegen acht Uhr bei der _____ sein.
11. Susanne spielt schon sechs _____ Klarinette.
12. Katrin und Renate sind Susannes _____.
13. Sie _____ schon vor der Disko.
14. Die Band _____ erst um halb neun.
15. Alle vier _____ in die Disko hinein.

Beantworte diese Fragen!

1. Von wem hat Oliver seinen Computer bekommen?
2. Warum ist er heute unruhig?
3. Was macht er am Telefon?
4. Was muß Susanne noch machen?
5. Warum muß sie heute üben?
6. Hat Susanne lange vor der Disko gewartet?
7. Spielt Susanne schon lange Klarinette?
8. Um wieviel Uhr wird die Band spielen?
9. Warten Oliver, Susanne, Renate und Katrin vor der Tür?

Übung macht den Meister!

1. *Spielst du ein Musikinstrument?* Inquire about your classmates' interest in musical instruments. Your questions should include such details as:

   Was für ein Musikinstrument spielst du?
   Wo, wie lange und wie oft übst du?
   Hast du Musikunterricht? (music lessons)
   Wie lange spielst du dieses Musikinstrument schon?
   Mit wem übst du manchmal zusammen?

2. *Kommst du mit zur Disko?* You and your classmates will make up a list of why or why not you do or don't want to go to the disco this weekend. Give as many reasons as possible.

3. *Wir haben einen Schultanz.* Imagine that your committee has been put in charge of making the necessary preparations for the next school dance. Make a list of questions that need to be addressed and then ask others in your class. Some of your questions might be:

Wann und wo soll der Tanz stattfinden?
Wen sollen wir einladen?
Was brauchen wir alles?
Wieviel soll eine Karte kosten?

Erweiterung

16. *Was macht Spaß?* Using the phrases below, describe what is fun to do.

❑ Schlittschuh laufen
   Schlittschuh laufen macht Spaß.

   1. tanzen
   2. Klavier spielen
   3. Auto fahren
   4. Sport treiben
   5. Karten spielen
   6. Briefmarken sammeln

17. *Was ist logisch?* Find the appropriate verbs from the list below that best match the words on the left.

essen   aufmachen   einladen   trinken   wählen
lesen   schreiben   bezahlen   tanzen   anprobieren

   1. ein Glas Milch
   2. eine Zeitschrift
   3. eine Jacke
   4. an der Kasse
   5. Ansichtskarten
   6. in der Disko
   7. die Tür
   8. ein Eis
   9. die Telefonnummer
   10. Gäste

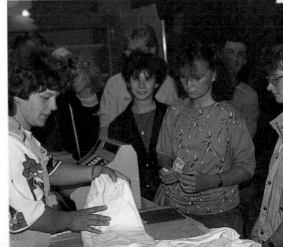

Was machen sie an der Kasse?

18. Provide an appropriate response in German. Be sure the conversation ties together and becomes meaningful.

1. Von wem hast du die Gitarre bekommen?
2. Wann hat er dir die Gitarre gegeben?
3. Kannst du denn spielen?
4. Dann mußt du bestimmt viel üben.

19. Beantworte diese Fragen!

1. Was machst du am Sonnabend?
2. Gehst du gern tanzen?
3. Was für Musik hörst du gern?
4. Wann hast du Geburtstag?
5. Was möchtest du zum Geburtstag bekommen?

20. Group the following words into these four categories: *Musikinstrument, Schule, Körperteil* and *Kleidungsstück.*

1. die Blockflöte
2. die Lippe
3. der Rock
4. die Landkarte
5. das Akkordeon
6. der Radiergummi
7. das Lineal
8. der Kopf
9. das Ohr
10. die Krawatte
11. die Trompete
12. das Heft
13. das Bein
14. der Hals
15. die Strümpfe

Sie spielen ein paar Musikinstrumente.

21. Beende diese Sätze!

1. Geht ihr heute _____?
2. Nein, wir haben _____.
3. Was macht ihr ____?
4. Wir werden _____.
5. Habt ihr denn _____?
6. Wir können nicht ohne _____.

Sprachspiegel

22. *Kannst du ihnen helfen?* Imagine that you are in charge of a disco. Many young adults are lining up in front and are asking you a number of questions. Can you help them out?

1. Um wieviel Uhr machen Sie auf?
   _____
2. Wer spielt denn heute?
   _____
3. Sind die gut?
   _____
4. Wie viele Jugendliche kommen immer zur Disko?
   _____
5. Haben Sie jede Woche eine Band?
   _____
6. Haben Sie dann einen Diskjockey?
   _____

23. *Was ist denn heute bei Gisela los?* The following words when put in sequence describe what is going on at Giselas.

1. es / am / Freitag / gibt / Party / eine
2. hat / Jugendliche / Gisela / eingeladen / zwanzig
3. werden / was / sie / machen / dort
4. bestimmt / Gitarre / Gisela / spielt
5. alle / dann / singen / werden
6. immer / Spaß / macht / das / viel

24. *Wie sagt man's?*

ansehen	Trompete	gesehen	Ausflug
Musik	langsam	Party	Uhr
gemacht	bei	tanzen	Jahr
fahren	Zimmer	sein	vor
gern	laut	kommt	gibt
weiß	los		

1. Gehst du _____ zu Rainer?
   Ja, da ist immer viel _____.
   Wann beginnt die _____ denn?
   So gegen sechs _____.
2. Warum mußt du wieder so _____ spielen?
   Ich habe eine neue _____ bekommen.
   Geh doch in ein anderes _____!

3. Ich kann mit Tina nicht _____.
   Gefällt ihr diese _____ nicht?
   Ja, aber sie ist zu _____.
4. Willst du dir einen Film _____?
   Was für einen Film _____ es denn?
   Der Film _____ aus Italien.
   Er soll sehr gut _____.
5. Was hast du am Mittwoch _____?
   Das _____ ich heute noch nicht.
   Willst du mit uns einen _____ machen?
   Wohin werdet ihr denn _____?
6. Ich habe sie schon lange nicht _____.
   Sie ist ein _____ in Europa gewesen.
   Was hat sie dort _____?
   Sie hat _____ ihrem Onkel gewohnt.

25. *Schreibe einen Dialog oder ein Lesestück!* **Write a dialog or a narrative using the following details. Call your friend...ask him or her to go to a dance...provide information about where and when this takes place... where to meet...who is playing. Be as creative as possible.**

26. Wie heißt das auf deutsch?

1. Let's play piano.
2. What kind of musical instrument do you play?
3. I have to practice.
4. What is your hobby?
5. He is calling up his girlfriend.
6. Would you like to dance?

Rückblick

I. Change these sentences from the present to the present perfect tense.

❏ Wir trinken gern Apfelsaft.
  Wir haben gern Apfelsaft getrunken.

1. Der Tourist fragt den Beamten.
2. Wann bist du im Kaufhaus?
3. Mein Vater kommt um fünf Uhr nach Hause.
4. Haben wir heute viele Aufgaben?
5. Sprechen die Gäste Deutsch?
6. Bringen sie ihm Geschenke?
7. Ich sage das nicht.
8. Mein Freund fährt nach Deutschland.
9. Wir tanzen oft in der Disko.
10. Bezahlst du für diese Karten?
11. Wie gefällt dir das Turnier?
12. Ich esse heute schon früh.

II. Supply the proper forms in the present, future or present perfect tense. Use the verbs provided in parentheses. Make sure that each sentence is meaningful.

1. (gehen) Die Mädchen _____ gestern zur Disko _____.
2. (sehen) Wir _____ diesen Film nächste Woche _____.
3. (kommen) Wann _____ du zu uns?
4. (kaufen) Was _____ ihr ihm morgen zum Geburtstag _____?
5. (fahren) Heute ist der 15. Mai. Schmidts _____ am 19. Mai nach Österreich _____.
6. (gefallen) Dieser Mantel _____ mir nicht.
7. (warten) Erika kommt immer spät. Ich _____ das letzte Mal lange auf sie _____.
8. (sein) Es ist sechs Uhr. Der Zug _____ bald hier _____.
9. (helfen) Warum _____ du ihm nicht?
10. (wissen) Köln liegt am Rhein. Das _____ ich nicht _____.

Der Bus steht da drüben. (Bad Homburg)　　　　　　　　　　　*Was kann man hier kaufen?*

III. **Supply the proper plural forms of all the nouns.**

   ❑ Kennst du (Junge)?
     Kennst du die Jungen?

    1. Die Verkäuferin zeigt ihr (Hemd, Bluse, Zeitung, Buch, Mantel).
    2. Wir fahren zu (Stadt, Haus, Café, Kino).
    3. Ich brauche die Karten für (Lehrer, Junge, Mädchen).
    4. Kaufst du (Heft, Karte, Hemd, Ball)?
    5. (Straßenbahn, Fahrrad, Bus, Zug) stehen da drüben.
    6. Die Besucher kommen aus (Bahnhof, Büro, Museum, Disko).

IV. **Supply the proper forms of the nouns followed by the dative or accusative prepositions. The singular or plural forms in parentheses are given in the nominative case.**

   ❑ Sprichst du mit (er) _____?
     Sprichst du mit ihm?

    1. Er kommt aus (die Schule) _____.
    2. Wir spielen gegen (euere Klasse) _____.

3. Warum geht ihr nicht ohne (ich) _____?
4. Er erzählt viel von (seine Reise) _____.
5. Nach (das Spiel) _____ können wir ins Café gehen.
6. Müßt ihr um (der Bahnhof) _____ fahren?
7. Sie wohnt bei (ihre Eltern) _____.
8. Hat er etwas Geld für (wir) _____?
9. Die Touristen gehen durch (das Museum) _____.
10. Spielst du gern mit (dein Bruder) _____?
11. Sie fahren zu (ihre Freunde) _____.
12. Außer (ich) _____ spielt auch Ursula Klavier.

V. **Provide the correct forms of the possessive adjectives in each sentence.**

1. Er geht mit (his girlfriend, her brother, my sister) _____ einkaufen.
2. Ich habe (my parents, his mother, our teacher,) _____ gefragt.
3. (Her blouse, his suit, my coat, your pair of shoes) _____ ist sehr teuer.
4. Wir spielen (our clarinet, your piano, her guitar) _____ sehr gern.
5. Wir essen bei (your uncle, my grandmother, their aunt, our brother) _____.
6. Kauf (your sisters, his girlfriends, my grandmother) _____ ein schönes Geschenk!

Zungenbrecher

Der Potsdamer Postkutscher putzt den Potsdamer Postkutschkasten.

(The Potsdam stagecoach driver is cleaning the Potsdam stagecoach.)

Foreign Influence in Germany

A first-time visitor arriving in Germany may be surprised to see many non-German words on store fronts, billboards and in the media. Foreigners have had a tremendous influence on the German economy during the last few decades. The Americans have had the greatest impact. The American love of fast food has found its way to Germany. Now you can satisfy a craving for hamburgers and french fries from fast-food franchises that are well known to American and German consumers alike. Well-known American soft drinks are also popular among Germans of all ages.

A variety of American products from breakfast cereals to different brands of gum can be found in supermarkets. When you get in line to pay for your items, you'll find the German checkout system is very similar to what you find in America. German shoppers used to shop daily for their food items. Now many shop less frequently. American-style jeans have been in fashion for years. Every German city advertises jeans in their stores.

In Deutschland wohnen viele Ausländer.

Italienisches Eis schmeckt immer gut.

Jugoslawen

Was bekommt man hier?

American rock stars dominate the music industry and air waves. Germans buy the latest hits on LP records. Lately CDs are gaining in popularity.

Computer technology is highly advanced. PCs share shelf space with more sophisticated computers in many stores. Germans have adored the influence of America's Wild West for a long time. Occasionally, American rodeos perform in German cities and towns to the delight of their audience. American movies have always been popular. They can be seen at nearly every German movie theater.

The French influence has long been evident in the German clothes. German buyers eagerly await the spring and fall fashion shows in Paris for that season's first look at the newest French fashions. When it comes to fashion and perfume, the Germans look to their style-conscious neighbor to the west to set the trends. Even accessories with a French accent are considered stylish by German standards.

If you have a taste for international food, you won't have to look for long. Italian cafés feature delicious ice creams, espressos, and rolls or sandwiches with different fillings. Germans don't have to travel to Italy for a

In einem Kaufhaus kann man Kleidungsstücke kaufen.

eine bekannte Firma aus Amerika

taste of authentic Italian-style pizza. An interest in Oriental food has been growing. And many German restaurants boast Greek culinary influences as well.

Foreign workers and their families make up about 4.5 million people — the largest minority in the Federal Republic. More than 60 percent have lived in Germany for 10 years and longer. More than two out of three foreign children have been born in the country. Turks, Yugoslavs, Italians, and Greeks make up the majority of foreign workers living in Germany.

In einem Fotogeschäft gibt es Kameras aus anderen Ländern.

Manchmal sieht man französischen Einfluß (influence).

Hier gibt es auch Süßigkeiten aus dem Ausland.

Vokabeln

ach oh
das **Akkordeon,-s** accordion
allein(e) alone
anfangen to begin, start
anrufen to call up
begleiten to accompany
die **Begleitung,-en** accompaniment
beiseite aside, apart
Spaß beiseite. Fun aside. Be serious.
die **Blockflöte,-n** recorder
die **Disko,-s** disco
Auf zur Disko! Let's go to the disco.
draußen outside
euer your (familiar plural)
die **Flöte,-n** flute

die **Frage,-n** question
die **Geige,-n** violin
ihr her, their
informieren to inform
klappen to go smoothly
Das klappt. That works out.
die **Klarinette,-n** clarinet
das **Klavier,-e** piano
klingeln to ring
an der Tür klingeln to ring the doorbell
kompliziert complicated
manchmal sometimes
das **Musikbuch,-er** music book
das **Musikinstrument,-e** musical instrument

der **Musiklehrer,-** music teacher
reinkommen to come inside
die **Stelle,-n** spot, place
sich **treffen** to meet
Treffen wir uns! Let's meet.
die **Trompete,-n** trumpet
trotzdem nevertheless, in spite of it
überzeugen to convince
unruhig restless
versuchen to try
wählen to select, dial (phone)
zusammen together

Teppiche (rugs) aus dem Orient sind bei den Deutschen sehr beliebt.

Rückblick

B

Ein Tag bei Schuhmanns

Familie Schuhmann wohnt in Fürstenfeldbruck, einer Stadt nicht weit von München entfernt. Herr und Frau Schuhmann haben einen Sohn, Christopher, und eine Tochter, Ulrike. Christopher ist 15 Jahre alt und geht auf eine Realschule. Seine Schwester, zwei Jahre älter, besucht ein Gymnasium.

Der Tag beginnt um halb sieben. Um diese Zeit stehen Herr und Frau Schuhmann auf°. Eine halbe Stunde später stehen Christopher und Ulrike auf. In der Küche deckt Frau Schuhmann den Tisch und bereitet das Frühstück° zu. Viertel nach sieben sitzen alle am Tisch und essen Frühstück. Was gibt's heute? Brot mit Butter, Marmelade, Milch und Kaffee.

Um halb acht geht Herr Schuhmann ins Büro. Sein Büro ist gleich in der Stadt. Deshalb kann er zu Fuß gehen. Etwas später verlassen Christopher und Ulrike das Haus. Christophers Schule ist ganz in der Nähe. Ulrike muß mit der S-Bahn° zur Schule fahren.

Frau Schuhmann arbeitet von neun bis ein Uhr bei der Post. Sie ist immer zu Hause, wenn Christopher und Ulrike aus der Schule kommen. Dann macht sie ihnen das Mittagessen°. Beide haben großen Hunger. Frau Schuhmann bringt auch bald das Essen. Es ist meistens warm. Heute gibt es Bratwurst, Kartoffeln° und Sauerkraut.

Nach dem Essen machen Ulrike und Christopher ihre Hausaufgaben°. Ulrike hat heute besonders viel zu tun. Sie muß einen Aufsatz° schreiben. Das ist nicht so leicht. Später ruft sie Maria, ihre Freundin, an. Sie kann ihr beim Aufsatz nicht helfen. Sie hat heute nachmittag° keine Zeit. Sie kann Ulrike nicht besuchen. Ulrike hat viele Kassetten. Sie hört gern Musik.

Christopher sitzt in seinem Zimmer. Er muß Matheaufgaben machen. Die Aufgaben sind heute sehr leicht. Deshalb geht es schnell. Dann spielt er gern Gitarre. Oft kommt Toni rüber. Dann fahren sie manchmal zum Tennisplatz und spielen Tennis.

Um sechs Uhr steht das Abendbrot auf dem Tisch. Meistens essen Schuhmanns Kalte Platte — Brot mit Butter, Wurst°, Käse° und Tomaten°. Dazu° trinken sie Tee° oder Milch. Frau Schuhmann stellt alles auf den Tisch.

Am Abend sitzen Herr und Frau Schuhmann im Wohnzimmer. Was gibt's denn heute im Fernsehen? Herr Schuhmann möchte die Nachrichten° im Ersten Programm sehen. Das interessiert Frau Schuhmann sehr wenig. Sie liest oft die Zeitung oder ein Buch. Manchmal gibt es im Fernsehen einen spannenden Film aus Amerika. Den möchte sie natürlich sehen.

Christopher geht heute zu Toni. Er bringt seine Briefmarken mit. Beide sammeln Briefmarken und haben ein paar hundert von vielen Ländern.

Maria kommt am Abend zu Ulrike rüber. Sie sitzen in Ulrikes Zimmer und sprechen über die Party am Freitag. Sie wird bei Anneliese, einer Freundin von Maria, stattfinden. Anneliese wohnt in einem großen Haus. Es kommen immer viele Jugendliche zu Anneliese. Es wird bestimmt wieder toll sein.

(*stehen...auf* get up, *Frühstück* breakfast, *S-Bahn* city train, *Mittagessen* lunch, *Kartoffeln* potatoes, *Hausaufgaben* homework, *Aufsatz* essay, *heute nachmittag* this afternoon, *Wurst* sausage, *Käse* cheese, *Tomaten* tomatoes, *dazu* with it, *Tee* tea, *Nachrichten* news)

Fragen

1. Wo liegt Fürstenfeldbruck?
2. Wie alt sind Christopher und Ulrike?
3. Um wieviel Uhr stehen alle auf?
4. Was essen sie zum Frühstück?
5. Geht Ulrike zu Fuß zur Schule?
6. Wo arbeitet Frau Schuhmann?
7. Wie viele Stunden arbeitet sie dort am Tag?
8. Was gibt es heute zum Mittagessen?
9. Was muß Ulrike nach der Schule machen?
10. Warum kann Maria Ulrike heute nachmittag nicht besuchen?
11. Wie sind Christophers Aufgaben heute?
12. Wohin fahren Christopher und Toni?
13. Wann essen Schuhmanns Abendbrot?
14. Was machen Herr und Frau Schuhmann nach dem Abendbrot?
15. Was sammeln Christopher und Toni?
16. Was machen Ulrike und ihre Freundin Maria?

Übungen

1. **Provide an appropriate response in German. Be sure the whole conversation ties together and becomes meaningful.**

   A: Heute habe ich wirklich Lust, an den See zu fahren.
   B: Ich habe heute leider keine Zeit.
   A: _____
   B: Ich muß mit meinen Eltern zum Bahnhof fahren.
   A: _____
   B: Mein Onkel und meine Tante.
   A: _____
   B: Aus Stuttgart.
   A: _____
   B: Ungefähr drei Wochen.

2. **Form complete sentences using first the future and then the present perfect tense.**

   ❑ Film / beginnen / acht Uhr
   Der Film wird um acht Uhr beginnen.
   Der Film hat um acht Uhr begonnen.

   1. Jungen / spielen / Montag / Tennis
   2. Familie Holz / fahren / Sommer / Österreich
   3. Ich / kaufen / Hose / und / Hemd
   4. Sprechen / du / Deutsch / oder / Englisch
   5. Wir / Spiel / gewinnen
   6. Sehen / ihr / Film / aus / Deutschland
   7. Gäste / spät / nach Hause / gehen

3. *Was kannst du über diese Wörter schreiben?* **Describe each word with one complete sentence.** *Auf deutsch bitte!*

   ❑ das Kleid
   Das ist ein Kleidungsstück.

   1. der Zug
   2. der Mittwoch
   3. das Kino
   4. die Stadt
   5. das Klavier
   6. das Brot
   7. das Geld
   8. der Mund
   9. die Lehrerin
   10. der Apfelsaft

4. *Ergänze diese Sätze!* Supply the correct form of the possessive adjective indicated.

1. Hast du (my) _____ Bruder gesehen?
2. Wo habt ihr (our) _____ Karten gekauft?
3. Ich kann (his) _____ Schwester nicht verstehen.
4. Herr Schubert wird (his) _____ Schülern (their) _____ Bücher geben.
5. Wohin ist (your) _____ Schwester gefahren, Herr Bäumler?
6. Sie kommt mit (her) _____ Eltern nach Europa.
7. Tanja bekommt das Geschenk von (my) _____ Eltern.
8. Ich habe (your) _____ Onkel schon lange nicht gesehen, Erika.
9. Habt ihr von (your) _____ Freunden etwas gehört?
10. Was machen Sie denn nach (your) _____ Reise?
11. Haben Sie mit (my) _____ Mutter gesprochen?
12. Wolfgang hat (his) _____ Freund nichts von der Party gesagt.

5. **Welche Wörter passen hier zusammen?**

Körperteil	Kleidungsstück	Kino	Haus
Restaurant	Verkehrsmittel	Café	Sport
Jahreszeit	Musikinstrument	Monat	Tag

1. Herbst
2. Tischtennis
3. Essen
4. Zimmer
5. Blockflöte
6. Straßenbahn
7. Bluse
8. Eis
9. Film
10. Mittwoch
11. Fuß
12. August

Was ist eine Straßenbahn? (Bern)

Auf dem Weg in die Stadt

Frau Sender: Guten Tag, Frau Böll. Wohin gehen Sie denn so
früh am Morgen?

Frau Böll: Guten Tag, Frau Sender. Ich will in die Stadt
gehen und ein Geschenk für meinen Mann°
kaufen. Er hat morgen Geburtstag.

Frau Sender: Fahren Sie mit der Straßenbahn?

Frau Böll: Nein, ich gehe zu Fuß. Es dauert nur eine halbe
Stunde, bis ich in der Stadt bin.

Frau Sender: Was kaufen Sie Ihrem Mann denn?

Frau Böll: Das weiß ich noch nicht genau. Vielleicht ein
Hemd und eine Krawatte oder ein Buch.

Frau Sender: Das ist eine gute Idee. Mein Bruder hat nächste
Woche Geburtstag. Er liest auch sehr gern Bücher.

Frau Böll: Wollen Sie mitkommen?

Frau Sender: Nein, heute habe ich leider keine Zeit.

(*Mann* husband, man)

auf dem Weg in die Stadt (Würzburg)   Fährt Frau Böll mit der Straßenbahn? (Würzburg)

Was paßt hier?

1. Frau Böll will
2. Frau Bölls Mann hat
3. Frau Böll fährt
4. Frau Sender hat
5. Frau Senders Bruder hat
6. Frau Böll kauft
7. Frau Sender will
8. Frau Senders Bruder liest

a. nicht in die Stadt
mitkommen
b. heute keine Zeit
c. gern Bücher
d. in die Stadt gehen
e. nächste Woche
Geburtstag
f. morgen Geburtstag
g. vielleicht eine Krawatte
h. nicht mit der Straßenbahn

Wie kommen sie in die Stadt? (Neuß)   *Diese Stadt gefällt mir besonders gut. (Lüneburg)*

Beantworte diese Fragen!

1. Was will Frau Böll für ihren Mann kaufen?
2. Warum will Frau Böll etwas kaufen?
3. Wie kommt Frau Böll in die Stadt?
4. Was möchte Frau Sender kaufen?
5. Warum kann Frau Sender heute nicht mit Frau Böll in die Stadt gehen?

6. **Change the following sentences to the present perfect tense.**

1. Herr Schmidt spricht gut Deutsch.
2. Ich werde ein paar CDs spielen.
3. Seine Eltern sind nicht zu Hause.
4. Werden sie heute nach Köln kommen?
5. Wir besuchen unsere Tante.
6. Habt ihr die Karten?
7. Wie lange dauert die Reise?
8. Wo bleibt er denn nur?
9. Ich finde das Buch sehr schwer.
10. Warum fragst du ihn nicht?

7. **Supply the proper present tense of the verbs provided in parentheses.**

❐ (sprechen) _____ du Deutsch?
Sprichst du Deutsch?

1. (geben) _____ er dir sein Fahrrad?
2. (lesen) Paul _____ das Buch. Es ist toll.
3. (laufen) Der Film _____ schon lange im Kino.
4. (fahren) Familie Meier _____ in die Schweiz.
5. (sehen) _____ du das Flugzeug?
6. (sprechen) _____ Sie Deutsch?
7. (essen) Was _____ ihr denn?
8. (gefallen) Diese Stadt _____ mir besonders gut.

8. *Welche Wörter passen am besten in diesen Sätzen?* Supply the proper form of the selected verb.

❒ Meine Mutter ＿＿＿＿ heute einen Kuchen. (arbeiten, kommen, backen)
Meine Mutter bäckt heute einen Kuchen.

1. Sie ＿＿＿＿ zu Fuß in die Stadt. (fahren, gehen, sehen)
2. Ich möchte gern diesen Film ＿＿＿＿. (laufen, sehen, spielen)
3. Willst du die Karten ＿＿＿＿? (essen, sprechen, kaufen)
4. Wir können den Beamten nicht ＿＿＿＿. (verstehen, parken, kommen)
5. ＿＿＿＿ wir doch am Bahnhof! (holen, liegen, warten)
6. Die Touristen ＿＿＿＿ im Sommer gern die Stadt München. (wandern, besuchen, laufen)
7. In Mainz müssen wir in einen anderen Zug ＿＿＿＿. (umsteigen, anrufen, mitkommen)
8. Meine Freundin wird das Kleid ＿＿＿＿. (trinken, anprobieren, einsteigen)
9. Wir wollen meinen Onkel ＿＿＿＿. (glauben, stellen, besuchen)
10. Möchtest du in der Disko ＿＿＿＿? (tanzen, gratulieren, brauchen)

Welche Farben haben die Sweatshirts?

Hier gibt es Schuhe in allen Größen. (Wiesbaden)

Nützliche Ausdrücke

Here are some phrases that are particularly helpful when buying clothing items:

Bitte sehr?	May I help you?
Ich möchte ein Paar Schuhe, Größe 41, bitte.	I would like a pair of shoes, size 9, please.
Welche Größe haben Sie?	Which size do you wear?
Welche Farbe?	Which color?

Wollen Sie den Mantel anprobieren?	Do you wish to try the coat on?
Gehen Sie bitte in die Kabine.	Please go to the fitting room.
Die Jeans sind zu eng.	The jeans are too tight.
Was kostet das?	What does it cost?

Wie viele Kilometer sind es nach München?

Wieviel kostet ein Kilo Spare-Ribs?

Was kann man hier kaufen?

Cultural Notes

Metric Measurements

The metric system is used in almost all countries of the world . When traveling to Europe, the following measurements might come in handy to know.

German Metric		U.S.
1	Gramm (g)	0.035 ounce
28	Gramm	1 ounce
1	Pfund (Pfd)	1.1 pounds
1	Kilogramm or Kilo (kg)	2.2 pounds
1	Zentimeter (cm)	0.3937 inch
2,54	Zentimeter	1 inch
1	Meter (m)	3.281 feet
1609,3	Meter	1 mile
1	Kilometer (km)	1,094 yards
1	Liter (l)	2.113 pints

Metric Units		
1	Pfund	500 Gramm
2	Pfund	1 Kilogramm or 1,000 Gramm
1	Meter	100 Zentimeter
1,000	Meter	1 Kilometer

Thermometer Readings

German thermometers use the centigrade (Celsius) scale. To convert Fahrenheit to centigrade, subtract 32, then multiply by 5 and divide by 9. To convert centigrade to Fahrenheit, multiply by 9, divide by 5 and add 32. The chart below gives some sample readings with the conversion.

Wie warm ist es heute?

C°	F°
38	100.4
25	77
10	50
0	32
-15	5
-25	-13

Wieviel Pfund Brot willst du kaufen?

Wieviel Gramm bekommt man für DM 1,95?

Die Stadt Frankfurt

Die Touristen kommen in Hamburg an.

Origin of Town Names

Many town and city names in Germany have suffixes that can easily identify their origin. Once you know a little about the origin, you may look at these places with different eyes. Many town names go back to the Romans or the Germanic tribes.

The ending syllable *-furt* (as in *Frankfurt*) means that the town originated at a ford, where the river could be crossed by wading or with a wagon.

Some German town names end or begin with *reuth, reute, rode,* or *rath* (as *Bayreuth, Wernigerode* or *Benrath*). These towns originated in a wooded area that had to be cleared of trees and stumps (*roden*) before houses could be built and fields could be made arable.

Many towns in southern and western Germany originated as Roman settlements in the earliest centuries A.D. The end syllable *-kastel* (as in *Bernkastel*) goes back to the Latin "castellum" (castle, fortified camp).

If a name ends with *-burg* (as *Hamburg*), this shows that the town grew near or around a *Burg*, a castle.

Towns originating around abbeys, convents, etc., often still carry the word *Kloster* (cloister) or *Mönch* (monk) in their names (*Klosterreichenbach, München*).

Town names ending with *-ingen* (*Sigmaringen*) usually lie in Swabia, those with *-ing* (*Dingolfing*) in Bavaria. The name *Sigmaringen* tells that the settlement was founded by a Teuton called Sigmar and his kin.

English Equivalents of Dialogs and Narratives

The following material represents the English version to the dialogs and narratives that appear at the beginning of Lessons 1 through 10. They are intended to assist you in clarifying the meaning. Keep in mind that these equivalents are not literal translations.

Lektion 1 — Where do you live?

Holger:	Hello, Claudia. How are you?
Claudia:	Quite well.
Holger:	What are you doing now?
Claudia:	I'm going home.
Holger:	So early?
Claudia:	It's already late.

Christine:	Where do you live?
Silke:	Downtown. And you?
Christine:	Not far from here.
Silke:	And where exactly?
Christine:	Near the park.
Silke:	Oh, how nice!

Alex:	Hello, Thomas.
Thomas:	Where is your girlfriend?
Alex:	Gabi?
Thomas:	Is there another one?
Alex:	Maybe.

Lektion 2 — At home

(on the phone)

Tina:	Tina Schiller.
Steffie:	Hello, Tina. This is Steffie. Do you have time?
Tina:	Why are you asking?
Steffie:	Rolf is coming at seven. He's bringing many cassettes along.
Tina:	Good. I'll come, too.
Steffie:	OK, until then.

(at Steffie's)

Rolf:	I have cassettes and CDs.
Steffie:	We prefer to listen to cassettes.
Rolf:	Say, the rock music here is great.
Steffie:	The Wildcat Band is better.
Rolf:	Well, why don't you play it.
Steffie:	Just a moment. Tina is here.

(later)

Tina:	It's already nine o'clock. I have to go home.
Rolf:	Me too.

Steffie:	We're taking a test tomorrow.
Tina:	Don't worry. It's easy.
Steffie:	You always say that.
Rolf:	She is just smart.

Lektion 3 — Going to school

Jens:	Do you know Jürgen?
Sven:	Is he new here?
Jens:	Yes, he is from Köln. Quite athletic and also intelligent.
Sven:	You know a lot.

Sven:	The exercises are quite hard again.
Jens:	For English or Math?
Sven:	The English exercises. Here on page 89.
Jens:	But English is easy.
Sven:	Well, you're also a genius.

Jens:	It's already five to eight. Let's hurry.
Sven:	Take it easy. Mr. Erhard is never on time.
Jens:	But today we're taking a test.
Sven:	That's right. Then, lets' go!

Lektion 4 — Let's go to the movie theater!

(on the phone)

Peter:	What are you doing today?
Jens:	I would like to go to a movie.
Peter:	Good idea. What's playing at the Union Theater?
Jens:	*Frantic*, a movie from America. Really super.
Peter:	When does the movie start?
Jens:	Just a moment. Here it is. At 3:30.
Peter:	I'll come over right away.
Jens:	OK. Hurry up!

(at the movie theater)

Gerd:	Hello, Peter and Jens.
Sven:	Where are you going?
Jens:	To a movie. Why don't you come along.
Gerd:	The tickets are nine marks. I don't have enough money.
Jens:	That doesn't matter. I have enough. Let's go!

(in the movie theater)

Jens:	Four tickets, please.
Saleslady:	That comes to 36 marks.
Jens:	Here are 40.
Saleslady:	And four marks back. Hurry! The movie is already playing.

(later)

Peter:	The movie is fantastic. What do you think, Jens?
Jens:	Yes, it's quite thrilling.
Sven:	For me it's a little boring.
Gerd:	You're much too critical. I would like to go again.

English Equivalents

Lektion 5 — Ice cream, please.

(on the way)

Marc:	Should we have some ice cream?
Gabi:	Good idea.
Ali:	I'll come along too.
Gabi:	Why don't we go to Café Rialto.
Marc:	Yes, they have Italian ice cream.
Ali:	That tastes especially good.

(in front of the café)

Marc:	The selection here is always large.
Ali:	But, it's not cheap. Oh, I don't have enough money.
Marc:	It doesn't matter. I can lend you a few marks.
Ali:	It's already 3:30.
Gabi:	So what? Heike can wait.
Marc:	I think so, too.
Ali:	Well, whatever you think. Then, let's go!

(in the café)

Gabi:	I would like a milk shake.
Ali:	And a *Hawaiibecher* (kind of ice cream sundae) for me.
Waiter:	May I help you?
Marc:	Please bring us a milk shake, a *Hawaiibecher* and some chocolate ice cream with whipped cream.
Waiter:	I'll bring it right away. (later) Here you are. I hope you enjoy it.

(later)

Ali:	What are you going to do later?
Marc:	Well, you're going to Heike's. Gabi, why don't you come over.
Gabi:	OK, I'm not planning anything.
Marc:	There's a quiz show on TV today.
Gabi:	Great! Then I'll come for sure.
Ali:	Mmmm, the ice cream tastes very good.
Marc:	The check, please.
Gabi:	Do you ever eat fast.

Lektion 6 — Who's birthday is it?

Two weeks from Wednesday is a special day for Sabine. On this day, she has a birthday. Sabine will be 15. For her birthday, she would like to invite a few boyfriends and girlfriends. She is writing the invitations today. Uschi, Sabine's best girlfriend, receives the invitation the next day. She will come for sure.

Finally, the day is here. Sabine's grandma bakes a cake already in the morning. She decorates it beautifully. Then, she sets the table and places the cake on the table in the living room. The guests are coming at four o'clock.

Uschi:	Happy birthday, Sabine!
Anne:	Finally you're fifteen.

Uschi:	Here, a present for you.
Sabine:	Many thanks.
Anne:	I hope you like my present.
Sabine:	I'm sure. Let's eat. We can sit down here.
Anne:	Mmmm, this cake tastes delicious.
Uschi:	Cheers! This lemonade quenches your thirst.
Sabine:	There is a cold buffet on the table. You can take what you like.
Anne:	Your grandma always bakes so well.
Sabine:	Say, Uschi, come here quickly. Otherwise everything will be gone.
Uschi:	Don't worry. I'll get something.

After the meal they sit in the living room. Anne plays guitar and the young people sing a few folk songs. Later, they play cards. It's a lot of fun. At about seven they all leave the house. A few ride with their bikes, others walk home. Sabine thanks her friends for the presents. What a beautiful birthday!

Lektion 7 — At the train station

(in front of the station)

Manfred:	It's almost eleven o'clock.
Willi:	That's not quite correct. Look at the clock there. It's already three minutes after eleven.
Manfred:	My watch is slow again.
Willi:	Come, let's look at the schedule.
Manfred:	Here it is. From Bremen to Freiburg. The train leaves at 11:14 A.M.
Willi:	We won't make that one. Let's go with the Intercity at 12:11 P.M. We'll transfer in Hannover and arrive in Freiburg at 7:00 P.M.

(in the station)

Willi:	There is the traveler's information.
Manfred:	Let's go inside.
Willi:	It says on the monitor here whether the trains are departing on time.
Manfred:	Yes, the Intercity is departing on time.
Willi:	How much do we have to spend for the tickets?
Manfred:	I don't know exactly. Why don't we ask. Two tickets to Freiburg, please.
Official:	Round trip?
Willi:	One-way and second class, please.

(at the newspaper stand)

Manfred:	The trip will take almost seven hours.
Willi:	I'll buy a newspaper.
Manfred:	OK, good; and I'll buy a magazine. I'll pay for that.
Saleslady:	May I help you?
Manfred:	This newspaper and the magazine.
Saleslady:	That comes to 7.50.

Manfred:	Here are eight marks.
Saleslady:	And fifty pfennigs back.

(on the platform)

Willi:	There is the train already.
Manfred:	Why don't we get in.
Willi:	Dennis and Klaus won't come to Freiburg until three days from now.
Manfred:	Yes, but they're coming by car. Then we'll drive back together.
Willi:	Look, the official is giving the signal.
Manfred:	Here, we go finally.

Lektion 8 — In the department store

(in front of the department store)

Tanja:	The sweater there is chic.
Britta:	Don't you have many already?
Tanja:	But the colors are too dark.
Karin:	I need a sweater too.
Tanja:	Maybe the selection is good in the department store .
Britta:	Let's not stand here at the entrance.
Karin:	That's true. Let's go inside.

(in the department store)

Tanja:	This sweater looks good on you, Karin.
Karin:	No, it's much too large.
Britta:	And what do you think of this sweater here?
Karin:	Not bad.
Tanja:	I like the white sweater there.
Britta:	Quite reasonable.
Tanja:	And it fits me, too.
Britta:	Well, then the decision is simple.
Tanja:	Let's go to the cash register.
Karin:	You're lucky again. I can never find anything.
Tanja:	You're just too choosy.
Saleslady:	A beautiful sweater. So, that's 18 marks.
Tanja:	Here you are.
Saleslady:	And two marks back.
Britta:	Let's get out of the department store fast.
Karin:	Are you worried that I'm going to buy something?
Britta:	No, I have to go to the café. My parents are waiting there.

Lektion 9 — At the table tennis tournament

What's going on in Leipzig today? A table tennis tournament is taking place in the sports hall. The best players in town have come to the sports hall. At 16 tables they are showing what they can do. Klaus and Sascha have also come here.

Klaus:	Sascha, did you hear our names?

Sascha:	Yes, the announcer said we're supposed to go to table 11.
Klaus:	Let's practice a bit first.
Sascha:	I agree. "Practice makes perfect."
Klaus:	You're once again in good form.
Sascha:	But not quite as good as you. Well, let's go.

Klaus and Sascha play a game. Klaus is really good today. He wins against Sascha. Sascha congratulates Klaus. Then Sascha goes to a small table and announces the result to the judges.

Sascha:	If you continue playing like this, you'll have a good chance.
Klaus:	Today was not your day.
Sascha:	You're right. Last time I beat you.
Klaus:	Unfortunately, we played in the same group.
Sascha:	You're in the fifth round now.
Klaus:	There are still eight players until the final game.
Sascha:	I think you can make it.
Klaus:	I hope so.
Sascha:	The announcer called your name. Good luck, Klaus.

Lektion 10 — Let's make music!

Sonja likes to come to Bärbel's house. Both are good friends and are in the same class in school. Sonja rings the bell at the door. Bärbel is there and opens the door right away.

Bärbel:	Oh, it's you. I've already practiced the violin.
Sonja:	Without me? You need my accompaniment.
Bärbel:	Nevertheless, I have to practice a little alone.
Sonja:	Don't you think it works better together?
Bärbel:	I think so. Come inside. We won't make any music here outside.
Sonja:	Well, you're right. Let's play together inside.

Both are going into the living room and look at a few music books. Bärbel has been playing the piano many years already. That's why she has a large selection of books.

Sonja:	Let's play this piece.
Bärbel:	That's too complicated. I'll have to practice first.
Sonja:	You're being much too choosy again.
Bärbel:	Here, a piece by Mozart. You can accompany me well.
Sonja:	Why don't we try it.
Bärbel:	Sit down, please.

(at the piano)

Bärbel:	Do we start from here?
Sonja:	In the middle? Then we'll lose the rhythm completely.
Bärbel:	Well, do you have any at all?
Sonja:	Now, joking aside.
Bärbel:	From here it's going to go better for sure.
Sonja:	OK, let's begin now.

English Equivalents

Personal Pronouns

SINGULAR	Nominative	Accusative	Dative
1st person	ich	mich	mir
2nd person	du	dich	dir
3rd person	er sie es	ihn sie es	ihm ihr ihm
PLURAL			
1st person	wir	uns	uns
2nd person	ihr	euch	euch
3rd person	sie	sie	ihnen
formal form (plural or singular)	Sie	Sie	Ihnen

Definite Article

	Singular			Plural
	Masculine	Feminine	Neuter	
Nominative	der	die	das	die
Accusative	den	die	das	die
Dative	dem	der	dem	den

Question Words: *Wer? Was?*

Nominative	wer	was
Accusative	wen	was
Dative	wem	

Grammar

Indefinite Article

	Singular			Plural
	Masculine	Feminine	Neuter	
Nominative	ein	eine	ein	keine
Accusative	einen	eine	ein	keine
Dative	einem	einer	einem	keinen

Regular Verb Forms — Present Tense

	gehen	finden	heißen
ich	gehe	finde	heiße
du	gehst	findest	heißt
er, sie, es	geht	findet	heißen
wir	gehen	finden	heißen
ihr	geht	findet	heißt
sie, Sie	gehen	finden	heißen

Irregular Verb Forms — Present Tense

	haben	sein	wissen
ich	habe	bin	weiß
du	hast	bist	weißt
er, sie, es	hat	ist	weiß
wir	haben	sind	wissen
ihr	habt	seid	wißt
sie, Sie	haben	sind	wissen

Command Forms

Familiar (singular)	Geh!	Warte!	Sei!	Hab!
Familiar (plural)	Geht!	Wartet!	Seid!	Habt!
Formal (singular/plural)	Gehen Sie!	Warten Sie!	Seien Sie!	Haben Sie!
Wir-form (Let's...)	Gehen wir!	Warten wir!	Seien wir!	Haben wir!

Plural of Nouns

	Singular	Plural
no change or add umlaut	das Zimmer die Mutter	die Zimmer die Mütter
add -n, -en, or -nen	die Ecke der Herr die Freundin	die Ecken die Herren die Freundinnen
add -e or ⸚e	der Tag die Stadt	die Tage die Städte
add ⸚er	das Buch das Fach	die Bücher die Fächer
add -s (adopted foreign words)	das Café das Büro	die Cafés die Büros

Inverted Word Order

1. Formation of questions beginning with the verb
   Spielst du heute Fußball?
2. Formation of questions beginning with a question word
   Wohin gehen Sie heute nachmittag?
3. Command forms
   Hab keine Angst!
   Lauft schnell!
   Passen Sie auf!
   Gehen wir!

Negation

Verbs (*nicht*) Kommen Sie nicht zu uns?

Nouns (*kein*) Ich habe keine Karte.

Modal Auxiliaries

	dürfen	können	mögen	müssen	sollen	wollen
ich	darf	kann	mag	muß	soll	will
du	darfst	kannst	magst	mußt	sollst	willst
er, sie, es	darf	kann	mag	muß	soll	will
wir	dürfen	können	mögen	müssen	sollen	wollen
ihr	dürft	könnt	mögt	müßt	sollt	wollt
sie, Sie	dürfen	können	mögen	müssen	sollen	wollen

Future tense (*werden* + infinitive)

ich	werde
du	wirst
er, sie, es	wird
wir	werden
ihr	werdet
sie, Sie	werden

Sie werden nächstes Jahr nach Deutschland fahren.
Wirst du morgen ins Kino gehen?

Verbs with Stem Vowel Change (2nd & 3rd person singular only)

	a to ä	*e to i*	*e to ie*
ich	fahre	spreche	sehe
du	fährst	sprichst	siehst
er, sie, es	fährt	spricht	sieht
wir	fahren	sprechen	sehen
ihr	fahrt	sprecht	seht
sie, Sie	fahren	sprechen	sehen

Prepositions

Dative	Accusative	Contraction
aus	durch	durch das = durchs
außer	für	für das = fürs
bei	gegen	bei dem = beim
mit	ohne	—
nach	um	um das = ums
seit		—
von		von dem = vom
zu		zu dem = zum/zu der = zur

Verbs Followed by Dative Case

helfen   antworten   gefallen   passen   glauben

Gabi hilft ihrer Mutter.

Der Anzug gefällt mir.

The verb *glauben* may take either the dative or accusative. If used with a person, the dative follows *(Ich glaube ihm)*. If used with an object, the accusative is used *(Ich glaube das nicht)*.

Possessive Adjectives

	Singular			Plural
	Masculine	**Feminine**	**Neuter**	
Nominative	mein	meine	mein	meine
Accusative	meinen	meine	mein	meine
Dative	meinem	meiner	meinem	meinen

The endings of possessive adjectives are the same as those of the indefinite article (ein-words). Possessive adjectives are *mein, dein, sein, ihr, sein, unser, euer, ihr, Ihr.*

Comparison of Adjectives and Adverbs

Adjective/Adverb	schnell	warm	gut	hoch
Comparative	schneller	wärmer	besser	höher
Superlative	schnellst-	wärmst-	best-	höchst-

Numbers

0 = null	11 = elf	22 = zweiundzwanzig
1 = eins	12 = zwölf	30 = dreißig
2 = zwei	13 = dreizehn	40 = vierzig
3 = drei	14 = vierzehn	50 = fünfzig
4 = vier	15 = fünfzehn	60 = sechzig
5 = fünf	16 = sechzehn	70 = siebzig
6 = sechs	17 = siebzehn	80 = achtzig
7 = sieben	18 = achtzehn	90 = neunzig
8 = acht	19 = neunzehn	100 = einhundert
9 = neun	20 = zwanzig	101 = hunderteins
10 = zehn	21 = einundzwanzig	

Time

1:00   Es ist ein Uhr.

2:00   Es ist zwei Uhr.

3:30   Es ist halb vier Uhr.

10:15   Es ist Viertel nach zehn.

11:45   Es ist Viertel vor zwölf.

5:10   Es ist zehn Minuten nach fünf.

7:58   Es ist zwei Minuten vor acht.

Irregular Verbs — Present Perfect Tense (Past Participle)

The following list contains all the irregular verbs used in *Deutsch Aktuell 1*. Verbs with separable or inseparable prefixes are not included when the basic verb form has been introduced (Example: *kommen, ankommen*). If the basic verb has not been introduced, then the verb is included with its prefix. Verbs with stem vowel changes have also been indicated.

Infinitive	Stem Vowel Change	Past Participle	Meaning
abbiegen		abgebogen	to turn (to)
anfangen	fängt an	angefangen	to begin, start
anrufen		angerufen	to call (phone)
beginnen		begonnen	to begin
bekommen		bekommen	to get
bleiben		ist geblieben	to stay, remain
bringen		gebracht	to bring
einladen	lädt ein	eingeladen	to invite
einsteigen		eingestiegen	to get in, board
essen	ißt	gegessen	to eat
fahren	fährt	ist gefahren	to drive, to
finden		gefunden	to find
fließen		ist geflossen	to flow, run
geben	gibt	gegeben	to give
gefallen	gefällt	gefallen	to like
gehen		ist gegangen	to go, walk
gewinnen		gewonnen	to win
haben	hat	gehabt	to have
heißen		geheißen	to be called
helfen	hilft	geholfen	to help

Infinitive	Stem Vowel Change	Past Participle	Meaning
kennen		gekannt	to know (a person)
kommen		ist gekommen	to come
laufen	läuft	ist gelaufen	to run, walk
leihen		geliehen	to loan, lend
lesen	liest	gelesen	to read
liegen		gelegen	to lie
nehmen	nimmt	genommen	to take
scheinen		geschienen	to shine
schlagen	schlägt	geschlagen	to beat, hit
schreiben		geschrieben	to write
schwimmen		ist geschwommen	to swim
sehen	sieht	gesehen	to see
sein	ist	ist gewesen	to be
singen		gesungen	to sing
sitzen		gesessen	to sit
sprechen	spricht	gesprochen	to speak, talk
stehen		gestanden	to stand
tragen	trägt	getragen	to carry
treffen	trifft	getroffen	to meet
treiben		getrieben	to do (sports)
trinken		getrunken	to drink
tun		getan	to do
umziehen		umgezogen	to change clothes
verlassen	verläßt	verlassen	to leave
wissen	weiß	gewußt	to know

Vocabulary

All the words introduced in *Deutsch: Aktuell 1* have been summarized in this section. The numbers or letters following the meaning of individual words or phrases indicate the particular lesson in which they appear for the first time. The letters *A, B* and *E* are for Review Lessons A and B and for the introductory lesson entitled *Einführung*. In cases in which there is more than one meaning for a word or phrase and it has appeared in different lessons, both lesson numbers are listed. (Example: *gegen* about, around 3; against 7) Nouns have been listed with their respective articles and plural forms. Words preceded by an asterisk (*) are passive and appear in the margin of the *Land und Leute* reading sections. All other words are considered active and used frequently throughout the text.

A

abbiegen to turn (to) 7
der **Abend,-e** evening 6; *am Abend* in the evening 6
das **Abendbrot** supper 6
aber but 2
abfahren to depart, leave 7
ach oh 10
acht eight E
achtzehn eighteen E
das **Akkordeon,-s** accordion 10
alle all, everyone 4
allein(e) alone 10
alles all, everything 3
*die **Alpen** Alps 5
als than 5; *mehr als* more than 5
alt old E
Amerika America 4
an at,on 2; *am* (or: *an dem*) at the, on the 2
*das **Andenken,-** souvenir 7
ander(e) other, different 1
anfangen to begin, start 10
die **Angst,-e** fear 2; *(Hab) Keine Angst!* Don't worry! Don't be afraid! 2
anhaben to have on, wear 8
ankommen to arrive 7
anprobieren to try on 8
anrufen to call up 10

der **Ansager,-** announcer 9
sich **ansehen** to look at 7
die **Ansichtskarte,-n** picture postcard 7
antworten to answer 8
der **Anzug,-e** suit 8
der **Apfelsaft** apple juice 5
der **April** April 4
die **Arbeit,-en** work, test 2; *eine Arbeit schreiben* to take a test 2
arbeiten to work 6
der **Arm,-e** arm 9
auch also, too 1
auf on, to 3
die **Aufgabe,-n** problem, exercise, assignment 3
aufgeregt excited 4
aufhaben to have homework to do 3
aufmachen to open 4
der **Aufsatz,-e** essay, composition B
aufschlagen to serve (tennis) 9
aufsetzen to put on 8
aufstehen to get up B
die **Auge,-n** eye 9
der **August** August 4
aus from, out of, out 3
der **Ausflug,-e** excursion 7; *einen Ausflug machen* to go on an excursion 7
*der **Ausflugsort,-e** excursion area 9

ausgeben to spend 7
ausgezeichnet excellent 1
der **Ausländer,-** foreigner A
ausprobieren to try (out) 9
ausreichend sufficient 3
aussehen to look, appear 8
ausverkauft sold out 4
die **Auswahl** selection, choice 5
außer besides, except 8
das **Auto,-s** car 6

B

backen to bake 6
das **Bad,-er** bathroom 6
der **Bahnhof,-e** (train) station 7
bald soon 2
der **Ball,-e** ball 9
die **Band,-s** band 4
die **Bank,-en** bank 7
die **Bank,-e** bench 7
bar cash 8; *bar bezahlen* to pay cash 8
der **Basketball,-e** basketball 9
der **Beamte,-n** official (male) 7
die **Beamtin,-nen** official (female) 7
sich **beeilen** to hurry 4; *Beeil dich!* Hurry (up)! (singular) 4; *Beeilt*

euch! Hurry (up)! (plural) *4*

befriedigend satisfactory *3*

beginnen to begin *4*

begleiten to accompany *10*

die **Begleitung,-en** accompaniment *10*

begrüßen to greet *8*

bei at, near *1* with *B*; *beim Park* near the park *1*

beide both *4*

das **Bein,-e** leg *9*

beiseite aside, apart *10*; *Spaß beiseite.* Fun aside. Be serious. *10*

*das **Beispiel,-e** example *9*; *zum Beispiel* for example *9*

bekannt well-known *4*

bekanntgeben to announce *9*

bekommen to get, receive *3*

* **Belgien** Belgium *4*

* **beliebt** popular *5*

*der **Berg,-e** mountain *5*

* **bergig** mountainous *9*

besonders especially, special *3*

besser better *2*

best- best *6*

bestaunen to marvel at *7*

bestellen to order *8*

bestimmt definitely, for sure *2*

* **besuchen** to visit *5*

*der **Besucher,-** visitor *7*

bezahlen to pay *8*; *bar bezahlen* to pay cash *8*

* **bilden** to form *9*

*der **Bildschirm,-e** monitor, telescreen *7*

billig inexpensive, cheap *2*

die **Biologie** biology *3*

bis until *2*

bitte please *4*; *Bitte sehr.* Here you are. *5*; *Bitte?* May I help you? *5*

blau blue *8*

bleiben to stay, remain *7*

der **Bleistift,-e** pencil *3*

die **Blockflöte,-n** recorder *10*

die **Bluse,-n** blouse *8*

*der **Bodensee** Lake Constance *9*

das **Boot,-e** boat *7*

die **Bratwurst,-̈e** bratwurst *B*

brauchen to need *6*

braun brown *8*

breit wide *7*

die **Briefmarke,-n** stamp *A*

die **Brille,-n** glasses *8*

bringen to bring *5*

das **Brot,-e** bread *6*

der **Bruder,-̈** brother *6*

das **Buch,-̈er** book *3*

das **Büfett,-s** buffet *6*

*das **Bundesland,-̈er** Federal State *5*

*die **Bundesrepublik Deutschland** Federal Republic (of Germany) *3*

*die **Bundesstraße,-n** Federal Highway *7*

bunt colorful *8*

das **Büro,-s** office *6*

der **Bus,-se** bus *7*

die **Butter** butter *B*

C

das **Café,-s** café *7*

die **CD,-s** CD, compact disk *2*

die **Chance,-n** chance *9*

die **Chemie** chemistry *3*

die **Cola,-s** cola *5*

der **Computer,-** computer *3*

D

da there *1*; *da drüben* over there *1*

dafür for it *7*

* **Dänemark** Denmark *4*

der **Dank** thanks *6*; *Vielen Dank.* Many thanks. *6*

dann then *2*

das that *E*; *das* the *2*

* **daß** that *5*

dauern to take, last *A*

dazu with it *B*

decken to cover *6*; *den Tisch decken* to set the table *6*

dein your *1*

dekorieren to decorate *6*

denn used for emphasis *2*

der the *2*

derselbe the same *9*

deshalb therefore *9*

das **Deutsch** German *3*

*die **Deutsche Demokratische Republik** German Democratic Republic *3*

der **Dezember** December *4*

dich (form of **du**) you *3*

die the *2*

der **Dienstag,-e** Tuesday *2*

dieser this *3*; *diese* (form of *dieser*) this *3*

* **direkt** direct, straight *9*

der **Diskjockey,-s** disc jockey, DJ *5*

die **Disko,-s** disco *10*; *Auf zur Disko!* Let's go to the disco. *10*

doch used for emphasis *3*

der **Dom,-e** cathedral *7*

der **Donnerstag,-e** Thursday *2*

dort there *1*; *dort drüben* over there *1*

drängeln to push, shove *4*

dran sein to be one's turn *5*; *Ich bin dran.* It's my turn. *5*

draußen outside *10*

drei three *E*

dreizehn thirteen *E*

du you (familiar singular) *E*

dunkel dark *8*; *dunkelbraun* dark brown *8*

* **durch** through *5*

dürfen to be permitted to, may *5*

der **Durst** thirst *5*; *Durst haben* to be thirsty *5*

E

eben just *2*

die **Ecke,-n** corner *1*

ein(e) a, an *E*

einfach simple *4* easy, one-way ticket *7*

der **Eingang,-̈e** entrance *8*

einkaufen to shop *6*; *einkaufen gehen* to go shopping *6*

einladen to invite *6*

die **Einladung,-en** invitation *6*

einmal once *4*; *noch einmal* once more *4*

eins one *E*

einsteigen to get in, board 7

*der Einwohner,- inhabitant 3

die Einzelheit,-en detail 8

das Eis ice, ice cream 5

das Eiscafé,-s ice cream parlor, café 5

das Eishockey ice hockey 9

der Eistee ice tea 5

elf eleven *E*

die Eltern (pl.) parents 6

endlich finally 6

das Endspiel,-e final (game) 9

das Englisch English 3

der Enkel,- grandson 6

die Enkelin,-nen granddaughter 6

entfernt away, distant 7

*die Entfernung,-en distance 3

die Entscheidung,-en decision 8

* entspringen to originate (river) 9

er he *E*

erbauen to build, construct 7; *erbaut* built, constructed 7

das Erdbeereis strawberry ice cream 5

die Erdkunde geography 3

das Ergebnis,-se result, score 9

erst just 5

erzählen to tell 7

es it *1*

essen to eat 5

das Essen meal, food 6

das Eßzimmer,- dining room 6

etwas some, a little, something 4

euer your (familiar plural) 10

* Europa Europe 5

F

das Fach,-̈er (school) subject 3

fahren to drive, go 3

der Fahrplan,-̈e schedule 7

das Fahrrad,-̈er bicycle 3

die Familie,-n family 6

der Fan,-s fan 4

die Farbe,-n color 8

* fast almost 5

der Februar February 4

das Fernsehen television 5

fernsehen to watch TV 6

der Film,-e film, movie 4

finden to find 5; think 8; *Wie findest du...?* What do you think of...? 8

der Finger,- finger 9

* flach flat 5

*die Fläche,-n area 3

* fließen to flow, run 5

die Flöte,-n flute 10

das Flugzeug,-e airplane 7

*der Fluß,-̈sse river 5

die Form,-en form 9

fotografieren to take pictures 4

die Frage,-n question 10

fragen to ask 2

* Frankreich France 4

die Frau,-en woman, Mrs. *1*

der Freitag,-e Friday 2

der Freund,-e boyfriend *1*

die Freundin,-nen girlfriend *1*

froh glad 3

früh early *1*

der Frühling,-e spring 4

das Frühstück breakfast *B*

fünf five *E*

fünfzehn fifteen *E*

für for *E*

der Fußball,-̈e soccer, soccer ball 9

der Fuß,-̈e foot 3; *zu Fuß gehen* to walk 3

G

ganz quite *1*

der Gast,-̈e guest 6

geben to give 3; *es gibt* there is (are) 4

der Geburtstag,-e birthday 6

gefallen to like 6; *Wie gefällt dir...?* How do you like...? 6

gegen about, around 3; against 7

gehen to go *1; Wie geht's?* How are you? (familiar) *1*

die Geige,-n violin 10

gelb yellow 8

das Geld money 4

genau exact(ly) *1*

das Genie,-s genius 3

genug enough 4

geradeaus straight ahead 7

gern gladly, with pleasure 2; *gern hören* to like (enjoy) listening to 2; *gern haben* to like (someone, something) 4

das Geschenk,-e present, gift 6

die Geschichte history 3

das Geschirr dishes 6

der Geschmack taste 8

die Geschwister (pl.) siblings 6

gewinnen to win 9

die Gitarre,-n guitar 6

das Glas,-̈er glass 5

glauben to believe, think 5

gleich immediately, right away *1; gleich um die Ecke* right around the corner *1*

das Glück luck 3; *Glück haben* to be lucky 3

das Golf golf 9

gratulieren to congratulate 9

grau gray 8

*die Grenze,-n border 7

* grenzen an to border on 9

* groß big, large 3

die Größe,-n size 8

die Großeltern (pl.) grandparents 6

die Großmutter,-̈ grandmother 6

der Großvater,-̈ grandfather 6

grün green 8

die Gruppe,-n group 9

Grüß dich! Hi!, Hello! *E; Grüß Gott!* Hello! *E*

gut good, well, OK *1*

das Gymnasium,-sien secondary school 3

H

das Haar,-e hair 9

haben to have 2

halb half 3

Hallo! Hi! *E*

der Hals,-̈e neck 9

die Hand,-̈e hand 9

der Handschuh,-e glove 8

*die Hauptstadt,-̈e capital (city) 3

die **Hausaufgabe,-n** homework *B; Hausaufgaben machen* to do homework *B*

das **Haus,-̈er** house *1; nach Hause gehen* to go home *1; zu Hause sein* to be at home *2*

der **Hawaiibecher,-** kind of ice cream sundae *5*

das **Heft,-e** notebook *3*

heiß hot *4*

heißen to be called, named *E; Wie heißt du?* What's your name? *E*

helfen to help *8*

hell light *8; hellblau* light blue *8*

das **Hemd,-en** shirt *8*

der **Herbst,-e** fall, autumn *4*

herkommen to come here *6*

der **Herr,-en** Mr., gentleman *1*

herzlich sincere, cordial *6; Herzlichen Glückwunsch* Happy birthday! *6*

heute today *2*

hier here *1*

hin und zurück there and back, round trip (ticket) *7*

hineingehen to go inside *5*

sich **hinsetzen** to sit down *6*

der **Hit,-s** hit (song, tune) *4*

das **Hobby,-s** hobby *A*

 * **hoch** high *5; höchst-* highest *5*

hoffentlich hopefully *5*

*die **Höhe,-n** height *7*

holen to fetch, get *6*

 * **Holland** Holland *4*

hören to hear, listen to *2*

die **Hose,-n** pants, slacks *8*

das **Hotel,-s** hotel *7*

hundert hundred *2*

der **Hunger** hunger *7; Hunger haben* to be hungry *7*

I

ich I *E*

die **Idee,-n** idea *4*

ihr you (familiar plural) *1;* her *4;* their *10*

immer always *2*

in in *1*

informieren to inform *10*

die **Insel,-n** island *9*

intelligent intelligent *3*

interessant interesting *6*

 * **Italien** Italy *4*

italienisch Italian *5*

J

ja yes *1*

die **Jacke,-n** jacket *8*

das **Jahr,-e** year *6*

*die **Jahreszeit,-en** season *5*

der **Januar** January *4*

die **Jeans** (pl.) jeans *8*

jeder every, each *3; jeden* (form of *jeder*) *3*

jetzt now *1*

jubeln to cheer *4*

die **Jugend** youth *5*

der **Jugendklub,-s** youth club *5*

der **Jugendliche,-n** young-ster, teenager, youth *4*

 * **Jugoslawien** Yugoslavia *5*

der **Juli** July *4*

der **Junge,-n** boy *E*

der **Juni** June *4*

K

der **Kaffee** coffee *5*

*das **Kaisergrab,-̈er** emperor's grave *7*

*die **Kaisergruft,-̈e** emperors' tomb *7*

der **Kakao** hot chocolate *5*

kalt cold *4*

die **Karte,-n** ticket *4;* card *6*

die **Kartoffel,-n** potato *B*

der **Käse** cheese *B*

die **Kasse,-n** cash register *8*

die **Kassette,-n** cassette *2*

kaufen to buy *2*

das **Kaufhaus,-̈er** depart-ment store *6*

der **Kavalier,-e** gentleman *5*

kein no *2*

der **Kellner,-** waiter *5*

kennen to know (per-son, place) *3*

*der **Kilometer,-** kilometer *3*

das **Kinn,-e** chin *9*

das **Kino,-s** movie theater *4*

klappen to go smoothly *10; Das klappt.* That works out. *10*

die **Klarinette,-n** clarinet *10*

klasse super, fantastic *4*

die **Klasse,-n** class *6*

klatschen to clap, applaud *4*

das **Klavier,-e** piano *10*

das **Kleid,-er** dress *8*

das **Kleidungsstück,-e** cloth-ing item *8*

klein small, little *3*

klingeln to ring *10; an der Tür klingeln* to ring the doorbell *10*

der **Klub,-s** club *5*

klug smart, intelligent *2*

komisch comical, funny *8*

kommen to come *2*

kompliziert complicated *10*

können to be able to, can *5*

das **Konzert,-e** concert *4*

die **Konzerthalle,-n** concert hall *4*

der **Körperteil,-e** part of body *9*

kosten to cost *4*

die **Krawatte,-n** tie *8*

die **Kreditkarte,-n** credit card *8*

die **Kreide,-n** chalk *3*

*das **Kreuz,-e** cross *7*

kritisch critical *4*

die **Küche,-n** kitchen *6*

der **Kuchen,-** cake *6*

kühl cool *4*

der **Kuli,-s** (ballpoint) pen *3*

die **Kunst** art *3*

L

der **Laden,-̈** store *8*

*das **Land,-̈er** country *3*

die **Landkarte,-n** map *3*

lang long *5; längst-* longest *5*

lange long, long time *4*

*die **Länge,-n** length *9*

langsam slow *3*

langweilig boring *4*

laufen to run *4; Der Film läuft schon.* The movie is running already. *4*

laut loud 4
* leben to live 9
lecker delicious 6
der Lehrer,- teacher (male) 3
die Lehrerin,-nen teacher (female) 3
leicht easy 2
leider unfortunately 9
leihen to loan, lend 5
lernen to learn 3
lesen to read 3
letzt- last 4
lieber rather 2
das Lieblingsfach,-er favorite (school) subject 3
* Liechtenstein Liechtenstein 5
* liegen to be located, lie 3
die Limo,-s lemonade, soft drink 6
das Lineal,-e ruler 3
links left 7; nach links to the left 7
die Lippe,-n lip 9
los: Dann mal los! Then let's go! 3; losgehen to start 3; Wann geht's los? When will it start? 3; Da ist viel los. There's a lot going on. 4
* Luxemburg Luxembourg 4

M

machen to do, make 1; Das macht 5 Mark. That comes to 5 marks. 4; Das macht nichts. That doesn't matter. 4
das Mädchen,- girl E
der Mai May 4
mal times 5; mal wieder once again 5
das Mal,-e time(s) 9
man one, they, people 3
manchmal sometimes 10
mangelhaft inadequate 3
der Mantel,- coat 8
die Mark mark (German monetary unit) 4
die Marmelade,-n jam B
der März March 4

die Mathematik (short: Mathe) mathematics 3
mehr more 4; nicht mehr no more 4; mehr als more than 5
mein my 3
meinen to mean, think 4
meistens mostly 9
*der Mensch,-en person, human being 7
*der Meter,- meter 5
das Mietshaus,-er apartment building 6
die Milch milk 5
das Milchmix,-e milk shake 5
minus minus E
die Minute,-n minute 3
mit with 3
mitbringen to bring along 2
das Mitglied,-er member 9
mitkommen to come along 4
das Mittagessen,- lunch B
*die Mitte,-n center, middle 5
der Mittwoch,-e Wednesday 2
möchten to would like to 4; Ich möchte...I would like to... 4
die Mode,-n fashion 8
mögen to like 5
der Moment,-e moment 2
der Monat,-e month 4
der Montag,-e Monday 2
das Moped,-s moped A
morgen tomorrow 2
der Morgen,- morning 6
das Motorrad,-er motorcycle 7
der Mund,-er mouth 9
das Museum,-seen museum 7
die Musik music 2
das Musikbuch,-er music book 10
*das Musikfest,-e music festival 5
das Musikinstrument,-e musical instrument 10
der Musiklehrer,- music teacher 10
müssen to have to, must 5
die Mutter,- mother 6

N

na well 2
nach to, after 3
das Nachbarland,-er neighboring country 4
nachgehen to be slow (watch) 7
der Nachmittag,-e afternoon B; heute nachmittag this afternoon B
die Nachrichten (pl.) news B
nächst- next 5
* nächstgrößt- next largest 9
die Nähe nearness, proximity 7; in der Nähe nearby 7
der Name,-n name E
*die Nationalfahne,-n national flag 5
natürlich natural(ly), of course 8
nehmen to take 6
nein no 1
neu new 3
neun nine E
neunzehn nineteen E
nicht not 1
nichts nothing 4
nie never 3
*die Niederlande Netherlands 4
noch still, yet 1
*der Norden north 3
*die Nordsee North Sea 7
die Note,-n (school) grade, mark 3
notieren to note 9
der November November 4
null zero E
die Nummer,-n number 9
nur only 2

O

ob if, whether 7
die Oberschule,-n high school 6
oder or E
oft often A
* ohne without 3
das Ohr,-en ear 9
der Oktober October 4
die Oma,-s grandma 6
der Onkel,- uncle 6
der Opa,-s grandpa 6
der Optiker,- optician 8
orange orange 8

*der **Osten** east 3
Österreich Austria 4
*die **Ostsee** Baltic Sea 9

P

paar: ein paar a few 2
das **Paar,-e** pair 8
das **Papier** paper 3
der **Park,-s** park 1
parken to park 7
die **Party,-s** party 3; *eine Party geben* to give a party 3
* **passen** to fit 3
die **Pause,-n** intermission, break 4
die **Physik** physics 3
die **Platte,-n** platter, plate 6 *die Kalte Platte* cold-cut platter 6; table (top) 9
plus plus E
Polen Poland 4
populär popular 4
die **Post** post office 7
das **Poster,-** poster A
preiswert reasonable 8
das **Programm,-e** program 6
Prost! Cheers! 5
*das **Prozent,-e** percent 9
der **Pulli,-s** sweater, pullover 8
der **Pullover,-** sweater, pullover 8
pünktlich punctual, on time 3

Q

die **Qualität,-en** quality 8
die **Quizshow,-s** quiz show 5

R

das **Rad,-̈er** bike, bicycle 9
der **Radiergummi,-s** eraser 3
das **Rathaus,-̈er** city hall 7
recht right 9; *Du hast recht.* You're right. 9
rechts right 7; *nach rechts* to the right 7
regnen to rain 4
die **Reihe,-n** row 9; *Ich bin an der Reihe.* It's my turn. 9
reinkommen to come inside 10
die **Reise,-n** trip 7
*die **Reiseauskunft** traveler's information 7

Reisen traveling 7
die **Religion** religion 3
*die **Republik** Republic 5
das **Restaurant,-s** restaurant 7
das **Rezept,-e** prescription 8
*der **Rhein** Rhine River 7
der **Rhythmus** rhythm 4
*der **Richter,-** judge 9
richtig correct, right 8
*das **Riesenfaß** gigantic barrel 7
die **Rockband,-s** rock band 4
der **Rock,-̈e** skirt 8
das **Rockkonzert,-e** rock concert 4
die **Rockmusik** rock music 2
der **Roman,-e** novel A
rosa pink 8
rot red 5
rüberkommen to come over 4
*die **Runde,-n** round 9
die **S-Bahn,-en** city train, suburban express train B

S

sagen to say 1
sammeln to collect A
der **Samstag,-e** Saturday 2
die **Sängerin,-nen** singer 5
der **Satz,-̈e** set 9
das **Sauerkraut** sauerkraut B
schaffen to manage (it), make (it) 7
scheinen to shine 4
schick chic, fashionable 2
schicken to send 7
das **Schiff,-e** ship, boat 7
das **Schlafzimmer,-** bedroom 6
schlagen to beat, hit 9
der **Schläger,-** racket 9
die **Schlagsahne** whipped cream 5
schlecht bad 1
Schlittschuh laufen to skate 9
schmecken to taste 5
schneien to snow 4
schnell fast 3
das **Schokoeis** chocolate ice cream 5
schon already 1
schön beautiful, nice 1
schreiben to write 2

schreien to scream, shout, yell 4
der **Schuh,-e** shoe 8
die **Schulbank,-̈e** school desk 3
die **Schule,-n** school 3
der **Schüler,-** pupil, student (secondary school) 3
die **Schultasche,-n** school bag, satchel 3
die **Schulter,-n** shoulder 9
schwarz black 5
die **Schweiz** Switzerland 4
schwer hard, difficult 3
die **Schwester,-n** sister 6
schwimmen to swim 9
schwitzen to sweat 5
sechs six E
sechzehn sixteen E
*der **See,-n** lake 9
* **sehen** to see, look 5; *sehen auf* to look at 7
die **Sehenswürdigkeit,-en** sight(s) 7
sehr very 1
sein to be 1
sein his 4
seit since 8
die **Seite,-n** page 3; side 9
der **September** September 4
die **Show,-s** show 4
sie she E
Sie you (formal) E
sieben seven E
siebzehn seventeen E
das **Signal,-e** signal 7
singen to sing 4
sitzen to sit 5
der **Ski,-s** ski A; *Ski laufen* to ski A
so so 1
so...wie as...as 7
die **Socke,-n** sock 8
sofort right away, immediately 5
der **Sohn,-̈e** son 6
sollen to be supposed to, should 5
der **Sommer,-** summer 4
der **Sonnabend,-e** Saturday 2
die **Sonne** sun 4
der **Sonntag,-e** Sunday 2
sonst otherwise 6
* **Spanien** Spain 4
spannend exciting, thrilling 4
der **Spaß** fun 6; *Es macht Spaß.* It's fun. 6

spät late 1
das Spiel,-e game 9
spielen to play 2
der Spieler,- player 9
der Spielplan,-e game schedule 9
spitze hot, super 4
der Sport sport 3
die Sportart,-en kind of sport 9
die Sporthalle,-n sports hall 9
sportlich athletic 3
*die Sprache,-n language 7
sprechen to speak 5; sprechen über to talk about 3
spülen to wash, rinse 6; Geschirr spülen to wash dishes 6
*der Staat,-en state 3
die Stadt,-e city 1; in der Stadt downtown 1
stattfinden to take place 9
stehen to stand, be 4; Hier steht's. Here it is. 4; Es steht dir gut. It looks good on you. 8
die Stelle,-n spot, place 10
stellen to place, put 6
stimmen to be correct 3; Stimmt. That's right (correct). 3
die Stirn,-e forehead 9
die Straße-n street 7
die Straßenbahn,-en streetcar A
die Strecke,-n stretch, distance 9
der Strumpf,-e stocking 8
das Stück,-e piece 6
die Stunde,-n hour 4
der Stundenplan,-e class schedule 3
*der Süden south 3
super super, great 4
der Supermarkt,-e supermarket 6
das Sweatshirt,-s sweatshirt 2

T

das T-Shirt,-s T-shirt 8
die Tafel,-n blackboard, board 3
der Tafellappen,- rag (to wipe off blackboard) 3
der Tag,-e day E; Tag! Hello! (informal) E; Guten

Tag! Hello! (formal) E
die Tante,-n aunt 6
tanzen to dance 5
der Taschenrechner,- pocket calculator 6
die Tasse,-n cup 5
der Tee tea B
*der Teil,-e part, section 5; zum größten Teil for the most part 5
das Telefon,-e telephone 2
das Tennis tennis 9
der Tennisklub,-s tennis club 9
der Tennisplatz,-e tennis court 9
teuer expensive 8
der Tisch,-e table 5
das Tischtennis table tennis 9
das Tischtennisturnier,-e table tennis tournament 9
die Tochter,- daughter 6
toll great, terrific, smashing 2
die Tomate,-n tomato B
*der Tourist,-en tourist 7
tragen to wear 8
sich treffen to meet 10; Treffen wir uns! Let's meet. 10
treiben to do 9; Sport treiben to participate in sports 9
trinken to drink 5
die Trompete,-n trumpet 10
trotzdem nevertheless, in spite of it 10
*die Tschechoslowakei Czechoslovakia 4
Tschüs! See you! E
tun to do 3
die Tür,-en door 4

U

üben to practice 9
über across 8; über die Straße gehen to cross the street 8
überzeugen to convince 10
die Übung,-en exercise, practice 9; Übung macht den Meister! Practice makes perfect. 9

die Uhr,-en clock, watch 2; um neun Uhr at nine o'clock 2
um around, at 1; um die Ecke around the corner 1
*die Umgebung,-en surrounding, vicinity 5
umsteigen to transfer 7
umziehen to change clothes 9
und and 1
* Ungarn Hungary 5
ungefähr approximately 3
ungenügend unsatisfactory 3
unglaublich unbelievable 7
unruhig restless 10
unser our 10
die Unterhaltung entertainment 4

V

das Vanilleeis vanilla ice cream 5
der Vater,- father 6
*die Vereinigten Staaten von Amerika United States of America 3
die Verkäuferin,-nen saleslady, clerk 4
der Verkehr traffic 3
das Verkehrsmittel,- means of transportation 7
verlassen to leave 6
* verlaufen to run, extend 5
verstehen to understand 4
versuchen to try 10
viel much 2
viele many 2
vielleicht perhaps 1
vier four E
das Viertel,- quarter 3
vierzehn fourteen E
das Volkslied,-er folk song A
voll full 5
von from 1; of 8
vor before, in front of 3
vorhaben to plan, intend 5
der Vorort,-e suburb 6
die Vorstellung,-en performance 4

W

wählen to select, dial
(phone) 10
wählerisch choosy,
particular 10
* **während** during 5
* **wandern** to hike 7
wann when 3
war (past tense of **sein**)
was 4
warm warm 4
warten to wait 3
warum why 2
was what 1; *was für*
what kind of 5
der **Weg,-e** way 5; *auf dem
Weg* on the way 5
weg sein to be gone 6
* **weiß** white 5
weit far 1
* **weiter** further 7
weiterfahren to continue
on, drive on 7
weiterspielen to con-
tinue playing 9
welcher which 2
wenig little 3
wenn when 7; if 9
wer who E
werden will, shall 5
*der **Westen** west 3
das **Wetter** weather 4
wie how E; *Wie geht es
Ihnen?* How are you?
(formal) 1
wieder again 3
wiederkommen to come
again 8
**Wiedersehen: Auf Wie-
dersehen!** Good-bye! E
wieviel how much E
der **Winter,-** winter 4
*der **Wintersportler,-** winter
sports enthusiast 5
wir we 1
wirklich really 4
wissen to know 3
wo where 1
die **Woche,-n** week 4
woher where from 3
wohin where (to) 2
wohnen to live 1
die **Wohnung,-en**
apartment 6
das **Wohnzimmer,-**
livingroom 6
wollen to want to 5
die **Wurst,-̈e** sausage B

Z

zahlen to pay 5; *Zahlen,
bitte.* The check,
please. 5
der **Zahn,-̈e** tooth 9
zehn ten E
zeigen to show, point 8
die **Zeit,-en** time 2
die **Zeitschrift,-en**
magazine 7
die **Zeitung,-en** newspaper 6
das **Zimmer,-** room 6
das **Zitroneneis** lemon ice
cream 5
zu at, to, too 2
zubereiten to prepare (a
meal) 6
zuerst first 9
der **Zug,-̈e** train 7
zurück back 4
zurückfahren to drive
back 7
zurückgehen to go
back 7
zusammen together 10
zwanzig twenty E
zwei two E
zwölf twelve E

A

a ein(e) *E*
able: to be able to können *5*
about gegen, ungefähr *3*
accompaniment die Begleitung,-en *10*
to **accompany** begleiten *10*
accordion das Akkordeon,-s *10*
across über *8*; *to cross the street* über die Straße gehen *8*
after nach *3*
afternoon der Nachmittag,-e *B*; *this afternoon* heute nachmittag *B*
again wieder *3*
against gegen *7*
airplane das Flugzeug,-e *7*
all alles *3*; alle *4*
almost fast *5*
alone allein(e) *10*
Alps die Alpen *5*
already schon *1*
also auch *1*
always immer *2*
America Amerika *4*
an ein(e) *E*
and und *1*
to **announce** bekanntgeben *9*
announcer der Ansager,- *9*
to **answer** antworten *8*
apart beiseite *10*
apartment die Wohnung,-en *6*
apartment building das Mietshaus,-er *6*
to **appear** aussehen *8*
to **applaud** klatschen *4*
apple juice der Apfelsaft *5*
approximately ungefähr *3*
April der April *4*
area die Fläche,-n *3*
arm der Arm,-e *9*
around um *1*; gegen *3*; *around the corner* um die Ecke *1*
to **arrive** ankommen *7*
art die Kunst *3*
as...as so...wie *7*
aside beiseite *10*; *Fun aside. Be serious.* Spaß beiseite. *10*
to **ask** fragen *2*

assignment die Aufgabe,-n *3*
at bei, um *1*; an, zu *2*
athletic sportlich *3*
August der August *4*
aunt die Tante,-n *6*
Austria Österreich *4*
autumn der Herbst,-e *4*
away entfernt *7*

B

back zurück *4*
bad schlecht *1*
to **bake** backen *6*
ball der Ball,-e *9*
ballpoint pen der Kuli,-s *3*
Baltic Sea die Ostsee *9*
band die Band,-s *4*
bank die Bank,-en *7*
basketball der Basketball,-e *9*
bathroom das Bad,-er *6*
to **be** sein *1*; *to be one's turn* dran sein *5*; *It's my turn.* Ich bin dran. *5*
to **beat** schlagen *9*
beautiful schön *1*
bedroom das Schlafzimmer,- *6*
before vor *3*
to **begin** beginnen *4*; anfangen *10*
Belgium Belgien *4*
to **believe** glauben *5*
bench die Bank,-e *7*
besides außer *8*
best best- *6*
better besser *2*
bicycle das Fahrrad,-er *3*; das Rad,-er *9*
big groß *3*
bike das Rad,-er *9*
biology die Biologie *3*
birthday der Geburtstag,-e *6*
black schwarz *8*
blackboard die Tafel,-n *3*
blouse die Bluse,-n *8*
blue blau *8*
board die Tafel,-n *3*
to **board** einsteigen *7*
boat das Boot,-e, das Schiff,-e *7*
book das Buch,-er *3*
border die Grenze,-n *7*; *to border on* grenzen an *9*
boring langweilig *4*

both beide *4*
boy der Junge,-n *E*
boyfriend der Freund,-e *1*
bratwurst die Bratwurst,-e *B*
bread das Brot,-e *6*
break die Pause,-n *4*
breakfast das Frühstück *B*
to **bring** bringen *5*; *to bring along* mitbringen *2*
brother der Bruder,- *6*
brown braun *8*
buffet das Büfett,-s *6*
to **build** erbauen, bauen *7*; *built* erbaut *7*
bus der Bus,-se *7*
but aber *2*
butter die Butter *B*
to **buy** kaufen *2*

C

café das Eiscafé,-s *5*; das Café,-s *7*
cake der Kuchen,- *6*
to **call (up)** anrufen *10*; *to be called* heißen *E*
can können *5*
capital (city) die Hauptstadt,-e *3*
car das Auto,-s *6*
card die Karte,-n *6*
cash bar *8*; *to pay cash* bar bezahlen *8*
cash register die Kasse,-n *8*
cassette die Kassette,-n *2*
cathedral der Dom,-e *7*
CD (compact disc) die CD,-s *2*
center die Mitte,-n *5*
chalk die Kreide,-n *3*
chance die Chance,-n *9*
to **change clothes** umziehen *9*
cheap billig *2*
to **cheer** jubeln *4*; *Cheers!* Prost! *5*
cheese der Käse *B*
chemistry die Chemie *3*
chic schick *2*
chin das Kinn,-e *9*
chocolate ice cream das Schokoeis *5*
choice die Auswahl *5*
choosy wählerisch *10*
city die Stadt,-e *1*; *downtown* in der Stadt *1*

city hall das Rathaus,⸚er 7
city train die S-Bahn,-en B
to **clap** klatschen 4
clarinet die
Klarinette,-n 10
class die Klasse,-n 6
class schedule der
Stundenplan,⸚e 3
clerk (female) die
Verkäuferin,-nen 4;
(male) der Verkäufer,- 4
clock die Uhr,-en 2; at nine
o'clock um neun Uhr 2
clothing item das
Kleidungsstück,-e 8
club der Klub,-s 5
coat der Mantel,⸚ 8
coffee der Kaffee 5
cola die Cola,-s 5
cold kalt 4
to **collect** sammeln A
color die Farbe,-n 8
colorful bunt 8
to **come** kommen 2; to come
along mitkommen 4, to
come over
rüberkommen 4; to
come here herkommen
6; to come again
wiederkommen 8; to
come inside
reinkommen 10;
comical komisch 8
complicated
kompliziert 10
composition der
Aufsatz,⸚e B
computer der Computer,- 3
concert das Konzert,-e 4
concert hall die
Konzerthalle,-n 4
to **congratulate** gratulieren 9
to **construct** erbauen 7;
constructed erbaut 7
to **continue on** weiterfahren
7; to continue playing
weiterspielen 9
to **convince** überzeugen 10
cool kühl 4
cordial herzlich 6; Happy
birthday! Herzlichen
Glückwunsch zum
Geburtstag! 6
corner die Ecke,-n 1
correct richtig 8; to be
correct stimmen 3;
That's right. Das
stimmt. 3

D

to **cost** kosten 4
country das Land,⸚er 3
to **cover** decken 6; to set the
table den Tisch
decken 6
credit card die
Kreditkarte,-n 8
critical kritisch 4
cross das Kreuz,-e 7
cup die Tasse,-n 5
Czechoslovakia die
Tschechoslowakei 4

to **dance** tanzen 5
dark dunkel 8; dark brown
dunkelbraun 8
daughter die Tochter,⸚ 6
day der Tag,-e E; Hello!
(informal) Tag! E; Hello!
(formal) Guten Tag! E
December der Dezember 4
decision die
Entscheidung,-en 8
to **decorate** dekorieren 6
definitely bestimmt 2
delicious lecker 6
Denmark Dänemark 4
to **depart** abfahren 7
department store das
Kaufhaus,⸚er 6
detail die Einzelheit,-en 8
to **dial (phone)** wählen 10
different ander(e) 1
difficult schwer 3
dining room das
Eßzimmer,- 6
direct direkt 9
disc jockey der
Diskjockey,-s 5
disco die Disko,-s 10; Let's
go to the disco. Auf zur
Disko! 10
dishes das Geschirr 6
distance die
Entfernung,-en 3; die
Strecke,-n 9
distant entfernt 7
DJ der Diskjockey,-s 5
to **do, make** machen 1; That
comes to 5 marks. Das
macht 5 Mark. 4; That
doesn't matter. Das
macht nichts. 4
to **do** tun 3; treiben 9; to
participate in sports
Sport treiben 9

door die Tür,-en 4
dress das Kleid,-er 8
to **drink** trinken 5
to **drive** fahren 3; to drive
back zurückfahren, to
drive on weiterfahren 7
during während 5

E

each jeder 3
ear das Ohr,-en 9
early früh 1
east der Osten 3
easy leicht 2; einfach 7
to **eat** essen 5
eight acht E
eighteen achtzehn E
eleven elf E
emperor's grave das
Kaisergrab,⸚er 7;
emperors' tomb die
Kaisergruft,⸚e 7
English das Englisch 3
enough genug 4
entertainment die
Unterhaltung 4
entrance der Eingang,⸚e 8
eraser der
Radiergummi,-s 3
especially besonders 3
essay der Aufsatz,⸚e B
Europe Europa 5
evening der Abend,-e 6; in
the evening am
Abend 6
every jeder 3
everyone alle 4
everything alles 3
exact(ly) genau 1
example das Beispiel,-e 9;
for example zum
Beispiel 9
excellent ausgezeichnet 1
except außer 8
excited aufgeregt 4
exciting spannend 4
excursion der Ausflug,⸚e 7;
to go on an excursion
einen Ausflug machen
7; excursion area der
Ausflugsort,-e 9
exercise die Aufgabe,-n 3;
die Übung,-en 9
expensive teuer 8
to **extend** verlaufen 5
eye das Auge,-n 9

F

fall der Herbst,-e 4
family die Familie,-n 6
fan der Fan,-s 4
fantastic klasse 4
far weit 1
fashion die Mode,-n 8
fashionable schick 2
fast schnell 3
father der Vater,= 6
fear die Angst,=e 2; *Don't worry! Don't be afraid!* (Hab) Keine Angst! 2
February der Februar 4
Federal Highway die Bundesstraße,-n 7
Federal Republic (of Germany) die Bundesrepublik (Deutschland) 3
Federal State das Bundesland,=er 5
to **fetch** holen 6
fifteen fünfzehn E
film der Film,-e 4
finally endlich 6
to **find** finden 5
finger der Finger,- 9
first zuerst 9
to **fit** passen 3
five fünf E
flat flach 5
to **flow** fließen 5
flute die Flöte,-n 10
folk song das Volkslied,-er A
food das Essen 6
foot der Fuß,=e 3; *to walk* zu Fuß gehen 3
for für E; *for sure* bestimmt 2; *for it* dafür 7
forehead die Stirn,-e 9
foreigner der Ausländer,- A
form die Form,-en 9; *to form* bilden 9
four vier E
fourteen vierzehn E
France Frankreich 4
Friday der Freitag,-e 2
from von 1; aus 3
front: in front of vor 3
full voll 5
fun der Spaß 6; *It's fun.* Es macht Spaß. 6
funny komisch 8
further weiter 7

G

game das Spiel,-e 9
game schedule der Spielplan,=e 9
genius das Genie,-s 3
gentleman der Herr,-en 1; der Kavalier,-e 5
geography die Erdkunde 3
German das Deutsch 3
German Democratic Republic die Deutsche Demokratische Republik 3
to **get** bekommen 3; holen 6; *to get in* einsteigen 7; *to get up* aufstehen B
gift das Geschenk,-e 6
gigantic barrel das Riesenfaß 7
girl das Mädchen,- E
girlfriend die Freundin,-nen 1
to **give** geben 3; *there is (are)* es gibt 4
glad froh 3
gladly gern 2; *to like (enjoy) listening to* gern hören 2; *to like (someone, something)* gern haben 4
glass das Glas,=er 5
glasses die Brille,-n 8
glove der Handschuh,-e 8
to **go** gehen 1; *How are you? (familiar)* Wie geht's? 1; *to go* fahren 3; *to go back* zurückgehen 7; *to be gone* weg sein 6; *to go inside* hineingehen 5; *to go smoothly* klappen 10
golf das Golf 9
good gut 1
Good-bye! Wiedersehen: Auf Wiedersehen! E
grade (school) die Note,-n 3
granddaughter die Enkelin,-nen 6
grandfather der Großvater,= 6
grandma die Oma,-s 6
grandmother die Großmutter,= 6
grandpa der Opa,-s 6
grandparents die Großeltern (pl.) 6

grandson der Enkel,- 6
gray grau 8
great toll 2; super 4
green grün 8
to **greet** begrüßen 8
group die Gruppe,-n 9
guest der Gast,=e 6
guitar die Gitarre,-n 6

H

hair das Haar,-e 9
half halb 3
hand die Hand,=e 9
hard schwer 3
to **have** haben 2; *to have homework to do* aufhaben 3; *to have to* müssen 5; *to have on* anhaben 8
he er E
to **hear** hören 2
height die Höhe,-n 7
Hello! Grüß dich!, Grüß Gott! E
to **help** helfen 8
her ihr 10
here hier 1
Hi! Grüß dich!, Hallo! E
high hoch 5; *highest* höchst- 5
high school das Gymnasium,-sien 3; die Oberschule,-n 6
to **hike** wandern 7
his sein 4
history die Geschichte 3
to **hit** schlagen 9
hit *(song, tune)* der Hit,-s 4
hobby das Hobby,-s A
Holland Holland 4
homework die Hausaufgabe,-n B; *to do homework* Hausaufgaben machen B
hopefully hoffentlich 5
hot chocolate der Kakao 5
hot heiß, spitze 4
hotel das Hotel,-s 7
hour die Stunde,-n 4
house das Haus,=er 1; *to go home* nach Hause gehen 1; *to be at home* zu Hause sein 2
how wie E; *How are you? (formal)* Wie geht es Ihnen? 1; *how much* wieviel E

human being der
Mensch,-en 7
hundred hundert 2
Hungary Ungarn 5
hunger der Hunger 7; *to be
hungry* Hunger haben 7
to **hurry** sich beeilen 4; *Hurry
(up)! (singular)* Beeil
dich! 4; *Hurry (up)!
(plural)* Beeilt euch! 4

I

I ich *E*
ice cream das Eis 5; *ice
cream parlor* das
Eiscafé,-s 5
ice das Eis 5
ice hockey das
Eishockey 9
ice tea der Eistee 5
idea die Idee,-n 4
if ob 7; wenn 9
immediately gleich 1;
sofort 5
in in 1
inadequate mangelhaft 3
inexpensive billig 2
to **inform** informieren 10
inhabitant der
Einwohner,- 3
intelligent klug 2;
intelligent 3
to **intend** vorhaben 5
interesting interessant 6
intermission die
Pause,-n 4
invitation die
Einladung,-en 6
to **invite** einladen 6
island die Insel,-n 9
it es 1
Italian italienisch 5
Italy Italien 4

J

jacket die Jacke,-n 8
jam die Marmelade,-n *B*
January der Januar 4
jeans die Jeans (pl.) 8
judge der Richter,- 9
July der Juli 4
June der Juni 4
just eben 2; erst 5

K

kilometer der Kilometer,- 3

kitchen die Küche,-n 6
to **know** wissen 3; *to know
(person, place)* kennen 3

L

Lake Constance der
Bodensee 9
lake der See,-n 9
language die Sprache,-n 7
large groß 3
to **last** dauern *A*
last letzt- 4
late spät 1
to **learn** lernen 3
to **leave** verlassen 6;
abfahren 7
left links 7; *to the left* nach
links 7
leg das Bein,-e 9
lemon ice cream das
Zitroneneis 5
lemonade die Limo,-s 6
to **lend** leihen 5
length die Länge,-n 9
to **lie** liegen 3
Liechtenstein
Liechtenstein 5
light hell 8; *light blue*
hellblau 8
to **like** mögen 5; gefallen 6;
How do you like...? Wie
gefällt dir...? 6
lip die Lippe,-n 9
to **listen to** hören 2
little klein, wenig 3; *a
little* etwas 4
to **live** wohnen 1; leben 9
living room das
Wohnzimmer,- 6
to **loan** leihen 5
located: be located
liegen 3
long lang 5; *long time*
lange 4
to **look** sehen 5; aussehen 8;
to look at sich ansehen,
sehen auf 7
loud laut 4
luck das Glück 3; *to be
lucky* Glück haben 3
lunch das Mittagessen,- *B*
Luxembourg Luxemburg 4

M

magazine die
Zeitschrift,-en 7
to **make** machen 1; *to make it*

schaffen 7
many viele 2
map die Landkarte,-n 3
March der März 4
**mark (German monetary
unit)** die Mark 4
mark (grade) die Note,-n 3
to **marvel at** bestaunen 7
mathematics die Mathematik (*short:* Mathe) 3
May der Mai 4
may dürfen 5
meal das Essen 6
to **mean** meinen 4
means of transportation
das Verkehrsmittel,- 7
to **meet** sich treffen 10; *Let's
meet.* Treffen wir
uns! 10
member das Mitglied,-er 9
meter der Meter,- 5
middle die Mitte,-n 5
milk die Milch 5
milk shake das
Milchmix,-e 5
minus minus *E*
minute die Minute,-n 3
moment der Moment,-e 2
Monday der Montag,-e 2
money das Geld 4
monitor der
Bildschirm,-e 7
month der Monat,-e 4
moped das Moped,-s *A*
more mehr 4; *no more*
nicht mehr 4; *more than*
mehr als 5
morning der Morgen,- 6
mostly meistens 9
mother die Mutter,- 6
motorcycle das
Motorrad,-er 7
mountain der Berg,-e 5
mountainous bergig 9
mouth der Mund,-er 9
movie der Film,-e 4
movie theater das
Kino,-s 4
Mr. der Herr,-en 1
Mrs. die Frau,-en 1
much viel 2
museum das
Museum,-seen 7
music die Musik 2
music book das
Musikbuch,-er 10
music festival das
Musikfest,-e 5

music teacher der
  Musiklehrer,- 10
musical instrument das
  Musikinstrument,-e 10
must müssen 5
my mein 3

N

name der Name,-n E
named heißen E; *What's
  your name?* Wie heißt
  du? E
national flag die Nationalfahne,-n 5
natural(ly) natürlich 8
near bei 1; *nearby* in der
  Nähe 7
neck der Hals,⸚e 9
to **need** brauchen 6
neighboring country das
  Nachbarland,⸚er 4
Netherlands die
  Niederlande 4
never nie 3
nevertheless trotzdem 10
new neu 3
news die Nachrichten
  (pl.) B
newspaper die
  Zeitung,-en 6
next nächst- 5
nice schön 1
nine neun E
nineteen neunzehn E
no nein 1; kein(e) 2
north der Norden 3
North Sea die Nordsee 7
not nicht 1
to **note** notieren 9
notebook das Heft,-e 3
nothing nichts 4
novel der Roman,-e A
November der November 4
now jetzt 1
number die Nummer,-n 9

O

October der Oktober 4
of von 8
of course natürlich 8
office das Büro,-s 6
official (female) die
  Beamtin,-nen 7; *official
  (male)* der Beamte,-n 7
often oft A
oh ach 10
OK gut 1

old alt E
on an 2; auf 3; *on the* am
  (or: an dem) 2; *on time*
  pünktlich 3
once einmal 4; *once more*
  noch einmal 4
one eins E; man 3
one-way ticket einfach 7
only nur 2
to **open** aufmachen 4
optician der Optiker,- 8
or oder E
orange orange 8
to **order** bestellen 8
to **originate (river)**
  entspringen 9
other ander-1
otherwise sonst 6
our unser 10
out aus 3
outside draußen 10

P

page die Seite,-n 3
pair das Paar,-e 8
pants die Hose,-n 8
paper das Papier 3
parents die Eltern (pl.) 6
park der Park,-s 1; *to park*
  parken 7
part der Teil,-e 5; *for the
  most part* zum größten
  Teil 5
part of body der
  Körperteil,-e 9
particular wählerisch 10
party die Party,-s 3; *to give
  a party* eine Party
  geben 3
to **pay** zahlen 5; *The check,
  please.* Zahlen, bitte. 5;
  bezahlen 8; *to pay cash*
  bar bezahlen 8
pencil der Bleistift,-e 3
people man 3
percent das Prozent,-e 9
perhaps vielleicht 1
**permitted: to be permitted
  to** düfen 5
person der Mensch,-en 7
physics die Physik 3
piano das Klavier,-e 10
picture postcard die
  Ansichtskarte,-n 7
piece das Stück,-e 6
pink rosa 8
place die Stelle,-n 10; *to*

place stellen 6
to **plan** vorhaben 5
platter die Platte,-n 6;
  cold-cut platter die
  Kalte Platte 6
to **play** spielen 2
player der Spieler,- 9
please bitte 4; *Here you
  are.* Bitte sehr. 5; *May I
  help you?* Bitte? 5
plus plus E
pocket calculator der
  Taschenrechner,- 6
to **point** zeigen 8
Poland Polen 4
popular populär 4;
  beliebt 5
post office die Post 7
poster das Poster,- A
potato die Kartoffel,-n B
practice die Übung,-en 9;
  Practice makes perfect.
  Übung macht den
  Meister! 9; *to practice*
  üben 9
to **prepare (a meal)**
  zubereiten 6
prescription das
  Rezept,-e 8
present das Geschenk,-e 6
problem die Aufgabe,-n 3
program das
  Programm,-e 6
pullover der Pulli,-s, der
  Pullover,- 8
punctual pünktlich 3
pupil der Schüler,- 3
to **push** drängeln 4
to **put** stellen 6; *to put on*
  aufsetzen 8

Q

quality die Qualität,-en 8
quarter das Viertel,- 3
question die Frage,-n 10
quite ganz 1
quiz show die
  Quizshow,-s 5

R

racket der Schläger,- 9
**rag (to wipe off black-
  board)** der
  Tafellappen,- 3
to **rain** regnen 4
rather lieber 2
to **read** lesen 3
really wirklich 4

reasonable preiswert 8
to **receive** bekommen 3
recorder die
   Blockflöte,-n 10
red rot 5
religion die Religion 3
to **remain** bleiben 7
Republic die Republik 5
restaurant das
   Restaurant,-s 7
restless unruhig 10
result das Ergebnis,-se 9
Rhine River der Rhein 7
rhythm der Rhythmus 4
right sofort 5; rechts 7;
   richtig 8; recht 9; *right*
   away gleich 1; *right*
   around the corner
   gleich um die Ecke 1; *to*
   the right nach rechts 7;
   You're right. Du hast
   recht. 9
to **ring** klingeln 10; *to ring*
   the doorbell an der Tür
   klingeln 10
to **rinse** spülen 6
river der Fluß,¨sse 5
rock band die
   Rockband,-s 4
rock concert das
   Rockkonzert,-e 4
rock music die
   Rockmusik 2
room das Zimmer,- 6
round die Runde,-n 9
round trip (ticket) hin und
   zurück 7
row die Reihe,-n 9; *It's my*
   turn. Ich bin an der
   Reihe. 9
ruler das Lineal,-e 3
to **run** laufen 4; fließen,
   verlaufen 5; *The movie*
   is running already. Der
   Film läuft schon. 4

s

saleslady die
   Verkäuferin,-en 4
satchel die
   Schultasche,-n 3
satisfactory
   befriedigend 3
Saturday der
   Sonnabend,-e, der
   Samstag,-e 2
sauerkraut das

Sauerkraut B
sausage die Wurst,¨e B
to **say** sagen 1
schedule der Fahrplan,¨e 7
school die Schule,-n 3
school bag die
   Schultasche,-n 3
school desk die
   Schulbank,¨e 3
score das Ergebnis,-se 9
to **scream** schreien 4
season die Jahreszeit,-en 5
section der Teil,-e 5
to **see** sehen 5; *See you!*
   Tschüs! E
to **select** wählen 10
selection die Auswahl 5
to **send** schicken 7
September der
   September 4
to **serve (tennis)**
   aufschlagen 9
set der Satz,¨e 9
seven sieben E
seventeen siebzehn E
shall werden 5
she sie E
to **shine** scheinen 4
ship das Schiff,-e 7
shirt das Hemd,-en 8
shoe der Schuh,-e 8
to **shop** einkaufen 6; *to go*
   shopping einkaufen
   gehen 6
should sollen 5
shoulder die Schulter,-n 9
to **shout** schreien 4
to **shove** drängeln 4
show die Show,-s 4; *to*
   show zeigen 8
siblings die Geschwister
   (pl.) 6
side die Seite,-n 9
sight(s) die Sehens-
   würdigkeit,-en 7
signal das Signal,-e 7
simple einfach 4
since seit 8
sincere herzlich 6
to **sing** singen 4
singer der Sänger,-, die
   Sängerin,-nen 5
sister die Schwester,-n 6
to **sit** sitzen 5; *to sit down*
   sich hinsetzen 6
six sechs E
sixteen sechzehn E
size die Größe,-n 8

to **skate** Schlittschuh
   laufen 9
ski der Ski,-s A; *to ski* Ski
   laufen A
skirt der Rock,¨e 8
slacks die Hose,-n 8
slow langsam 3
small klein 3
smart klug 2
smashing toll 2
to **snow** schneien 4
so so 1
soccer der Fußball,¨e 9
soccer ball der
   Fußball,¨e 9
sock die Socke,-n 8
soft drink die Limo,-s 6
sold out ausverkauft 4
some etwas 4
something etwas 4
sometimes manchmal 10
son der Sohn,¨e 6
soon bald 2
south der Süden 3
souvenir das Andenken,- 7
Spain Spanien 4
to **speak** sprechen 5; *to talk*
   about sprechen über 3
special besonders 3
to **spend** ausgeben 7
sport der Sport 3; *kind of*
   sport die Sportart,-en 9
spot die Stelle,-n 10
spring der Frühling,-e 4
stamp die Briefmarke,-n A
to **stand** stehen 4; *Here it is.*
   Hier steht's. 4; *It looks*
   good on you. Es steht dir
   gut. 8
to **start** anfangen 10; losgehen
   3; *When will it start?*
   Wann geht's los? 3
state der Staat,-en 3
station (train) der
   Bahnhof,¨e 7
to **stay** bleiben 7
still noch 1
stocking der Strumpf,¨e 8
store der Laden,¨ 8
straight direkt 9; *straight*
   ahead geradeaus 7
strawberry ice cream das
   Erdbeereis 5
street die Straße-n 7
streetcar die
   Straßenbahn,-en A
stretch die Strecke,-n 9
student (secondary school)

der Schüler,- *3*
subject (school) das
Fach,:er *3*
suburb der Vorort,-e *6*
sufficient ausreichend *3*
suit der Anzug,-e *8*
summer der Sommer,- *4*
sun die Sonne *4*
Sunday der Sonntag,-e *2*
super klasse, super,
spitze *4*
supermarket der
Supermarkt,:e *6*
supper das Abendbrot *6*
supposed: to be supposed
sollen *5*
surrounding die
Umgebung,-en *5*
to **sweat** schwitzen *5*
sweater der Pulli,-s, der
Pullover,- *8*
sweatshirt das
Sweatshirt,-s *2*
to **swim** schwimmen *9*
Switzerland die Schweiz *4*

T

T-shirt das T-Shirt,-s *8*
table der Tisch,-e *5; table
(top)* die Platte,-n *9*
table tennis das
Tischtennis *9*
table tennis tournament
das Tischtennis-
turnier,-e *9*
to **take** nehmen *6; to take
(time)* dauern *A; to take
pictures* fotografieren *4;
to take place*
stattfinden *9*
taste der Geschmack *8; to
taste* schmecken *5*
tea der Tee *B*
teacher (female) die
Lehrerin,-nen *3; teacher
(male)* der Lehrer,- *3*
teenager der
Jugendliche,-n *4*
telephone das Telefon,-e *2*
telescreen der
Bildschirm,-e *7*
television das
Fernsehen *5*
to **tell** erzählen *7*
ten zehn *E*
tennis club der
Tennisklub,-s *9*
tennis court der
Tennisplatz,:e *9*

tennis das Tennis *9*
terrific toll *2*
test die Arbeit,-en *2; to
take a test* eine Arbeit
schreiben *2*
than als *5; more than*
mehr als *5*
thanks der Dank *6; Many
thanks.* Vielen Dank. *6*
that das *E; daß 5*
the der, die, das *2; the
same* derselbe *9*
their ihr *10*
then dann *2; Then let's go!*
Dann mal los! *3*
there da, dort *1; over there*
da drüben, dort drüben
1; there and back hin
und zurück *7; There's a
lot going on.* Da ist viel
los. *4*
therefore deshalb *9*
they man *3*
to **think** meinen *4;* glauben *5;*
finden *8; What do you
think of...?* Wie findest
du...? *8*
thirst der Durst *5; to be
thirsty* Durst haben *5*
thirteen dreizehn *E*
this dieser *3;* diese *(form
of* dieser*)* *3*
thousand tausend *2*
three drei *E*
thrilling spannend *4*
through durch *5*
Thursday der
Donnerstag,-e *2*
ticket die Karte,-n *4*
tie die Krawatte,-n *8*
time die Zeit,-en *2; times*
mal *5; once again* mal
wieder *5; time(s)* das
Mal,-e *9*
to zu *2;* auf, nach *3*
today heute *2*
together zusammen *10*
tomato die Tomate,-n *B*
tomorrow morgen *2*
too auch *1;* zu *2*
tooth der Zahn,:e *9*
tourist der Tourist,-en *7*
traffic der Verkehr *3*
train der Zug,:e *7*
to **transfer** umsteigen *7*
traveler's information die
Reiseauskunft *7*
traveling Reisen *7*

trip die Reise,-n *7*
trumpet die
Trompete,-n *10*
to **try** versuchen *10; to try on*
anprobieren *8; to try out*
ausprobieren *9*
Tuesday der Dienstag,-e *2*
to **turn (to)** abbiegen *7*
twelve zwölf *E*
twenty zwanzig *E*
two zwei *E*

U

unbelievable
unglaublich *7*
uncle der Onkel,- *6*
to **understand** verstehen *4*
unfortunately leider *9*
United States of America
die Vereinigten Staaten
von Amerika *3*
unsatisfactory
ungenügend *3*
until bis *2*

V

vanilla ice cream das
Vanilleeis *5*
very sehr *1*
vicinity die
Umgebung,-en *5*
violin die Geige,-n *10*
to **visit** besuchen *5*
visitor der Besucher,- *7*

W

to **wait** warten *3*
waiter der Kellner,- *5*
to **want to** wollen *5*
warm warm *4*
to **wash** spülen *6; to wash
dishes* Geschirr
spülen *6*
watch die Uhr,-en *2; to
watch TV* fernsehen *6*
way der Weg,-e *5; on the
way* auf dem Weg *5*
we wir *1*
to **wear** anhaben, tragen *8*
weather das Wetter *4*
Wednesday der
Mittwoch,-e *2*
week die Woche,-n *4*
well gut *1;* na *2*
well-known bekannt *4*
west der Westen *3*

what was *1; what kind of*
was für *5*

when wann *3;* wenn *7*

where wo *1; where to*
wohin *2; where from*
woher *3*

whether ob *7*

which welcher *2*

whipped cream die
Schlagsahne *5*

white weiß *5*

who wer *E*

why warum *2*

wide breit *7*

to **win** gewinnen *9*

winter der Winter,- *4*

winter sports enthusiast
der Wintersportler,- *5*

with mit *3;* bei *B; near the*
park beim Park *1; with*
it dazu *B*

without ohne *3*

woman die Frau,-en *1*

work die Arbeit,-en *2; to*
work arbeiten *6*

to **would like to** möchten *4;*
I would like to... Ich
möchte... *4*

to **write** schreiben *2*

Y

year das Jahr,-e *6*

to **yell** schreien *4*

yellow gelb *8*

yes ja *1*

yet noch *1*

Yugoslavia Jugoslawien *5*

you *(familiar singular)* du
E; you (familiar plural)
ihr *1; (formal)* Sie *E*

youngster der
Jugendliche,-n *4*

your dein *1; your (familiar*
plural) euer *10; your*
(formal) Ihr *10*

youth der Jugendliche,-n *4;*
die Jugend *5*

youth club der
Jugendklub,-s *5*

Z

zero null *E*

Abbreviations

Index

Acknowledgments

The author wishes to express his gratitude to the many people in Germany, Austria and Switzerland who assisted in the photography scenes for the textbook, the filmstrips and the videos. Special thanks should also go to those people who cooperated in setting up photography sessions in the other German-speaking countries: Friedrich-Wilhelm Becker (Rosdorf/Göttingen), Joachim Bubke and Family (Jever), Heinz Devrient and Family (Köln), Adolf Dürer and Family (Bremen), Rudi Elstner (Düsseldorf), Robert Frei (Zürich), Marie Garnhart (Madison, Wisconsin), Dr. Hans-Karl Gerlach and Family (Limburgerhof/Speyer), Joachim Groppler (Lüneburg), Monika Kamen (Großkrotzenburg), Dieter Messner and Family (Lienz), Horst Penner (Bergisch-Gladbach), Ingomar Stainer and Family (München), Peter Sternke and Family (Hamburg), Helmut Strunk and Family (Essen).

A special thank you goes to Donatus Moosauer (Altenmarkt/Osterhofen) who took several photography scenes in West Germany.

Furthermore, the author would like to pay tribute to those professionals who contributed in the creative effort beyond the original manuscript: Chris Wold Dyrud (illustrator), Owen Franken (cover photo), Design Team (design and layout), Carol Walsh and Sharon O'Donnell (editorial assistance).

Finally, the author would like to thank his wife, Rosie, and his two daughters, Heidi and Marci, for showing such tremendous patience during the development of the series and for their valuable contributions before, during and after the extensive trip throughout German-speaking countries.

The following German instructors provided valuable comments for the revision of *Deutsch Aktuell*:

Brenda Diane Anderson, Liberty High School, Bedford, Virginia; *Asta Aristov*, University High School, Los Angeles, California; *Edna Baker*, Peoria High School, Peoria, Illinois; *Kim Ball*, Lake Forest High School, Felton, Delaware; *Jewell B. Ballard*, Pleasant Valley High, Chico, California; *Mark Bland*, Bayside High School, Virginia Beach, Virginia; *Stephan Blumenschein*, Pacific Beach Middle School, San Diego, California; *Elizabeth Borysewicz*, Huguenot High School, Richmond, Virginia; *David Brewer*, Santiago High School, Garden Grove, California; *Dave Briner*, Monticello High School, Monticello, Minnesota; *Mary Bronfenbrenner Mateer*, DeWitt Middle School, Ithaca, New York; *LaVonne Carlson Moore*, Belle Plaine High School, Belle Plaine, Minnesota; *Dietlinde Cao*, Loma Linda Academy, Loma Linda, California; *Edward Carty*, Nelson Co. High School, Bardstown, Kentucky; *Deidre Chambers*, Vestal High School, Vestal, New York; *Richard Chan*, Glouster High School, Glouster, Massachusetts; *Neva M. Christensen*, West High School, Iowa City, Iowa; *Ruth Christensen*, Chisago Lakes High School, Lindstrom, Minnesota; *Christa M. Chope*, Linden High School, Linden, Michigan; *Judith Cohrs*, Brewen District #228, Midlothian, Illinois; *Rolf Daeschner*, Cathedral Prep., Erie, Pennsylvania; *Elisabeth Dangerfield*, El Camino High School, Sacramento, California; *Isle D. Denchfield*, Kennedy & Truman High School, Taylor, Michigan; *Mary M. Elliott*, Napoleon City Schools, Napoleon, Ohio; *Margaret A. Engebretson*, Cass Lake High School, Cass Lake, Minnesota; *Martha E. Ewan*, Manual High School, Peoria, Illinois; *Kathy Failing*, Castro Valley High School, Castro Valley, California; *Carole Farquhar*, Orland Jr. High, Orland Park, Illinois; *Rev. Dean Fleming*, Winnebago Lutheran Academy, Fond Du Lac, Wisconsin; *Karen L. Fowdy*, Monroe High School, Monroe, Wisconsin; *Leslie T. Foy*, South Davis Jr. High School, Bountiful, Utah; *Sharon Franke*, La Quinta High School, Westminster, California; *Lori Fredette*, Robinson School, Fairfax, Virginia; *Karl-Heinz Gabbey*, Buffalo Grove High School, Buffalo Grove, Illinois; *Agnes Gaertner*, Moreno Valley High School, Moreno Valley, California; *Karl-Heinz E. Gerstenberger*, Shenendehowa Schools, Clifton Park, New York; *Beth Gibb*, Capistrano Valley High School, Mission Viejo, California; *Dianne S. Gimbi*, Weatherly Area High School, Weatherly, Pennsylvania; *Linda M. Gurka*, Jefferson Jr. High School, Columbia, Missouri; *Sylvia Haase*, Truman Middle School, Tacoma, Washington; *Petra Hansen*, Liberty High School, Issaquan, Washington; *Myron Hassard*, Granite High School, Salt Lake City, Utah; *Ronald Hastreiter*, Canisius High School, Buffalo, New York; *Chuck Hawkins*, Lee-Davis High School, Mechanicsville, Virginia; *Don C. Henry*, McLean High

School, McLean, Virginia; *Deborah M. Hershman*, Broad Run High School, Ashburn, Virginia; *Ursula F. Hildebrandt*, Libertyville High School, Libertyville, Illinois; *Edde D. Hodnett*, Point Loma High School, San Diego, California; *Thomas Howe*, Colerain Jr. High, Cincinnati, Ohio; *Patricia Hughes*, Kelliher School, Kelliher, Minnesota; *Mary Hultgren*, Arlington-Green Isle, Arlington, Minnesota; *Heinz Janning*, Redwood Falls-Morton High School, Redwood Falls, Minnesota; *Wilfried Jarosch*, Thornwood, So. Holland, Illinois; *Robert Jenkins*, Deer Park High School, Cincinnati, Ohio; *Kaye F. Johnson*, Franklin County High School, Rocky Mount, Virginia; *Linda Johnson*, Dakota J.H.S., Rapid City, South Dakota; *Guido P. Kauls*, Minnehaha Academy, Minneapolis, Minnesota; *Kenneth J. Kelling*, Lane Technical High School, Chicago, Illinois; *Carole A. Kindell*, L'Anse Creuse High School, Mt. Clemens, Michigan; *Linda Klein*, Waupaca High School, Waupaca, Wisconsin; *Peter E. Klose*, Grand Blanc High School, Grand Blanc, Michigan; *S. Konopacki*, Notre Dame High School, Harper Woods, Michigan; *George Kopecky*, West Torrance High School, Torrance, California; *Richard G. Lamb*, MC High School, Hyrum, Utah; *Wesley Leiphart*, Parkland High School, Winston-Salem, North Carolina; *Lynne D. Lewis*, First Colonial High School, Virginia Beach, Virginia; *C. John Lontos*, Newton High School, Newton, New Jersey; *Jill Lowe*, Great Bridge Jr., Chesapeake, Virginia; *Bruce R. Malbon*, Haverhill Public Schools, Haverhill, Massachusetts; *Joyce McDonald*, Linton Stockton High School, Linton, Indiana; *Mary McDonough*, Wall High School, Wall, New Jersey; *Cynthia P. McIver*, West Springfield High School, Springfield, Virginia; *Gisela W. McKenna-Burke*, Horton Watkins High School, St. Louis, Missouri; *Edward W. McKenney*, George Washington High School, Philadelphia, Pennsylvania; *Bernard A. McKichan*, Sheboygan Falls Middle & Sr. High School, Sheboygan Falls, Wisconsin; *Carolyn A. Meister*, Milford High School, Milford, Ohio; *Barbara L. Metzger*, Glenbard West High School, Glen Ellyn, Illinois; *Spence Milne*, Madison High School, San Diego, California; *Larry R. Moore*, East Valley High School, Spokane, Washington; *Robert N. Mueller*, Jefferson Sr. High School, Cedar Rapids, Iowa; *JoAnn D. Nelson*, Jacksonville High School, Jacksonville, Illinois; *Mary L. Nienaber-Vosler*, Reese High School, Reese, Michigan; *Judy O'Bryne*, East High, Cheyenne, Wyoming; *Carl Olson*, Timberlane Regional High School, Plaistow, New Hampshire; *Paula Patrick*, Jefferson High School, Alexandria, Virginia; *Hans J. Paul*, Center High School, North Highlands, California; *Margaret Paul*, McCormick Jr. High School, Cheyenne, Wyoming; *Sister Mary Perpetua*, S.C.C., Central Catholic High School, Reading, Pennsylvania; *John Peters*, Cardinal O'Hara High School, Springfield, Pennsylvania; *Martha G. Piazza*, West Springfield High School, Springfield, Virginia; *Martha Pleggenkuhle*, St. Ansgar High School, St. Ansgar, Iowa; *Lois Purrington*, DRSH High School, Renville, Minnesota; *Caroline F. Redington*, Dunkirk Middle School, Dunkirk, New York; *Christa Renau*, Dana Hills High School, Dana Point, California; *David H. Renoll*, Tunkhannock Area High School, Tunkhannock, Pennsylvania; *Rev. Donald R. Rettig*, Elder High School, Cincinnati, Ohio; *Nancy Richards*, Camp Hill High School, Camp Hill, Pennsylvania; *Otto Rieger*, Claremont High School, Claremont, California; *Mary Beth Robinson*, Leuzinger High School, Lawndale, California; *Deborah Rose*, Scranton Preparatory School, Scranton, Pennsylvania; *Christine Rudolf*, Sycamore High School, Cincinnati, Ohio; *Don Ruhde*, Iowa Falls High School, Iowa Falls, Iowa; *Larry Scarpino*, Unesville High School, Unesville, Pennsylvania; *Erika Schirm*, Hanby Jr. High School, Wilmington, Delaware; *Shirley Schreiweis*, Wilson High School, Tacoma, Washington; *Peter K. Schwarz*, Winston Churchill Sr. High School, Potomac, Maryland; *John Scioli*, Archbishop Ryan High School, Philidelphia, Pennsylvania; *Kathryn L. Scott*, Midlothian Middle School, Chesterfield, Virginia; *Robert Schmid*, Oak Forest High School, Oak Forest, Illinois; *J. Carter Seibel*, North Harford High School, Pylesville, Maryland; *Thomas J. Sferes*, Kennebunk High School, Kennebunk, Maine; *Sigrid B. Shaw*, Clintonville Sr. High School, Clintonville, Wisconsin; *Dana Kent Shelburne*, Gompers Secondary, San Diego, California; *Hilke Sligar*, Marysville High School, Marysville, California; *Marcia Slosser*, Lloyd C. Bird High School, Chesterfield, Virginia; *Theresa M. Smejkal*, Wheeling High School, Wheeling, Illinois; *Kristy Snyder*, LaSalle-Peru Township High School, LaSalle, Illinois; *Paula Spedding*, Bell Jr. High, San Diego, California; *Larry B. Stell*, Crawford High School, San Diego, California; *Peggy Stuart*, T. H. High School, Dana Point, California; *Linda J. Swenson*, Severna Park Sr. High, Severna Park, Maryland; *Patrick Sylvester*, Socorro High School, Socorro, New Mexico; *Meredith E. Taylor*, Old Mill Senior High, Millersville, Maryland; *Rev. Don Thompson*, Kettle Moraine Lutheran High School, Jackson, Wisconsin; *Susi Tirmenstein*, San Clemente High School, San Clemente, California; *Glen A. Uhlenkott*, Moses Lake High School, Moses Lake, Washington; *Carol Van Abbema*, Withrow High School, Cincinnati, Ohio; *George Vaught*, Hayfield Secondary, Alexandria, Virginia; *Lisa Vielhauer*, Irvine High School, Irvine, California; *Jon Ward*, Malad High School, Malad, Idaho; *Judith K. Warner*, North Stafford High School, Stafford, Virginia; *Michael Wegener*, Hawthorne High School, Hawthorne, California; *Diane Wilcenski*, South High School, Sheboygan, Wisconsin; *Susan D. Wilkey*, Romeoville High School, Romeoville, Illinois; *Hildegard Willford*, Casa Roble High School, Orangevale, California; *Donald Keith Williams*, Skyline High School, Dallas, Texas; *Charlotte R. Woodley*, Cameran County High School, Emporium, Pennsylvania; *Kathy Young*, Union High School, Union, Missouri; *Hans R. Zumpft*, North High, Sheboygan, Wisconsin

Photo Credits

All the photos in *Deutsch Aktuell* (3rd edition) textbook not taken by the author have been provided by the following:

Austrian National Tourist Office: vi, (top left), xvi (all), xvii (all), 132 (bottom left), 133 (bottom), 162 (bottom right), 284 (top left), 319 (right)

Fremdenverkehrsverband Lüneburger Heide e.V.: v (top left), xiii (top left)

Fremdenverkehrsverband München-Oberbayern e.V.: xii (top left), 285(right), 311 (both)

Fremdenverkehrsverein Göttingen e.V.: 213 (left), 251 (left), 316 (right)

German Rail: 214 (bottom left), 215 (top), 240 (left), 244 (top left), 248 (left)

Harzer Verkehrsverband e.V.: 314 (right), 318 (right)

Informations- und Presseamt Dortmund: xi (bottom right), xii (bottom right)

Landeshauptstadt München: vi (bottom left), x (top right), xi (top right), xii (bottom left), xiii (bottom left)

Moosauer, Donatus: 17 (bottom), 182 (top and bottom left), 183 (top left) 184 (both), 186 (both), 187 (both), 198 (top)

Musik + Show: 117 (left), 118 (both), 123 (top), 294 (left)

Nash, Rod: 165 (top right and bottom left), 166 (right)

Owen Franken/German Information Center: vii (center left), xi (top left), 10 (both), 32 (left), 35 (top right), 46 (top), 98 (bottom left), 99 (bottom), 103 (both), 120 (center), 126 (bottom right), 130 (left), 151 (bottom), 164 (both), 167 (right), 169 (top right and bottom left), 178 (bottom right), 183 (right), 244 (bottom right), 279 (left), 280 (right), 294 (right), 317 (right), 320 (bottom left), 324 (both), 338 (center), 346 (left), 350 (bottom left)

Presse- und Informationsamt der Bundesregierung (Bildstelle): 247 (top), 347 (left)

Simson, David: x (bottom left), 183 (bottom left), 199 (all), 203 (left)

Stadt Augsburg (Amt für Öffentlichkeit): 234 (right), 318 (left)

Stock Boston: 132 (right), 350

Swiss National Tourist Office: vii (bottom left), xviii (top left, bottom right and left), xix (all), 213 (right), 240 (right), 241 (all), 243 (right), 284 (bottom left and right), 314 (left), 316 (left), 317 (left)

Tourismus-Zentrale Hamburg GmbH: v (bottom left), x (bottom right), xi (bottom left), xii (top right)

Touristenverband Siegerland-Wittgenstein e.V.: 319 (left)

Verkehrsamt der Stadt Frankfurt/Main: xiii (bottom right)

Verkehrsverein Augsburg: 234 (right)